ONE TIME AROUND

A Solo World Bicycle Journey

Alan Thompson

Published by APT Publishing Co.
1927 Mansfield, Toledo, Ohio 43613

Library of Congress Catalog Card Number: 91-93068

Edited by Ruth Thompson and Janet Rogolsky
Photographs by Alan Thompson
Typesetting by Marie Murrell, Executive Support Services
Dust jacket design by Dill Murrell, Special Characters
Dust jacket photograph by Jeff Davis, Emporia Gazette
Dust Jacket photograph enhancement by Prestige Studio, Toledo, OH

Printed by Braun-Brumfield, Inc.
Ann Arbor, Michigan

ISBN 0-9630747-0-9

CONTENTS

To my parents, Ruth and Charlie!

Prologue

The two young friends sat lazily on the bank of the sluggish stream that snakes its way through one of West Toledo's neighborhood parks. They were happy, and there was good reason to feel so on this particular day. The weather was warm and sunny. School was out, and a whole summer's vacation stretched enticingly before them. The end of school meant the beginning of baseball, and already their Cleveland Indians were off to a great start on what promised to be one of their best seasons ever.

The two nine-year-olds had been friends as long as either could remember. Living on opposite sides of the street in one of the comfortable neighborhoods of midwestern Toledo, Ohio, they were constant companions; where one could be found, the other would not be far behind. They dangled their bare feet in the cooling waters of the small creek and surveyed the dandelion carpeted field before them that would host many a neighborhood baseball game this coming season. But their minds were not really on baseball on this first day of summer. Instead, they dreamt of far away places—places like Indiana, Iowa, Colorado, and even California. These were places they had seen on maps before, and heard spoken of, but they could only imagine what strange and wonderful sights each dot on the map represented. They dreamt and carefully laid their plans as to how they would travel to these exotic lands in order to satisfy a growing lust for adventure.

The summer before, the Adventures of Tom Sawyer and Huckleberry Finn had fired their imaginations and inspired them to begin in earnest the construction of a sturdy raft that would carry them down the Maumee River, out into Lake Erie, and then to unknown destinations beyond the eastern horizon. Progress had proceeded nicely that summer. After all, by the end of the season they already had put the finishing touches on one of the paddles that would propel them into the unknown.

However, with the present summer at hand and their interest in an extended water journey on the wane, a new plan began to take shape. Both had ridden bicycles for many years—at least to them it seemed like many years—and their skills atop their two-wheeled chariots were certainly second to none. What better way to see new places than by bicycle? Out in the open, fresh air, sunny skies, gliding silently and effortlessly through the countryside.

Well then, why not a cross country bicycle trip? Yes, even all the way to California! What better adventure? They would camp out under the stars—rough it—or stay in youth hostels which were part of the young and growing American Youth Hostels organizations that one of the two friends had recently heard about. This would be the plan. This was the way to visit all those places that were just now names on a map. And they would visit them all!

The boys rushed home to tell their parents of their exciting adventure. Their Moms and Dads greeted the news of their impending long distance bicycle ride with a serious nod and a twinkle in their eyes. They agreed that this was certainly a wonderful idea, but why not take a trial ride first to a slightly closer destination—just to work out the bugs.

This seemed like wise counsel indeed to the two young adventurers. In fact, it was agreed a ride out to the local racetrack five miles distant on the outskirts of the city would surely allow them to work out any bugs and give them a feel for "long distance" bicycling.

Late in the day that had been chosen for their trial run, the two young, extremely exhausted cyclists wheeled into their respective backyards on their one-speed Schwinns with coaster brakes, no longer thinking of Indiana, Colorado, or California. No, their minds no longer dwelled on far away places, but on things a little closer to home: things like the Cleveland Indians, tomorrow's neighborhood baseball game, and especially what would be on the evening dinner table. Their aching legs and rather tender bottom sides had convinced them that California would not be going anywhere and it would surely make good sense to wait until they came out with a more comfortable bicycle seat. Bicycling could wait, and besides, their services were desperately needed on the neighborhood ball team this season. Yes, the cross-country bicycle trip would be saved for another day. For now it would be relegated to the bottom of that treasure chest of ideas that young boys seem always to rummage through on a regular basis. But for one of the two friends, a seed had been planted, and in later years it would grow into an adventure that it would be difficult for even a nine-year-old to imagine.

* * *

November 26, 1986—Bombay, India

The steady chop-chop-chop of the helicopter's rotor beat a constant rhythm as we swung low over the prison yard. I was gripped by a fear that attuned my ears to the least irregularity in this mechanical symphony that kept me and my pilot aloft. Far in the distance stretched the teeming metropolis of Bombay, home for eight million of the 900 million souls who inhabit the Indian subcontinent. Below me was a scene of pandemonium as the prison compound rose in revolt—flashes of gunfire, men struggling in hand-to-hand combat, and tear gas bombs laying down an irritating blanket of fumes and smoke. For a brief instant my mind flashed back to the events that had led up to this unenviable seat in the prison's helicopter—a vision of a time and place 10,000 miles and half a lifetime away when two young friends had dreamt of a cross-country bicycle trip; and also that day only five months before when I had said goodbye to my family and friends as I set out on my own, hoping to see the world from atop my 18-speed Miyata touring bicycle. I had looked at those faces as though I might not see them again and it turned out that the worried expressions were not unjustified. But my brief reverie was interrupted by the pilot who signaled me to open the helicopter's door and unleash the first of my grenades upon the heads of those poor beasts below. Could I do it? I had no choice. As if observing someone else, I struggled to open the door of the chopper, slowly extended my arm that held the deadly piece of explosive metal, paused for what seemed an interminable instant, and let it plummet to the earth below.

ONE

Setting Out

June 14, 1985 – Toledo, Ohio

I had little inkling on this day that in a few months I would find myself in a helicopter circling low over a prison camp in rebellion on the outskirts of Bombay, India. I knew the road ahead of me would not be easy with many an unpredictable obstacle and detour, but some possibilities one just doesn't consider.

This was the day I had chosen for my departure from the safety and security of my familiar surroundings and the care and concern of the people I am close to. I was riding—temporarily I hoped—out of their lives into the unknown to see and experience the world as most people will never have the chance to—close to nature, close to the elements, closer to the people of the lands through which I might ride.

At 35 years of age, I had been teaching junior high world history for 13 years in Sylvania, Ohio on the outskirts of Toledo. Junior high school teachers are a fairly easy breed to recognize. They are the ones who walk around as if in a daze with a slightly crazed look on their faces which is often accompanied by some sort of a nervous twitch which indicates to all who have contact with them that here is someone who spends a great deal of time with 12- and 13-year old adolescents. They say a junior high teacher has only so many good years to give. Could I have been reaching my upper limit?

In spite of the telltale signs, I had always enjoyed working with young people, in and out of the classroom. For a number of years I had coached our school wrestling team which in time I gave up in order to take over the 7th grade basketball position.

In the classroom each year my teaching colleagues and I tried to instill in our students an interest in and appreciation for the foundations of our Western Heritage—not an easy task when it seems the sole concern on the minds of most 7th graders is who is "going with" whom in the always changing romantic world of the junior high school scene. Our topics were usually the same in our world history course— the Cradles of Civilization, the Golden Age of the Greeks, the Glory of Ancient Rome, the Rise of Medieval Europe—but we always attempted to inject new ideas and materials that would grab our students' attention and maybe even fire their imaginations.

I'd always been a firm believer in the maxim that experience is the best teacher. Well, maybe it was time to practice what I believed. Having taught my students about the immense grandeur of the pyramids, the beauty of the Parthenon high atop the Acropolis, and the great engineering achievements of the Romans, I had a keen desire to experience these wonders myself first hand. Now was the time, and too, after 13 years of teaching—the set pattern, the daily routine—it was time to shake up my life a little.

I'd always had a touch of the wanderlust. My first experience with real independent travel was by motorcycle during my junior summer at the University of Toledo back in 1969. Inspired by the late 60's TV series *Then Came Bronson,* I purchased a one-cylinder BSA motorcycle and traversed the country from Ohio to California and back again, marveling at the immense size and great beauty of our own country. The summer of 1978 found me four years into my teaching career and looking towards the European continent as a new place to explore. Again by motorcycle, I fell in love with the old world charms of England, France, Germany, Austria, and Italy. It was on this five-week European excursion that bicycle touring first caught my attention. As I motored effortlessly up and down the sides of Europe's hills and mountains, I would smile as I roared past those poor souls who were huffing and puffing for all they were worth on their 10-speed bicycles loaded down with packs and camping gear. But there was something about it that intrigued me and I began thinking more and more about trading in my motorcycle for a bicycle. It was then and there that I vowed I would come back to Europe to travel once more by cycle, but the next one would be of the motorless variety.

That vow was fulfilled only two years later when I purchased a 10-speed touring bicycle—my first bicycle since my one-speed Schwinn of so long ago—and headed once more across the Atlantic. Though I couldn't cover as much ground as I had on my first trip to Europe, I enjoyed the slower pace and physical challenges that bicycle touring offered. I reveled in the feeling of freedom and independence and the sense of satisfaction that came from being self contained and having everything I required packed on my bicycle—no gasoline to buy; no train compartment or window to shield me from the environment of which I wanted to be a part; just my own energy, determination, and self-reliance that would get me to where I wanted to go.

Though it was only a short tour of three weeks, I was hooked on the joys and exhilaration of bicycle touring. The next few summers found me cycling in various locations throughout the United States and Canada. There was an American Youth Hostels tour down spectacular Highway One along the California coastline followed the next year by a Bikecentennial ride through the majestic Canadian Rockies. Not to ignore the pleasures of the East, a summer ride along the Blue Ridge Parkway proved to be a beautiful and challenging experience.

During these rides in and around the United States, I began to dream of the ultimate tour—a trek around the world that would take me through strange and exotic lands. I'd heard of people doing such a thing before, but I always thought they had to be the Christopher Columbus or Sir Edmond Hillary type. Now here I was actually contemplating a grandiose scheme of my own. Was it possible to cycle in places like Africa, India, and South East Asia? Were there even any roads other than mud tracks? How would the people react to a white-faced, carefree, Western cyclist bicycling through their homeland? Could a bicyclist ever survive the Third World with its poverty, hunger, and very different cultures? I began to look for some sources of information that would answer my many questions. I eagerly poured through travel brochures and books, especially those few written by world cyclists. Lloyd Sumner's book The Long Ride which detailed his four-year journey around the globe proved to be an inspiration, as well as Miles From Nowhere which was the fascinating account of Barbara and Larry Savage's two-year ride. However, I finally decided that no matter how much one reads about the experiences of someone else, the only way to really find out is to do it yourself. 1985 was to be my year or not at all!

With my fate now cast to the winds, there remained the small matter of figuring out a way to convince my school system to allow me to wander the world for a year and then happily surrender my job to me upon my return. My world history teaching position offered me a unique position from which to do this. I sat down and began work on a proposal to the school board that explained how the school system and my students would benefit from the multitude of first-hand experiences I would have and all the materials and pictures that I would send back to be used in our world history classroom. I also contacted the University of Toledo and arranged for my trip to count as an eight-hour independent study towards my masters degree. In addition, because the famine in Africa was currently reaping its harvest of death and I planned to travel close to some of these devastated areas, I received the blessing of our local Red Cross Chapter to solicit pledges for famine relief as I traveled. This reason alone seemed to justify the trip and made me feel good about being able to do something positive to help relieve some of the suffering.

To my amazement and joy, tempered with apprehension, the proposal was accepted and I was granted a one-year sabbatical leave which meant I would actually be making half pay while traveling. What could be better—to travel the world and be paid for doing it! There was now only one minor problem—I had to do it! That fact hit me in the face like a sledge hammer. I had actually severed my ties with everything that was familiar to me—to all that I knew, loved, and cherished. I would now embark on the life of a cycling vagabond for a year or more—no roots; no place to call home.

For me there had always been something stimulating about striking out on your own, going it alone, being out on a limb—maybe the element of danger or the challenge of facing the unknown. But could I do it for a whole year? With the acceptance of my proposal, it seemed that I had no choice.

The final days before my departure on the 14th of June, 1985, were busy ones filled with equipment checks, trial runs on my heavily laden, 18-speed touring bicycle, packing and repacking to find just the right balance for 40 to 50 pounds of clothing and gear, saying good-bye to friends, and tying up all those loose ends of one's life that cannot be left unattended for a year or more.

Friday, June 14 was probably one of the strangest days of my life. It was an emotional day filled with excitement, sadness, fear, and a growing apprehension about what the next 12 months held in store for me. Saying farewell to my family and friends was one of the most difficult things I've ever had to do. I'd always been close to my parents who are the kind of people who always are there when they are needed. To not see them and my sister and her family and my brother for a year or longer was hard to imagine. The setting for our final, tearful good-byes was in downtown Toledo at the summer, weekly Rally by the River, a kind of huge TGIF for all of Toledo held on the downtown banks of the Maumee River. My family, many of my friends, and some of the local news media had gathered for a final toast and grand sendoff. As the moment for my departure approached, I embraced my parents and brother, not wanting to let go, afraid that this might be the last time I would ever see or touch them. I climbed aboard my bicycle which would be my home for the next year and took one last look at all those people who meant so much to me. As I pedaled slowly out of their lives, I kept glancing over my shoulder, not wanting to lose sight of those faces. Finally, they were gone and I was on my own. My world tour had begun!

* * *

My plan was to bicycle to New York by way of Ohio, Pennsylvania, and New Jersey and then catch the plane for Lisbon, Portugal at which point I would begin my journey across southern Europe. From there it would be across the Mediterranean to Egypt and the Dark Continent, and then on to the Indian subcontinent and so work my way eastward around the globe. That plan seemed like a bizarre fantasy as I struggled through those first difficult miles. It appeared highly unlikely that I would even make Fremont, Ohio, only 35 miles east of Toledo on this first day's ride. My bicycle lumbered along under the most weight I had ever carried before—front and rear panniers chocked full of clothes and equipment, sleeping bag, tent, sleeping pad, cookstove, spare parts, tools. "Was it too late to turn around?" I thought sheepishly to myself—a thought that would plague me constantly over the next couple of weeks. I decided it was, at least for this day. My parents had wisely made reservations for me at a small motel, suspecting that I might need a soft bed at the end of this emotional and stressful day. Again, they were right on the money. I settled into my first night's accommodation with a sigh of relief and then called my parents just to hear their voices again and to let them know that I had survived the first day. After watching my departure on the 11 o'clock news, I switched off the lights and drifted off into a well deserved slumber, thinking of this day that had been like no other.

* * *

Drip . . . drip . . . drip . . . splash . . . slosh . . . drip . . . drip . . . drip . . . "God, have I made the most terrible mistake of my life?" was the only thought that occurred to me as I splashed and sloshed my way through the first full day of my world tour. I decided that Mother Nature had stayed up all night thinking to herself, "Well, how can we really stick it to old Al on his first full riding day tomorrow? Ah yes, I think I have just the thing!"

As I peeked my head outside my cozy motel room on this second day, I cast a wary eye at the gray, overcast skies above and I almost convinced myself that maybe it was a good day to just stay inside—you know, relax, read a good book, and recuperate from my first 35 miles last evening. After all, I had been riding into a headwind those first few miles. My conscience finally got the better of me and I gingerly began to load up my two-wheeled mount—a process that I would eventually be able to accomplish in my sleep. Who knows, maybe it was just a gray day and the rain would hold off.

It turned out I was correct on both counts—it definitely was a gray day and the rain did hold off—for about the first five minutes. Then, for the next nine hours I slithered my way along the roads of central Ohio listening to the rain maintain its steady beat on my helmet and cursing the countless cars and trucks that pelted me with their backwash—and cursing my decision to have set out on a journey such as this for a whole year.

I'd also forgotten the pain that goes along with bicycling, especially those first few days of any kind of tour. By mid-afternoon I felt as though every muscle in my body and especially my poor posterior were crying out, "Mercy, Please!" As the five o'clock hour rolled around I convinced myself it was time to find a place of rest for my weary and drenched body for that night. A cemetery that I passed looked inviting, but then I decided that maybe I would be pushing my luck just a little. At last I selected a friendly looking dwelling and in my slightly shriveled condition asked the inhabitants if they wouldn't mind converting their side yard into a mini campground. Secretly, I was hoping they might take pity on this soggy cyclist before them and invite me in to some small dry corner of their house, but no such luck was forthcoming. They did, however, agree to the mini campground idea and I set to work pitching my tent in-between the raindrops and was soon settled in for a sumptuous dinner of a can of beef soup with bread, peanut butter, and honey. A change of warm clothes and my cozy sleeping bag helped improve my attitude considerably and as I drifted off, I uttered a small prayer that Mother Nature too would enjoy a good night's sleep and look kindly on me in the days to come.

* * *

Not everyone can say they've been to the River Styx. In Greek mythology the River Styx is that river one must cross over to reach the land of the dead. It is a land of half light—half dark, and the waters of the Styx are black—a land of shadow-like travelers who are passing from this world into the next. As I proceeded into eastern Ohio I was quite surprised to see a sign welcoming me to River Styx. I paused and carefully surveyed the winding road beyond the sign, half expecting to see some wraith-like apparition beckoning me to join him in his nether world. As none appeared, I decided that maybe they were busy with other things and it was safe to pass through this Land of the Dead. I must admit to a slightly quickened pace through the tiny hamlet and a cautious glance or two over my shoulder.

It seemed as if Mother Nature had heard my prayer because she now provided me with vastly improved weather conditions—a smiling sun and crystal blue canopy—and comfortable riding conditions that buoyed my spirits. The gently undulating terrain of eastern Ohio sent me scudding across the landscape, rushing down one hillside and half way up the next with a brisk tailwind ushering me along. As I pulled into the National Park Campground in Deerfield, Ohio, I was greeted by a friendly ranger and a $7.00 camping fee that, to me, seemed a bit steep.

"Excuse me, Sir", I said. "I have just set out on a world bicycle tour which I've deemed a Ride For World Hunger since I'm taking pledges for African Famine Relief. How would you feel about cutting your camping fee in half since this is such a worthy cause?"

"Is that so?" the friendly ranger replied. "That certainly is a worthy cause, but I can't really make that decision. Be glad to send you up to the office, though, to see what they say there. Just follow the road around till you come to the main park building."

At the park administration building I encountered another amiable looking ranger with obviously more authority and again explained the worthwhile nature of my trip.

"Well now," said the ranger, "that surely is a good cause, but this is an important decision that I just can't make at this level. I would have to contact my superiors to get their

OK and then we'd have to fill out Form DD-40-1935 in triplicate to properly allow a discounted camping fee and then..."

"Stop. Don't bother," I interrupted. "I think I get the picture."

In spite of the "tremendous flexibility" of the park rangers and the $7.00 camping fee, it proved to be a lovely site located right on a lake that played early evening reflections of the surrounding hills across its surface. The hot shower seemed to be just what the doctor ordered and a batch of sloppy joes put a dent in my considerable appetite. After dinner, a walk along the twisting shoreline of the lake and a soothing breeze—a sunset that stretched its crimson fingers across the soft azure sky—somehow, it all did seem worthwhile!

* * *

As all touring bicyclists know, one's general attitude is a direct function of the skies overhead and the tilt of the road passing beneath your wheels, not to mention whether or not the wind is kissing you in the face or patting you on the behind. This was to be the case in 400 of the longest miles across the constantly up and down state of Pennsylvania.

I paused briefly at the Ohio-Pennsylvania border to celebrate my first real milestone of the trip. I glanced back at relatively flat Ohio and then looked in the opposite direction at not so relatively flat Pennsylvania and told myself that maybe there would be just a few small mountains to climb over and then easy sledding into New Jersey and New York. This was to prove quite a miscalculation on my part. Not too far from the border the hills began in earnest. The brooding skies darkened, along with my mood, and sent the first raindrops spattering across the pavement causing me to again reflect upon the wisdom of my decision. As I struggled up and down the hills of western Pennsylvania in and out of the intermittent rain showers, I thought to myself that no one who has not bike toured can really understand the physical demands—it's like an eight-hour workout when you're in the hills: pump, sweat, cool down; pump, sweat, cool down—it takes its toll.

On this first day in Pennsylvania, it was not hard to convince myself that my body deserved a comfortable room with a hot shower that just might help soothe my sagging spirits. This I was able to do in short order. I approached the motel manager of one roadside sanctuary in my drenched condition and with a pathetic look on my face—a look that I was becoming quite accomplished at—I explained the nature and purpose of my trip and was pleasantly surprised when he cut the price of the room by a third. I soon found myself tucked snugly away in my room, happy to be out of the rain and chilly temperatures at least for this day.

* * *

The truckers out on I-80 east of Clarion, Pennsylvania probably talked about Tuesday, June 18, for quite a spell. That was the day they saw that crazy bicyclist with stuff hanging off his "rig" every which way, cruising down that long, lonely ribbon of highway. It's probably a good thing that crazy cyclist didn't run into Ol' Smokey that day. I became so frustrated with the hills that I decided to take a short jaunt on the interstate which usually features a more manageable grade and sometimes a more direct route. I soon found that, though it might have been quicker, it really was not too enjoyable with the huge semi trailer rigs blowing past and all the other high-speed traffic. So, it was back to the smaller roads; but somehow I didn't really mind. I was beginning to feel that my initial break-in period was coming to an end. My legs felt stronger, becoming conditioned to the constant punishment of the Pennsylvania mountains, and my overall conditioning seemed to be on the upswing.

Mother Nature, too, came to my aid periodically, at first testing me with a day wrapped in misty, gray clouds only to be followed by a sun-alive day where She would spread her magic across the ever changing Pennsylvania countryside. One morning in particular in central Pennsylvania dawned fresh and clean, and the sun painted the rolling landscape in bright hues of green, yellow and blue. Even the hills didn't seem to matter much on this morn. Freshly plowed and planted fields stimulated the senses—the smells of the country. I took lunch on this day in "Podunk", Pennsylvania—really a little hamlet called Elmonton—at the local pub. Just a hamburger for me, and a little old fellow two stools down with a story to tell about his fighting days in World War II. I'd always had a keen interest in the Big War, so I just sat back and listened:

> "Yes, Siree, I was one of them grunts in the First Division—you know—the Big Red One— the Bloody One. Yup, I saw it all: North Africa, Sicily, and a place called Omaha Beach. Yes sir, laddy, I was one of them there forward observers—those guys out on a limb. Hell, we was 'in' before the first wave even hit the beach. From there it was on to St. Lo, the breakout, and then I got captured at that there Falaise Gap. Now, don't ya know that those German guards liked their wine and when my guard uncorked one too many bottles, I hightailed it out of there. Nothin' special, laddy—just doin' my job—just a survivor."

As my storyteller slipped back into a silent reverie of his WW II days of glory and excitement, I toasted him and all the many young men who were not as lucky as he to end up in the survivor's category.

As the hour was getting late, I pushed on into the early evening until the lengthening shadows reminded me it was time to find a place to pitch my tent for the night. Enter the Staley Family with their comfortable country home and huge yard and their friendly hospitality. Mr. and Mrs. Staley and their two children invited me to pitch my tent anywhere I pleased and then invited me in for a scrumptuous dinner and breakfast. In the evening we all settled in to their family room and I told them of my travels thus far and of my plans for the future. Their amazement and interest in what I was doing was probably outdone only by their kindness shown to this stranger from Toledo, Ohio.

The following evening I pulled in to Moshannon State Park, a beautifully forested region of central Pennsylvania, with tall, stately pine and hardwood trees that whispered softly in the early summer breezes. It had been another long day—77 tortuous miles of terrain that did not know the meaning of the term "level." My legs were a good approximation of jello pudding and my weariness was matched only by my appetite. Earlier in the day I had raided one of the country groceries anticipating the hunger that was gnawing away at my insides at that moment. I fired up my cookstove and commenced preparation of an Italian feast of spaghetti and garlic bread. As I was standing over my mini caldron of boiling, aromatic spaghetti sauce, I couldn't believe what my eyes beheld; marching down the middle of the camp road only 25 to 30 yards away was one of those very large, black, furry critters that are also known for their insatiable appetites. Slightly smaller than a bull elephant (or at least it seemed so), Mama or Papa bear marched right up the road as if she/he owned it. As the large animal slowed to glance in my direction, I stood frozen in my tracks, my eyeballs searching frantically left and right for a tree that was climbable. As mentioned before, these trees were all tall and stately, and so the lowest branches were in reach only if one happened to be a giraffe. With no escape route apparent, I remained motionless, hoping that I would blend in with the surrounding forest, trying for all I was worth to resemble a small sapling. I also uttered a small prayer that this was not a bear with Italian ancestry in her/his background with a taste for pasta. Our uninvited campground guest knew exactly where it wanted to go and luckily continued on up the camp road to the camp dumping site where the cuisine was more to its liking. With the crisis over, I sat down to my Italian banquet, trying not to pay too much attention to the tremendous racket coming from the direction of the camp garbage site. As I zipped myself into my "bearproof" tent that night, I sincerely hoped the intruder would not return for leftovers or, worse, a Homo sapien dessert!

* * *

Many of the people I had met so far on my journey wanted to know what it was like to do long distance bicycling. How did I feel after riding for eight to nine hours through all kinds of weather and all types of terrain? I would usually reply that it was like riding a roller coaster both figuratively and literally. One minute your spirit can be higher than a kite, and an hour later that kite can come crashing to the ground. Thursday, June 20, 1985, seemed to be a day that was a microcosm in the life of this touring cyclist:

> A predawn chorus of cheeps and chirps, announcing the arrival of a new day; clinging to those last few moments in my down cocoon; unwilling muscles stiff from yesterday's punishment; breaking camp and dreading what lies ahead; that first climb and a body that's not yet ready to climb; dread turning to delight as the route levels out; the forest highlands, wet with the morning dew, unaware of the cyclist's passage, but still offering their gifts for his enjoyment; the steady click-click-click of the freewheel; a five-mile downhill and whistling wind—and then, Nittany Mountain! Climbing, straining, sweating, close to the top, and the sky opening up; huddling on the side of the road with my 2-wheeled companion, under a tarp; torrents of rain, thunder, lightening, hail and falling temperatures; uncaring semis thundering past, and their spray finding its mark; the passing storm, the warming rays of the sun and a level stretch; the afternoon—bright, green, and alive with the promise of the late summer harvest; early evening, and a quiet campsite nestled in the hills of Appalachia; lengthening shadows, and the evensong of the forest.

* * *

Believe it or not, there really is a part of Pennsylvania that could qualify as flat. As I headed up the Susquehanna River Valley, I reveled in the level stretches and friendly tail winds that afforded me easy sledding and also allowed me to take stock of the first days of my world tour. I had now covered about two-thirds of the distance to New York and it really seemed as if I was on a spiritual roller coaster. Sagging lows would be followed by those sweet highs that make you feel as though you are in tune with the world and everything around you. It seemed difficult, though, to maintain any level of contentment. I was beginning to suspect that maybe I wasn't cut out for this type of life. I'd always enjoyed reading about people who struck out on their own on some grand adventure, but reading about it and actually doing it on your own were two vastly different things. My bike tours of the past were different. If the going got tough, you knew it was going to last only a short time—three or maybe four weeks. But here I was facing a stretch of weeks and months on end. How would I stand up to the constant challenge and stress of never knowing what lay around the next bend? Also, one of the real attractions for me in the past had been the group camaraderie of an organized tour—becoming close to new friends who shared the same experiences, even though one does give up some independence in such a group. My hope had been to meet some fellow cyclist along the way and join forces for a while, but amazingly, I'd only met one cyclist coming in the opposite direction thus far. True, it was still very early in my tour and that possibility was always there. But there was one motivation that always prevented me from turning around and admitting defeat, and that was my "Ride for World Hunger" theme. I had been passing out a number of my pledge cards to the people who expressed a curiosity and interest in my trip, and every time I did, I experienced a nice feeling inside. I really felt that this was worthwhile. I didn't know how much money would find its way back to the Red Cross African Relief Fund, but I felt good about being able to contribute in a small way to help alleviate some of the terrible suffering. Additionally, this trip was for my students so that I could share my experiences with them in my class-room, thereby helping them to know a little more about the world and its many different, but wonderful cultures. This was justification and there would be no turning around!

I tried to keep these thoughts in my head as I headed up into the Pocono Mountains. I tried to focus on the great beauty of the surrounding countryside and less on the pump-ing and exertion that had to propel me up, over, and through that same countryside. As I traversed the Poconos, land of honeymoon retreats—I was also reminded that in my 35 years, I still had not found that special person with whom to share the special things in life—things such as this great adventure on which I was embarking. This had always been a source of loneliness for me, but my independent nature had always overshadowed this empty part of my life. Well, there still would be time to look to this aspect of life when I returned from my travels.

I had always marveled at the number and variety of brief but interesting contacts one encounters in travel such as mine—people, often traveling in the same or similar manner, who touch your life for a short instant, but leave it richer because they have shared their own story and experiences with you. As I was walking my bike across the Delaware River—no, not on the water, but on a bridge—I met up with a hiker who was walking the Appalachian Trail. He was a fellow who had been in the construction trade for a number of years—a carpenter I think—and then just decided that he had had enough for a while; just decided to quit, buy himself a backpack, and begin walking. We traded stories of our good and bad fortunes so far and then bade each other best wishes and farewell.

Later that same day, I came upon Ira Wiss, the first cyclist I'd met who happened to be riding in the same direction. Ira was an attorney who lived in New Jersey and he was just out for a day ride. I was glad to have his company, if only for a short time, and he gladly guided me to a state park campground, where I arrived after the office was closed. I arose early the next morning and did not feel too guilty about not paying the $6 camping fee for a campsite that had no showers. As I glided past the still closed camp office with a small degree of guilt, I pondered whether or not Davey Crockett and Daniel Boone knew how lucky they were, not having to pay camp fees.

On the 24th of June I pulled into Sparta, New Jersey, only about 24 miles from New York City, and knocked on the door of Laurel Kozacek. Laurel had been my group leader the summer before when I had joined nine other American Youth Hostel bicyclists for a six-week tour of Europe. I had pleasant memories of that previous summer and I was happy to see her smiling and familiar face, and in turn, she was happy to see mine. We sat down with a couple of cold beers and I related the highlights of my 750 mile journey from Northwest Ohio. She was eager to hear of my experiences and was half tempted to join me for at least part of my ride through southern Europe. Laurel would put me up for the next couple of days in her comfortable and stylish home and help me prepare myself and my bicycle for the flight to Europe.

After a good night's sleep in a more than comfortable bed, I set to work the next day cleaning and lubricating my bike. Laurel had made a run to a local bike shop to pick up a bicycle box that would be home for the next couple of days for my two-wheeled friend. As Laurel unloaded the box from her car, I thought to myself, "How am I going to fit this very large bike into that very small box?" I had flown with my boxed-up bike before, but those boxes had seemed twice as big. Nervously, I began tearing apart my bike, unscrewing what seemed to be just about every nut and bolt on the machine. Before too long I had lying before me a pile of wheels, cables, tubes and racks that did not seem to resemble a bicycle very much at all. I was seized by a sudden panic that when I arrived in Lisbon, I would never be able to get everything back in its appropriate spot.

"Don't worry," said Laurel. "You've done OK this far in your trip, and you'll cross that bridge too when the time comes."

Though I didn't share her quiet confidence, I began stuffing it all into that very small box, and to my amazement, everything fit. The rest of the day was spent in relaxation and that evening Laurel and I shared a pizza at the local pizza parlor. We talked and reminisced about the last summer and how much fun the ten of us had had cycling the highways and byways of England, France, Germany, and Switzerland. That had been a special time, just as this now was also a special time for me. Staying with Laurel in her comfortable home in the hills of New Jersey for a very brief two days also made me realize once again how much I missed the comforts of my own home, and how much I would be giving up over the months ahead.

Laurel got me to the bus stop the following morning for the short ride into New York City. We hugged goodbye over my pile of packs, camping gear, and boxed-up machine; I was sorry to see her go. As I was standing on the wrong side of the street when the bus arrived, I practically had to throw myself and a couple of my packs in front of the bus to keep it from taking off without me. The none-too-friendly New Jersey bus driver gave me a menacing look as I responded with my best Midwestern smile.

"What the hell was ya doin' on that side of the street?" said the burly fellow.

"Well, sir," I replied, "I wasn't exactly certain where your fine bus was going to stop. You see, I'm on a world bicycle tour and I have all this..."

"Yea, yea—come on now buddy, I gots a schedule to keep. Hurry up and get all that crap loaded underneath."

Again I pleaded my ignorance, began wildly tossing packs, gear, and bulky box into the baggage compartments, and then away we sped to the Big Apple—my first visit ever to the Big City!

All the stories I'd heard about New York City and its army of thieves, muggers, and pickpockets appeared to be true when I arrived at the Port Authority Bus Terminal in the heart of the city. Situated at various locations in the terminal were shady-looking, streetwise entrepreneurs who seemed to have staked out their territory. Looking this way and that, they kept a wary eye on the continuous flow of travelers, business people, and shoppers in front of them. It was odd that all the thieves seemed to be on this floor while all the police seemed to have staked out the floor below. Putting on my meanest "Don't mess with me face," I puzzled over how I was going to find the baggage check and keep my worldly belongings safe at the same time. I just couldn't lug all this equipment with me—but there was no choice. I'd have to if I didn't want to find a very empty spot where my equipment had been. So, with a superhuman effort, I picked up my bulky boxed-up bicycle, the heavy rear panniers, my sleeping bag, tent and sleeping pad, my handlebar bag and backpack, and the slightly less heavy front panniers and made a beeline for a spot about 10 feet away. Then, again...and again...and again...until I finally made it to the baggage check area, which was not too far away after all; if only it hadn't been for that flight of stairs no one told me about....

With my bike and packs safely stowed away at the baggage check area, I ventured out onto the streets of New York to find Grand Central Station and a train to Rye, New York which was about 20 miles northeast of the city. When I arrived at the station in Rye, one of my old fraternity brothers, Gary Kranz, met me and spirited me away to his home located in one of the comfortable old neighborhoods of this suburban community. It just so happened that Gary and his family were in the middle of their move back to our home state, so this was definitely not the most opportune time for a visiting bicyclist. Even so, Gary and Sally rolled out the red carpet—which had not been packed up yet—and told me to make myself as comfortable as possible amid all the packed boxes and furniture.

During the three days I spent in Rye, I made two trips into the City and the impression this forest of skyscrapers left on me was a lasting one: New York—the Big Apple—an exciting and sometimes sad place to be. It is a city of contrasts—block upon block of towering buildings that touch the sky, and a beautifully landscaped park tucked right in the middle; business people in their button-down suits who always look five minutes late, and tourists strolling the avenues and taking in the sights, looking for that ideal snapshot; limousines with their shaded windows, transporting the rich and famous from one plush setting to the next, and the homeless with all their worldly possessions in a pushcart or a plastic bag—no place to go, no appointments to keep— the empty blank stares that look out on a world that tries not to stare back—to look the other way—a world of which they are not a part, and which doesn't seem to really care. It is a city always in a perpetual motion—constant surges of humanity moving up one street and down the next; traffic jams and the ubiquitous cabbies weaving their way in and out; street vendors hawking everything from purses to pot; street entertainers and musicians attracting passers-by with their impromptu performances, trying to make a living, and some not doing too badly; the hustle and bustle of this cosmopolitan metropolis—a city that never sleeps.

One afternoon I had set aside especially for visiting the New York Metropolitan Museum. I marveled at their collection of Egyptian antiquities and became lost in the Middle Ages as I stood face to face with shining suits of full armor. Their collection of medieval arms and armor is the best in the country and so I had a field day of camera work, the results of which I would send back home to become an enriching part of our school curriculum that deals with the Age of Chivalry. My only regret about this day was that I had not allowed myself enough time to wander through the Met's many galleries of wonderful treasures.

My final night in Rye I spent alone staring at the four blank walls of Gary's empty house. Gary and his family had packed off back to Ohio the day before, but he graciously offered me the use of his empty house, leaving me a spare set of keys. How strange it was—just the empty house, the carpet, and me. As I spread my sleeping bag out for my last night's sleep in the USA for quite a while, I thought about the next day's flight to Europe and what surprises the future held in store for me. There would be many.

The next day I checked in at the Peoples Express counter at Newark Airport with plenty of time to spare. While waiting for my flight time to arrive, I encountered a group of young cyclists—about high school age—who were on their way to a European cycling vacation. I chatted with their group leader and explained the purpose of my trip.

"Hey, how'd you like to give me a handful of those Red Cross pledge cards and I'll pass them out to my kids?" asked the group leader.

I readily agreed to his thoughtful suggestion and eagerly dug out a bundle of my cards from one of my packs. About five minutes later, a pretty little high school gal came over with her card in hand and greeted me.

"I really like what you're doing," she said, referring to my Ride For World Hunger. "I think it's neat and I wish you the best of luck; I hope you make it!"

Again I felt good inside and was happy that I had not given in to the temptation to turn around. I thanked this sensitive little gal and wished her a wonderful time on her cycling adventure, thinking of my own happy experience with last summer's AYH group.

As our 747 lifted off the surface of the runway, I looked down on the shores of my own country and wondered if everything would turn out OK, and if I would see those same shores once again.

TWO

Iberian Peninsula, Sun and Sweat

"Whadaya mean I can't take my fuel bottle with me. My God—I'm going to be traveling in the Third World and I've got to boil my water! Do you want me to die of dysentery?" I shouted at the guard at the British Airways check-in at London's Gatwyck Airport for my connecting flight to Lisbon, Portugal.

"I'm sorry, sir," said the guard, "but that fuel bottle has kerosene in it and there is no way you can take it on the plane."

Deep down I knew he was right. Like a fool, I hadn't even thought about emptying the bottle before my flight. In desperation I tried again. "Oh, come on, I've got to have that fuel bottle. At least let me empty it out."

"I'm sorry, sir, if you try to empty it out in the WC, it will just pollute the groundwater. No, we'll have to confiscate your fuel bottle."

I knew I was fighting a losing battle, so I tossed the guard one last look of Yankee outrage and disgust and reluctantly boarded my flight for Lisbon with visions of some strange Egyptian stomach disorder eating away my insides because I had not been able to boil my water for lack of a fuel bottle.

I arrived on continental Europe in a very poor frame of mind, still angered at the unaccommodating British Airways guard. To make matters worse, my flight didn't arrive in

Lisbon until 6:00 P.M. This meant I would have to assemble my extremely broken down bicycle, find my way into Lisbon, and then find a place to stay all with only a couple of hours of daylight left. Not having any time to fret and feel sorry for myself, I tore into the box of jumbled up cables, tires, frame, and racks and began slapping things together. To my utter amazement, everything seemed to find its way back to its appropriate functioning location and soon I was ready to head into the capital of Portugal. As I pulled onto the main road I headed in what I hoped was the right direction. It was, and soon I found myself entering the heart of a very large and totally unknown city. A feeling of desperation came over me as my daylight ran out quickly. Where would I stay? I had the address of the International Youth Hostel, but I had no idea where it was and I didn't see what appeared to be a hotel in this section of town. Darkness, tired and still fuming about my fuel bottle, no place to stay, pushing up one hill and down the next, searching for a place to lay my weary head—again the question: "What in God's name was I doing here?" At last I came upon a section of the city that appeared to be the economy hotel district. My first fruitless attempts found all accommodations full, but finally I was able to locate a Pensoe (room) near the heart of the city. As I pulled my bike and all my gear into my room and closed the door, I collapsed on the bed that almost sank to the floor and thanked the Lord for the end of a long and frustrating day.

A good night's sleep can do wonders for your attitude and this was the case as I awoke the next morning. I stepped out into the sunshine and the streets that had looked so forbidding the night before now looked interesting and inviting. I joined the multitude of early summer tourists and city inhabitants and wandered up and down the Avenu du Liberdad which was reminiscent of Paris's Champs Elysees. I explored the Alfama, a tangled mass of narrow streets and balconies, full of old world charm and small restaurants tucked away in the most unexpected places; up to the castelo (castle) which overlooks the city and the Tagus River as it threads its way to its union with the Atlantic Ocean. Here was spread before me a panoramic view of this charming, old world city made all the more romantic by the gentle, pastel colors of the evening sky. Again a feeling of contentment swept over me, and I knew I was doing the right thing.

After picking up my mail at the American Express office which I eagerly read with more than a few pangs of homesickness, I placed a call to the United States and soon I was listening to the sweet but sleepy voices of my Mom and Dad. It was 3:00 A.M. Toledo time, but that made no difference to them. I assured them everything was going well and asked them to send me another fuel bottle if they could swing it. Our time was all too short, and I promised them I would try to call again in three or four weeks.

* * *

I was eager to start riding. I was starting out from the westernmost point of the Iberian Peninsula. It was here that those first tentative steps were taken by the explorers of five centuries ago who sought a new route to the exotic treasures of the East, never expecting to find a New World. Now, I would be retracing in the opposite direction the flow of our Western Heritage. Moving from West to East, the culture and history of the land and its people would become more ancient. From Medieval to Roman to Greek to Egyptian—I felt as though it was a journey through time.

However, my start on this journey through time was not very auspicious. Getting out of Lisbon was no easy task, and it took most of a morning to accomplish it. There were only two ways to get across the Tagus—by ferry boat or across a high level suspension bridge which was part of the super highway. Of course, I made the wrong choice and tried the bridge first, which proved impossible because there was just no room, not to mention the fact that I wasn't supposed to be there in the first place. I attracted the strangest stares and all forms of honking and hand gesticulations that seemed to say, "Get off this bridge, you silly ass!" So, it was back down to the ferry where I should have gone in the first place. Once across the Tagus, I was completely lost and burned up more time climbing steep hills that led in every direction but the right one. It was a small miracle that I found my way out, but I did. I soon found that the routes were poorly marked and that it was better to look for the name of the town or village towards which you wanted to travel. At last I was heading in the right direction but by this time I was growing weary which was accompanied again by the feeling of being alone in a strange land. I wished more than ever that I had one or two companions to ease the strain. I was propositioned by some roadside prostitutes, but that was not exactly my idea of a "riding companion." It seems that they do business right on the side of the road—an enterprising idea to be sure. As I entered the village of Vendrado Novas, I knew I could go no farther. A brief search turned up a nice Pensoe for 500 Escudos or about $3. After I washed the day's sweat and grime from my body, I ventured out into this small village in search of food. Not having taken the time to learn my Portuguese, the menu of the small restaurant I located was definitely Greek to me. The old eeny, meeny style of choice, however, resulted in a pleasing meal of pork, salad, bread, and french fries with a fried egg on top. The owner of the establishment watched in amazement as I devoured the dishes before me but smiled widely when he realized that his preparations had indeed hit the spot.

On the 4th of July I paused to silently wish my own country a happy birthday. I thought of my ride through Ohio which now seemed like ages ago. I couldn't imagine the feeling of being on the road for three or four months. The frustrations of my departure from Lisbon melted away as I pushed farther into Portugal. The countryside was gently rolling, and the sun and a cloudless sky were my constant companions. In fact, the sun became too much of a close companion about midday, but then I had to remind myself that this was a Mediterranean land. Portugal reminded me a bit of Southern California—quite dry and parched, with groves of olive or citrus trees dotting the land. I arrived in the historic town of Evora whose cathedral dates back to 12th century. Close by were the ruins of a Roman temple which was constructed in the first or second century A.D. Evora is one of the oldest towns in the Iberian Peninsula, and as a Roman outpost it was known as *Liberalitas Julia*. It was captured from the Moors in 1165 and soon became the second most important city in the kingdom next to Lisbon during the Middle Ages.

As I pushed farther inland toward the Spanish border, the continental climate began to take over from the coastal climate. The sun beat down mercilessly from a cloudless sky; temperatures climbed into the high nineties; long stretches of brick or cobblestone roads rattled my teeth and made my bike sound as though it would fall apart; stretches of uphill seemed twice as long as they really were as the sun sapped my energy. I was beginning to wonder if I would survive even this trip across the Iberian Peninsula. The roads in Portugal were proving to be horrendous, too, especially from the cyclist's viewpoint. Even roads that were major routes could seem like the bombed out Ho Chi Minh Trail during the Vietnam War. It was impossible to tell, no matter what the maps might say.

In spite of the heat and rotten roads, it was not hard to enjoy the quiet beauty and pastoral calm of the countryside. Here and there were situated little villages with their whitewashed walls and red tiled roofs. As I entered the main square of most any village, I might be greeted by the sight of the town's little old men, sitting all in a row on a bench in a shady spot, probably talking of Miguel's cow that recently died or Enrique's wife who hit him over the head with the washbowl. My passage through these sleepy little hamlets probably furnished conversation for days on end, for I'm sure they rarely saw anything like my loaded down, space age bicycle. In fact, I attracted stares and waves from just about everybody—from the town police to the little old ladies dressed completely in black, who sometimes carried bulky baskets on top of their heads.

It had not taken me long to traverse the width of Portugal, it being a rather small country, especially from east to west, and neatly tucked into the western coast of the Iberian Peninsula. From the heavily fortified city of Elvas where I discovered a 600-year old aqueduct that still brings water to the city, I gazed off into the distance and could easily see into neighboring Spain. This would be no quick and easy ride, for I'd heard and read of Spain's wide open plains and her searing midsummer temperatures.

I was finding that those temperatures were not a myth in this sun drenched land. It seemed that the heat would start with a vengeance every day between 11 and 12 o'clock. By mid afternoon the thermometer would climb above 100°F with ease, and the air seemed to shimmer above the land. This did not bode well for me as I crossed the Spanish border and headed for the city of Badahoz. Here I located the youth hostel, but I was a little disconcerted when I saw that there were hundreds of small and some not so small children running this way and that. In Spain, their youth hostel association utilizes school dormitories that apparently function as hostels during the tourist season. I was assigned a room which was also occupied by an older student, but at night it was so stifling hot that I soon found myself out in the much cooler hallway reading a Robert Ludlum novel, dozing off with every other paragraph.

I was also finding that bicycle touring in Spain in the summer was like a desert of discomfort, punctuated here and there with an oasis of pleasure and satisfaction that made my journey through this hot land seem worthwhile—at least I had to tell myself that. I happened on a couple of these oases one morning unexpectedly. The early morning ride had been cool and flat. A rare cloud cover had helped to keep the sun's rays from doing their dirty work so early in the day. The flat terrain made for easy cycling, and my wheels eagerly clicked off the miles. By 11:00 A.M. I'd already counted 35 miles on my odometer.

As I wheeled into the town of Merida for a bit of nourishment, another surprise oasis awaited me. On the walls of the hotel-restaurant were some photographs of Roman ruins. Looking at the innkeeper and drawing on my extensive high school Spanish, I pointed to the pictures and said, "Aqui?" (Here?). He nodded eagerly and explained in broken English that all these ruins could be found in the town. As I soon was to discover, the whole town was covered with Roman ruins— relics of another age and time. Most people when they think of the glory of ancient Rome think only of the city itself and the Italian peninsula. Many do not realize that the tentacles of Roman civilization reached all throughout the Mediterranean world, binding together a multitude of civilized and uncivilized cultures under the banner of one Roman law and society. A look at today's map will reveal that over 30 modern day countries are encompassed within the borders of the old Roman Empire—quite a feat of unification and administration. And here, 1300 miles from the city of Rome, was an excellent example of that pervasive Roman culture. Merida was established in the year 25 B.C. by the order of the Emperor Augustus, also known as Octavian, in order to provide a colony for the veterans of his Legions in the Roman army. It came to be thought of as a "Small Rome" and it featured all the amenities of a typical Roman city: a beautiful theater, an arena that could seat 14,000 people, aqueducts for their water supply, the circus—not the P.T. Barnum type, but a track for the infamous charioteers—and villas for the rich and tenements for the poor.

For the next three to four hours I climbed over and through the crumbling walls, seats, and passageways of the arena where gladiators once fought each other to the death for the glory of their emperor, stood where they once stood gazing nervously up at the provincial governor to pronounce their solemn oath, "Ave Imperator – te morituri te salutant" (Hail Emperor – we who are about to die salute you.) Not far from the arena were the remains of the great theater where Greek and Roman tragedies and comedies were once performed. A few steps more brought me to the remains of a Roman house that featured beautiful mosaics still covering the floors. And then a brief ride over to the circus where chariots and charioteers thundered around the elongated oval with the roar of a frenzied crowd sounding in their ears. Close by stood the remains of an aqueduct that brought water into the center of the city to be distributed to public drawing points or piped into the homes of the rich. A ride across town took me to a Roman bridge that spans the River Guordiana. But here was no ruin, for this is still a functioning bridge that carries modern day traffic. Yes, the Romans built things to last!

By the time I finished exploring this treasure of classical antiquity, it was already well into the afternoon and the heat was making me feel as though I was on "slow bake." I decided that Merida would be my stop for the night, and a half hour's search turned up a room in a hostel for a reasonable price. Unfortunately that reasonable price didn't include the price of a shower which was an extra 100 pesetos. I had a better solution. I imagine the citizens of Merida thought it a peculiar sight as they passed an "Americano" clad only in a brief pair of shorts standing in front of a hostel in the center of the city holding a portable shower bag over his head "oohing" and "aahing" as the water washed away the heat of the day.

In all my years of cycling I had never ridden more than 100 miles in one day. It's kind of a magical mark that all cyclists shoot for sooner or later. It becomes a little more of a challenge when you're carrying 40 to 50 pounds of extra weight. I had just never had the occasion to do it—at least up until now.

I headed northeast out of Merida toward Toledo and Madrid, gliding easily over a broad, level plain. As my wheels gobbled up huge chunks of Spanish countryside, I had time to reflect on the pleasures of the previous day. Yesterday evening in Merida a wonderful aspect of Spanish life had been revealed to me. Earlier in the afternoon, as I had searched for a hostel where I could retreat from the sweltering heat of the midday sun, I took note of the central plaza of the city. As in most European towns, the central plaza or square is a communal meeting spot with outdoor cafes, booths selling ice cream and other delicious treats, and usually a fountain shooting streams high into the air. But the plaza at this time of day was devoid of souls. In fact, the streets seemed deserted—only a few hardy persons ventured out into the heat of the Spanish sun that shimmered and danced on the pavement. Then, in the waning hours of the day as the sun sank below the western horizon, it was as if someone pulled a switch that unlocked a thousand doors. The streets were filled with the residents of Merida, all seeming to migrate toward the central plaza of the city where the sidewalk cafes were now filled and the booths were doing a nonstop business. In the shopping district, which is really a kind of outdoor mall, people walked and window shopped. Some of the shops were open on this Sunday evening, but most were closed. However, they still had all their lights turned on so the window shoppers might have a good view of the merchandise inside. Señors and señoritas strolled arm in arm, sharing an ice cream cone or a fresh limonada. All seemed relieved that the heat of the afternoon had taken a backseat to the cool of the evening. I had joined the wandering throngs and tasted the most heavenly fresh limonada. A fitting conclusion to that exceptional day.

My reflections of the previous day were interrupted by a glance at my odometer which announced the fact that I had covered 55 miles and it was just 12:00. Could this be my first century? As the miles continued to pass beneath my wheels, I could see in the distance the city of Trujillo. This had been the home of Francisco Pizzaro, the conquistador who had subdued the great Incan Empire of South America. Situated atop the highest point in Trujillo was an interesting looking castle that appeared to be a blending of Islamic and Medieval architecture—a remnant of Moorish influence in this part of Spain. This was too much to resist, even with my desire to close in on that magic 100, and so I took a couple of hours to explore the towers and battlements of this imposing structure.

Before I climbed back on my bike, I decided a midday shower would help cool me down. I filled up my water sack and located an alleyway away from the eyes of any curious Truhillians. And then, fully clothed, I performed my North American water dance, fully drenching myself and putting out the fires that seemed to be engulfing my body. My wet clothing provided me with a little natural air conditioning when I began pedaling once again, but only for a short time, for the blistering temperatures soon rendered me dry as a bone. If someone had told me at the 75-mile mark that I had a little bit of a mountain range to cross over, I might have said to myself, "Well, Al, we'll think about 100 miles another day." But, I still felt strong and I traversed the small range with ease. As I closed in on the magic mark I counted it down: 99.5 .. 99.6 .. 99.7 .. 99.8 .. 99.9 .. 100 miles! I gave myself a hearty congratulations and was pleased to find right at the century mark a clean and modern hostel that had another bonus—it was about the most reasonable price for lodging I had encountered thus far in Spain.

Though the temperatures of central Spain were formidable, I was enjoying my ride across this sunbaked piece of earth. Each day I seemed to be carried along on the crest of the wind, swept over the landscape of central Iberia by a breeze that proved to be my friend and not an adversary. The landscape, too, was on my side—flat and rolling plains stretching away as far as the eye could see, reminiscent of our own central and western United States. And always mountains off in the distance, now to the left and then to the right, never daring to approach. The main roads in Spain seemed excellent, with wide margins on either side, making them ideal for bicycling. This was in contrast to Portugal, where even the roads can be a pain in the derriere. Portugal had seemed to be a much poorer country and that had been reflected in the upkeep of their highways.

Every now and then I would have to deal with the sometimes scary feeling of being totally on my own. This could be accentuated by the beautiful but desolate nature of the countryside. Once in a while, on a long day's ride, not having anyone to talk with began to weigh heavily. So, in order to spice things up on those long downhills, I'd sit bolt upright on my bike, as on a throne, sometimes with my arms folded, sometimes outstretched as the wings of an airplane, now doing an imitation of Hawaiian hula dancing, always waving vigorously at oncoming traffic and those passing me and shouting "Hola!" to all. Oh, the looks and doubletakes from my fellow denizens of the highway as they pointed, laughed, and waved back at one crazy cyclist. These were definitely not safe riding practices, but the silliness seemed to combat that feeling of being by myself.

In addition to enjoying the riding, I was finding the Spanish people to be warm and friendly. One evening in the small town of Porta de Montalbon, I was having a bit of a problem locating a room for the night. A kindly Spanish gentleman approached me and indicated to me that he would like to help. I did my best to explain to the fellow in my high school Spanish the nature of my trip and became slightly amazed at myself when he seemed to understand what I was saying. Soon he was guiding me across town to a room that he knew of and when that proved unsuccessful, we marched right back to the same location where we had met. This kind Spaniard seemed genuinely concerned that I find a room for the night and would not rest until I had done so. A few more attempts produced the desired room and I warmly shook his hand and expressed my sincere gratitude, for he had done me a service that I might not have accomplished on my own!

* * *

"Toledo—30 kilometers" read the sign. A brief wave of homesickness tempered with a little déjà vu washed over me. How strange to see a sign telling me I was not too far from my hometown, here, half way round the world. Of course, this was not Toledo, Ohio but Toledo, España, our sister city and namesake. The city fathers of my own hometown made an excellent decision when they chose Toledo for the name of our All-American city at the western tip of Lake Erie, for it is named after one of the most beautiful and romantic cities of the Old World!

Seen from a distance, Toledo, Spain radiates a warmth and an almost golden color that stands in deep contrast to the blue Spanish sky. Situated on a rocky promontory that consists of seven small hills, it overlooks the Tagus River and the surrounding countryside. Its beautiful Gothic cathedral and mighty fortress, the Alcazar, dominate the vistas and beckon one to come explore. For two days I wandered the narrow and twisting streets that resound with the echoes of old Spain, visiting the churches, museums, and monuments which abound. Here also can be found the house of El Greco, the famous Greek painter who adopted Toledo as his own city and created beautiful renderings of it in his painting. On one street corner I paused and looked up at a street sign that said "Calle de Toledo de Ohio" (Street of Toledo, Ohio). Our two cities have had many cultural exchanges and I was warmed by the thought that they had named one of their streets after my own hometown. I felt like shouting out to the residents of this colorful city, "Hey, everyone, I'm from Toledo, Ohio!"

* * *

Protecting your worldly belongings from the legions of thieves that inhabit the great cities of Europe is always a challenge for anyone who travels, be it by bicycle or Lear jet. However, most things that are lost or lifted by Europe's sticky-fingered thieves can be replaced and only present a minor inconvenience, although it may not seem that way at the time. But if one happens to be on a world bicycle tour and your bicycle disappears, then that could very well be the end of the whole show. This was almost my fate in Madrid, Spain's busy capital city!

The ride up to Madrid from Toledo was pleasant but uneventful. However, the closer I came to the city the more crowded and congested things became and the more I had to be on my guard against those would-be bicycle head hunters who seem to abound on the streets of the larger cities. It took me most of the afternoon to thread my way into the heart of the city to the Puerto Del Sol, one of the huge main plazas that in some ways resembles a Spanish Times Square. I soon discovered that the tourist season was in full swing, for my efforts to locate a room met with failure after failure.

I had almost accepted the idea that I would be spending my first night in Madrid on the street along with the other destitute and homeless, but literally at the 11th hour, I was able to find a hotel with a vacant room. Now it's a peculiarity of hotels in many of Europe's larger cities that more than one hotel may be located in the same building. You may find four or five hotels in one building, each one occupying a different floor. My hotel happened to be located on the fourth floor, so I secured my bike with cable and lock down in the lobby, confident that it would be fairly secure. After all, the lobby was not visible from the street and the only people using the lobby would be those who were guests of one of the hotels. I settled in for the night, feeling that sense of relief and ease that comes when you know you have met the challenge of another day and you are in a spot where you can just relax.

The following morning I geared up for an exploration of the city. Before leaving my hotel, I checked my bicycle, cable, and lock to make sure that all was in order. It was, and so I set out for the day. I found Madrid pretty much like other capital cities—cosmopolitan, crowded, fast, exciting, and in some ways depressing. It has the huge monuments, grand boulevards, and the grandiose state buildings that serve as reminders to citizens and visitors alike of Spain's glorious past and its hope for a somewhat uncertain future. And always the destitute, the deformed, the evicted, the old and tired—sitting or lying there pathetically with a bowl in front of them into which passers-by can throw a peseta or two, so maybe they can make it through another day. I wandered up and down the streets and through the huge plazas taking in the flavor of Spain's capital city. I even relieved the pain of the Big Mac attack that I had been suffering periodically by stopping at—you guessed it—McDonald's. I could just have easily stopped in at Burger King, for the hamburger wars are taking place on many different fronts all over the world!

The afternoon was entering its final stages and I decided it was time to return to my hotel. As I entered the hotel lobby, I was startled to see a shady looking Spaniard standing only a couple of feet from my 18-speed Miyata, staring intently at my bicycle. He jerked his head in my direction with a nervous look in his eyes. I glanced at him and then at my bicycle which was still in the spot I had left it, but then I noticed with alarm that the lock had been opened and was no longer securing my bike to the pillar in the lobby. As I advanced toward him, not sure whether I should threaten him with my nonexistent Kung Fu background, he back-peddled a few steps, muttered under his breath in broken English that he was looking for a hotel and then was gone in a flash.

"Whew, that was a close one!" I said to myself. I was positive that had I come back two minutes later, my bike would have been gone, on its way to becoming a permanent resident on the streets of Madrid, and my world tour could very well have come to an inglorious end. Of course, it had been my own carelessness. I had purchased that lock the year before, and it was the kind with only three numbers that could be mixed in only 1,000 combinations. A patient thief with enough privacy could work through all the combinations and eventually hit the right one. This had been a patient thief. I immediately ran out to buy a more secure lock and also determined that from now on, whenever possible, my bicycle would also become my roommate! This had been my first experience with theft on my trip so far, and I had been lucky. It would not be my last, and I would not be as fortunate the next time around!

* * *

"God, nothing seems to be going right!" I cursed at myself as I lay sprawled across the floor of the train compartment in a pile of my packs, camping gear and bicycle. It had just been two days since the almost theft of my transportation and here again I had almost lost my bike along with most of my packs and camping equipment. It seemed as if evil forces were at work trying to separate the two of us. This time, however, a thief was not the culprit, but the Spanish Rail System.

I had decided while staying in Madrid that I would visit the town of Segovia about 40 miles to the northwest, even though it was in the opposite direction from that I was traveling. Here can be found one of the most amazing structures to be seen anywhere in Europe—the Roman aqueduct which has been standing for almost 2,000 years.

Since Segovia was in the opposite direction of my travel, I was allowing myself the luxury of a train ride there and back to Madrid from where I would continue pedaling toward the border of Spain and France. Madrid is a huge city with a number of train stations that send trains off in all directions, so rather than end up in the wrong station I rode northwest out of the city in the direction of Segovia, hoping to hop the train somewhere along the way. Looming in front of me were a substantial series of "bumps" on the surface of the earth, the Guadarama Mountains. I eyed them a little suspiciously for if I were not able to find a train station, I would come to know them much more than I really cared to from atop the seat of my bicycle. At last, in the small village of Pinar de las Rosas, I located the small railway station and prepared to board the approaching train, wondering if the conductor would take kindly to my two-wheeled traveling companion. When the doors opened automatically, I threw all of my equipment and my unloaded bicycle on the train into one of the passenger compartments, falling over a passenger or two, and pretty much making the way impassable for anyone who might want foolishly to pass through.

As my fellow passengers sneaked curious glances at me and my pile of paraphernalia, the compartment door swung open and there, with a look of abject horror on his countenance, was the conductor. His wild facial expression told me that I might be able to stay, but the bicycle would have to go.

"Señor, your bicycle—it must go in de baggage car at de end of the train," he explained in a worried tone. "When de train stops, please take to de back!"

This I readily agreed to, and when the train came to a halt I leaped out the door with bike on shoulder and sprinted for the baggage compartment six cars back, not really certain how long I would have before the doors automatically slammed shut. To my dismay, the baggage car was overflowing and so, in desperation, I tossed myself and machine onto the next passenger car which thankfully was deserted. As the train slowly gathered speed once again, I realized in panic that now I and my bike were in the back of the train while all my other equipment was still five cars forward, totally unattended. As the train slowed for the next stop and the doors swung open, I again leaped and made a mad dash for the front where I found all of my equipment as I had left it. I cast a thankful eye at the honest Spaniards who smiled and pointed to my equipment as if to say "Yes, we were watching it all the time you were gone."

But now, the reverse was true—I and my equipment were in the front of the train and my bicycle sat unattended five cars back. I knew what was coming next. As the train slowed and the doors swung open one more time, I made my third and final leap. In the middle of my 50-yard dash, equipment hanging off every appendage of my body, I heard the whistle signaling the start of the train. With less than a half-second to spare, I literally dove in the nearest door just as it sealed shut—another close call! I lay there a moment in a daze, contemplating the image of me standing there on the side of the tracks waving good-bye to my bicycle as it proceeded merrily on its way to Segovia, minus its rider!

When I caught the first sight of the aqueduct in Segovia, I knew all the hassle had been worth the effort. This aqueduct, just one of the mighty engineering achievements of the Romans, had brought precious water to the people of this city for close to two millennia. It was still in use only a couple of decades ago. It was constructed sometime between the 1st and 2nd century A.D., possibly during the reigns of the emperors Trajan and Hadrian. The Romans did not invent the arch, but it is almost as if they had perfected its use in this engineering marvel. It is an imposing sight, constructed of huge blocks of stone without the aid of mortar or cement and it consists of 167 arches reaching a height of nearly 90 feet in the middle and running a length of nearly 900 feet. It was partially destroyed by one of the Moorish leaders of Toledo, Spain in 1052, but was restored during the reigns of Ferdinand and Isabella. The only modern restoration has been to reinforce the base of the aqueduct where the wheels of chariots have now been replaced by the wheels of 20th century traffic, causing considerable road vibration and potential damage to the structure. This tremendous achievement, unlike some of the darker aspects of Rome's legacy, attests to the ability of man in any age to build something lasting and good—something that contributes to life, and does not degrade or destroy it!

* * *

"Say, why don't you give me one of your Red Cross pledge cards; I'd be glad to send $20 to my Red Cross chapter when I get home to California."

This was Tony, a psychology professor at Sonoma State College on the West Coast whose acquaintance I made during my brief one-night stay at Segovia youth hostel. He was touring the continent over his three-month hiatus and so far he had enjoyed every minute of it. He seemed to be a friendly and easy-going chap, and when I explained about the purpose of my trip, he willingly volunteered to contribute to the cause. Again I felt good about what I was doing and happy that I had endured my athletic train ride to Segovia.

"Best of luck on the rest of your trip; what you're doing is a real worthwhile thing," said Tony the next morning as we shook hands in farewell. This morning I was also going to learn a little bit of a lesson about buying less than the best equipment for a world bicycle tour. As I set out for the train station for the trip back to Madrid, my mood was in tune with the sunny skies over Segovia. As I sailed down a gentle downhill, without warning, my bicycle came to a screeching halt. In front of me there was no apparent reason for my sudden termination of forward flight, but looking behind me was a different story. There in the road, like a cart with no wheels, was my luggage rack with rear panniers still attached. The bracket under the seat that holds everything upright had broken clean off. With my mood no longer in tune with the aforementioned sunny skies, I sought out a shop that could drill a new hole for my bracket. In a foreign country it seems even the simplest things become difficult, and this was no exception. It took me most of the morning to accomplish the task and all the while I cursed myself for not having bought a sturdier rack. I had compromised when purchasing some of my equipment for my world tour, paying too much attention to price and not enough to quality. I was to learn this lesson again when I made it to Egypt, but the next time I would pay dearly for it and barely escape serious injury!

After my return to Madrid, I picked up my long awaited and treasured mail at the American Express office and then immediately headed northwest out of the city. I soon found myself in a desolate but beautiful region of the country, in some ways very much similar to our Dakota Badlands. It was here, on the ride from Alcala to Ariz, that I was to chalk up my second 100-miler. It was a day on which, even though I was becoming a little tired and crazed by the sun, it seemed that I could have gone on for hours. The terrain was a smorgasbord of variety featuring rolling plains, fields of wheat and barley whipped to and fro by the warm summer breezes, narrow valleys nestled between mountains on either side, and rocky gorges etched in deep colors of red, orange, and yellow. The miles kept mounting and then, a wonderful deep and narrow gorge with high cliffs surrounding it, offering their proof of centuries of erosion from the forces of nature.

It was on days like this that my thoughts would wander, and as I rode I would try to imagine what the land must have looked like a thousand years ago, or even two thousand, when it was an outlying province of the Roman Empire. Images of that time could be seen in the faces and lives of the people of the small villages— farmers out working their fields—the sheep herders marching their flocks from one pasture to the next, a symphony of bells announcing their passage—all performing their daily tasks that probably have not changed greatly over the centuries, content in the knowledge that the pattern of their lives is as it should be.

The little town of Ariz came into view just as my odometer clicked over 100 miles, and a brief search turned up an inn that looked as though it might have one guest each month. An elderly couple ran the establishment, and as I entered encrusted with 100 miles of sweat and road grime, they greeted me with a friendly smile. The kindly matron showed me to a comfortable room on the second floor and indicated that I should immediately fall right into the shower. After completing the no small task of cleaning myself up, I returned to the first floor dining room that contained all of two tables and asked if I might have a spot of food. My hostess nodded her agreement, but instead of showing me a menu, in a short time she brought out a plate heaped full of pork and the most heavenly plate of beans and potatoes cooked with stewed tomatoes. My hosts watched in quiet amazement as I devoured these and washed it all down with four beers and two cokes that were only partially successful in satiating my unquenchable thirst!

* * *

Holy Toledo! It just ain't true—the rain in Spain does not fall mainly on the plain! In fact, it didn't seem to fall at all. These were my thoughts as Northeastern Spain passed beneath my wheels. It was one hot and sunbaked land during the summer. But though the land was barren and brown, parched by the warm Spanish sun, it still had a great beauty all its own, and I was really enjoying the challenge of the temperatures and terrain.

The geography of this section of the country was quite fascinating. The land seemed to be a series of plateaus, one leading to the next through adjoining valleys. You could be riding on one level, and then drop down into the "basement", then back up again to the "first floor", and sometimes all the way to the second. It was almost as if you were standing on the landing of a stairway and you had the ability to see the floor below you and the floor above you at the same time. Additionally, there always seemed to be hills, some aspiring to be mountains, off in the distance which gave truth to the statement that Spain is the second most mountainous country in Europe.

Free camping was never a problem and really quite a joy in this arid and sparsely populated region. One evening I found myself standing stark naked in the middle of one of the vast plains that surrounds the city of Zaragosa, taking my evening shower with my handy-dandy water sack that I could just hold over my head. There were no camp fees; no hassles; complete privacy; totally self-contained. When it was time to set up camp for the night, I would stop to fill my water sack which was enough for a shower, cooking, and drinking. Then I would ride on a little farther and look for a deserted spot in the middle of nowhere, as far as possible off the highway—and that is where I would set up camp. I could see for miles and miles in every direction from the site I had chosen on this evening, and the sunset was a breathtaking show played out on the western stage. When the final curtain had fallen, I nestled down into my ringside seat to watch the nightly stellar parade across the dark Spanish sky that seemed to engulf all that was around me. Though I was alone, I didn't feel lonely, but instead privileged to be able to witness such an extraordinary sight!

This vast area of plains and plateaus seemed to go on forever, but I knew it would come to an end soon, for ahead of me now lay another milestone of my journey. It was in the shape of the massive mountain barrier that lies on the border of Spain and France. As the snow crested peaks of the Pyrenees Mountains gently came into focus, I felt the tingling sensation and the butterflies that a marathoner experiences as he stands at the starting line waiting for the start of his 26-mile ordeal. This would be a marathon, too, of sorts but more of the vertical rolling variety. It would be me against the mountains with only my strength, stamina and willpower to aid me in winning to the mountain pass that would send me sailing into Southern France. I was looking forward to the test.

The physical test was not the only reason for my anticipation, but also because these mountains had been the stage where so many of history's players had acted out their scenes. It was these very same mountains that the great Carthagenian general, Hannibal, had crossed 2,226 years before, leading his host of 90,000 soldiers and 37 war elephants down into the Italian boot to wreak havoc in Rome's backyard. And it was also here in the Pyrenees in the Vale of Renceveaux that Charlemagne's rear guard was ambushed by the Moors, and his brave but proud comrade, Roland, refused to blow his horn to summon aid before it was too late. This was one of the legends that became an inspiration for Europe's knightly class during the Age of Chivalry. It was exciting to think I would be crossing these mountains that had been witness to some of history's great events!

As I began climbing that first grade, however, I soon forgot about Hannibal's elephants and Roland's horn and became more concerned with Al's legs and knees and how they would stand up to the stress of some heavy-duty pumping. In addition to the physical exertion, I also had to battle the bumps and grinds of a terrible road that was home to a number of potholes that were happily lying in wait, ready to swallow one or both of my wheels. I bumped and bounced my way ever higher and soon ran into some dust-choking road construction, which at least indicated that the Spanish government was trying to remedy the road conditions, although I don't believe road construction and bicycling make the best of mates. Even all bad things must come to an end and, before long, the construction ended and the road smoothed. The grade of that first rugged climb leveled out and I then found myself pedaling easily into an Alpine wonderland.

I became lost in the beauty and majesty surrounding me. The Pyrenees seemed like jewels standing tall on the border between Spain and France—silent sentinels over one of nature's finest displays. They have witnessed the passing of eons, human history really only a day in their life span. Armies have come and gone, traversing these rugged slopes. It is not the tallest of mountain ranges, or the longest, or even the widest, but still a work of art by the Ultimate Artist. I guessed that this was a good reason for being here in this spot, to be doing what I was doing; to see this and to appreciate it in a way most people will never be able to—moving silently and slowly across the Artist's canvas, with time to look and wonder and reflect on how beautiful this world of ours can be!

Though the scenery was magnificent, I considered it a crime that most of the scenic pulloffs were cluttered with garbage and litter. I couldn't understand why anyone, be they native or tourist, would want to spoil such natural beauty which should be a source of pride and enjoyment for all who pass this way. Another drawback to this idyllic setting was the all too typical European motorists who all seem to drive these mountain roads as if they were on the Grand Prix Circuit. I decided that there must be some code of the highway that says a driver must round all curves on two wheels and flail away at the horn at every ten second interval whether someone is in the way or not.

In spite of the rugged mountain terrain, I had logged 75 miles on this first day in the Pyrenees, and my body was pointing that fact out to me as I pedaled into a campground located in a picturesque valley tucked in-between tall mountain peaks. The temperatures were much cooler now at these upper elevations and it was welcome relief from the torrid climate of central Spain. This campground also had the added bonus of a swimming pool, and a soothing soak helped relax muscles that had been put to the test. Feeling clean and refreshed, I slipped into a set of snug, warm clothing and settled back to watch the final rays of sunlight dance across the mountain tops. As the alpine twilight took hold, small campfires sprung up around me, adding their special aroma to the clean mountain air. The rumblings in my stomach told me I was not paying it the proper respect it deserved and so I headed over to the camp canteen where a king-size Spanish hamburger, fried potatoes, and three quick beers turned me into one mellow fellow! As I floated back to my tent, I contemplated all that Spain and Portugal had thrown at me over the last month and I was happy that I had met the challenge. I now looked forward to the beauty and history of Southern France, especially its famed Côte d' Azur —the French Riviera.

THREE

La Côte d'Azur

"Bon jour, Monsieur! Comment Alles-vous?" said the French border crossing guard. I figured someone had thrown another one of those switches, for everyone was now speaking French while only a few yards away, they were all speaking Spanish. That was one of the amazing things about traveling in Europe—the variety of languages and cultures that exist side by side. In the border areas many of the people are bilingual, but here, language is more than just a means of communication—it is a source of national pride. It was too bad though, because I was just beginning to feel I could make myself understood in Spanish and even understand what was being said to me.

While standing at the border crossing station the congregating clouds above me sent their message of forewarning. My rain gear had not seen the outside of my packs since Pennsylvania, but I guessed that would change very soon. But sure enough, I looked back into Spain and there the sun was still shining brightly. I smiled to myself and supposed that maybe even the sun needed a passport to cross the border into France.

I had also assumed that the border crossing was located at that long-sought-after mountain pass that would catapult me out of the Pyrenees down into the verdant fields of French Languedoc. There I was wrong again. The road seemed to lead only upward and so I resumed my climb as the first rain drops announced their presence on my helmet and panniers. Before long, I was engulfed in a swirling mist that floated across the alpine meadows. Soaked and chilled to the bone,

I reminisced about the dry heat of central Spain and thought that maybe it wasn't quite that bad after all! I sought refuge in a small mountain village where a quaint restaurant/inn provided me with the hot chocolate that my insides required. It was still early in the afternoon, but I just couldn't make myself move, not wishing to descend to another level of discomfort by venturing out into the cold mountain shower. For two hours I sat and watched the rain-laden clouds roll across the mountain sides and debated whether or not I really had the pioneer camping spirit for that night. An hour later I had my answer as I soaked in a steaming hot tub that was down the hall from a snug room with a comfortable bed that soon would contain one weary cyclist.

For three days I had been climbing up, up, and up—not a really steep grade, mind you, but I knew I wasn't on a downhill. For three days I had been looking for that downhill out of the Pyrenees. I found it at about noon on July 24. Over the next two hours and thirty miles I had one of the greatest rides of my life. As I crested the col or mountain pass, I paused to take in the spectacular vista spread before me, tighten the strap on my helmet, batten down the hatches, and I let her rip. Downward, ever downward on a downhill that seemed to know no end. What a magnificent ride through alpine meadows, forests of pine and birch, and narrow water-hewn gorges! It was a feast for the senses: the wind whistling through my helmet, the scent of the pine forests, the sun-drenched mountains contrasting with a deep azure sky. I found myself braking quite often, not from the dangerous descent, but because I wanted to—needed to—capture the moment, savor it, and keep it for the times ahead when things would get rough and my resolve might weaken. It was the memory of times like these that I hoped would keep me going!

About midway in my descent there appeared a picture-book mountain village that seemed to be an excellent spot to seek some appeasement for my protesting belly. I leisurely wandered from shop to shop buying some French bread, a little fromage (cheese), a few slices of jambon (ham), a big, red, juicy pomme (apple), and a couple of bottles of Orangina, that heavenly citrus soda drink that can really wet your whistle. I sat down with my impromptu feast in the village square to enjoy the warm sunshine filtering down through the tall trees overhead and the parade of tourists and travelers passing by. Before resuming my downward plunge, I made the first of many, many stops at a patisserie to select at least two of those sinful baked goods that the French are noted for. I was reminded of my bike tour three years before in the Canadian Rockies when our group of hungry cyclists raided one of the mountain bake shops. On that day I had walked out with no less than six different sweet delights, all of which I devoured within the next hour. I was getting better, but my sweet tooth was still my Achilles Heel!

I was now well into the lower elevations and with the lower elevations came the increase in temperature. In fact, I was finding the temps of southern France to be on a par with those of central Spain. It was downright hot!

Luckily, my choice of campground for the night had a swimming pool which seemed to be a standard feature of campgrounds hereabouts. Camping and caravaning is a favorite way for Europeans to spend their holiday, and so most of the campgrounds have excellent facilities that provide for some of the creature comforts. After a dip in the ol' swimming hole, I fired up my stove and began preparing my dinner of rice and vegetables.

"Bon jour, Monsieur," said the small voice behind me. This was Etienne, my little neighbor from the adjoining campsite. He was soon joined by his smaller brother and they became very interested and absorbed in my preparations for dinner. We conversed, they in French and I in English, and it was almost as if we understood what the other was saying. I threw in a few French words that I knew to give our conversation some kind of meaning, and we all got on famously.

After I finished my dinner, Etienne again appeared and invited me over to his campsite for an apéritif. His parents were waiting for me with a bottle of wine and a comfortable chair in front of their campfire. Their English was much better than my French so we were able to communicate semi-easily. They expressed to me their love of this part of their country and then pulled out their maps to show me all the highlights that I had to visit. I soon felt as comfortable as I did with my own family, and so we passed the evening in easy conversation and relaxation. Before I returned to my own campsite, I pulled a couple of balloons from the pack I was carrying in my pannier for just this purpose. When I blew them up, I could see my two little friends' eyes light up, and they thought that this small gift was really quite wonderful. I bade them all good night and thanked them for a more than pleasant evening!

This area of southwestern France through which I was now traveling historically was called Languedoc, which took its name from the language that was spoken here. The prize jewel of this region for which I set my course is the medieval, walled city of Carcassonne. And what a jewel it was and is! Sometimes referred to as the Maid of Languedoc, "La Cité" is the largest and best preserved medieval town in all of Europe. When I first caught sight of this relic of the middle ages, I think my mouth was agape. It sits high and proudly on a hill overlooking the River Aude and the lower, newer city at its base. In its heyday it was a nearly impregnable fortress surrounded by not one, but two walls that are still punctuated with over fifty turreted towers. What an amazing sight!

Carcassonne had always had a strategic importance because of its location in the shadow of the Pyrenees Mountains on the border of France and Spain. Its history dates back to pre-Roman times when the hill on which Carcassonne sits was fortified. A colony of Roman veterans was established in the later stages of the empire, and it was they who began construction of the high, inner wall. After the Roman Empire fell, the area fell under the control of that jolly group of barbarians, the Visigoths, who ruled for a couple of hundred years. Next in line were the Saracens, or Moslems, but they only hung around for a short time before they were pushed back into Spain by the father of Charlemagne who went by the name of Pepin the Short.

During the twelfth century "La Cité" was ruled by the Viscounts of Trencavel, one of the many French baronial families who definitely had minds of their own and always thought it a bad idea to give anything more than lip service to the French king. It was during this period that the castle and beautiful basilica or cathedral within the walls of the town were built and this was one of the happiest and most prosperous times for the "Maid of Languedoc." Yes, this was the Age of Chivalry when the heavily armored, mounted knight reigned supreme on the battlefield and when wandering minstrels and troubadours visited towns such as Carcassonne and spread their musical tales of legend and lore—tales like that of the Song of Roland who met his end not far from here in the Vale of Thorns high in the Pyrenees.

The beginning of hard times for Carcassonne began in the thirteenth century with the spread of something called the Albigensian Heresy. Of course, all of Europe at this time was a Christian world and anyone who didn't see eye to eye with the Church was labeled a heretic. The Albigensians were a group of believers who definitely had one eyeball going in the opposite direction. They believed that the world was created by two forces: one for good and one for evil—in other words, God and the Devil. God ruled over the mind and the spirit while the devil controlled all the physical things of the world, including the body. Because ol' Satan owned your body, it was to be neglected. The most fanatic starved themselves, never washed, and never messed around or made babies, since procreation was considered sinful. In a nutshell, this was, without a doubt, not a fun group of people to hang around with.

Even Pope Innocent III thought they needed to lighten up a little. Actually he became pretty irate that they were trying to steal his show in the South of France, and so he sent out formal invitations to the French nobles of the north for an "all-expenses paid" crusade to the south of France to help besiege the city of Carcassonne which happened to be a stronghold of the Albigensian Heresy.

By 1226 "La Cité" had come under control of the French king, Louis VIII, and he and his successor, Louis IX, otherwise known as St. Louis, undertook the task of making this a mighty fortress, much as it appears today.

I located the clean and modern youth hostel right in the heart of the old city which is a maze of narrow, winding streets which still is home for eight hundred or so of Carcassonne's residents. I spent the next day and a half eagerly exploring the town and its formidable defense fortifications. "La Cité" consists of a lower outer wall and a higher inner wall, one third of which dates back to Roman times, and of course, the castle itself. This means you have a fortress within a fortress. In looking at the walls it's very easy to determine which parts were built by the Romans and which parts were constructed in a later period. Some of the towers within the walls were actually designed as fortresses in themselves with their own wells, ovens, and latrines in case they were cut off from the rest of the city. It was also interesting to see that most of the lower towers in the outer wall are open on the back so that if the outer wall was taken, the attackers would have no cover.

One of the favorite legends about Carcassonne concerns the great Frankish king, Charlemagne. He had been besieging the city for close to five years but couldn't quite seem to finish it off. Inside, the defenders were starving and down to their last provisions when a spunky little old lady called Dame Carcas came up with a brilliant idea. She chased down her last pig and stuffed it full of the last grain that could be found anywhere in the city. The old Dame, with a little help from her friends, hauled the bloated sow to the top of the walls and tossed the poor porker off where it landed at Charlemagne's feet and burst open, spreading grain hither and yon. Charlemagne concluded that if they had enough grain to do crazy things like that, then they had enough food to withstand the siege, and he called off the whole shooting match.

My two days here were exceptional and I considered it to be one of the highlights of my travels so far. Although much restoration work has been done, being in "La Cité" allowed me to take a step back into the middle ages and achieve a sense of what life must have been like in this impregnable medieval fortress!

In my many miles across Portugal and Spain, I had noticed not only a definite lack of precipitation, but also a paucity of other cyclists going my way or coming from the opposite direction. In truth, I seemed to be the only one crazy enough to brave the midsummer climate of the Iberian Peninsula. But now, as I loaded up my cycle in Carcassonne in preparation for the day's ride toward the Mediterranean coast, another touring cyclist emerged from the youth hostel and cast a friendly eye in my direction.

"Vous etes un Américan?"inquired the French cyclist, wanting to know if I was an American.

"Oui," I replied, just about exhausting my French vocabulary for this particular situation.

"Hey, that's great; if you're heading toward Narbonne, maybe we can ride together," was his unexpected response. It turned out that the "French cyclist" was really from Detroit, Michigan, about fifty miles north of my hometown, and he happened to speak some pretty fair French. Mark Gemerly was a big, friendly fellow with a curly shock of hair and he had been touring throughout France for most of the summer. He still had a couple more weeks to go on his tour before heading home to the States, and so we decided to head toward Narbonne and the coast as a twosome. Neither of us suspected that the next day would be the last day of his bike tour as we wheeled out of the gates of "La Cite."

Mark was using a better scale map than I, and so we were able to follow mostly the picturesque back roads through the lush fields of Languedoc. I had learned from previous bike tours that cycling almost anywhere in France is a joy because the secondary roads, even the small country lanes, are so smooth and well maintained. Every now and then we would stop at some old ruin or chateau that we saw indicated on the map to see if it was open to explore.

We pedaled leisurely into the coastal city of Narbonne early in the afternoon and immediately sought out a sidewalk cafe where Mark had a chance to practice his French with two little girls about twelve or thirteen years of age who seemed eager to talk to a couple of Americans. After provisioning ourselves for dinner, we headed out to the beach, past the official campground, and pitched our tents on a sandy dune overlooking the calm waters of "La Mer." It had been a good day, and we both slept well that night on our soft beds of sand.

The next morning we rose early and broke camp on our private sand dune overlooking the sea. We pushed out to the main road and headed east toward Avignon. Again the pace was leisurely, the skies sunny as they always seemed to be here in southern Europe.

About midmorning as we were winding our way up a gentle grade, Mark yelled over his shoulder to me, "Hold up, Al. Let's pull off to the side of the road for a minute."

As I pulled up alongside him, he had a perplexed look on his face and was down carefully inspecting his Fuji bicycle. "I don't know; something just doesn't feel right—it's really strange," he mused.

He continued his careful inspection and then, "God damn! Would ya' look at that! Just look at that! My frame is cracked clean in two! Can ya' believe that?" His frame had cracked just where the two down tubes come together at the bottom bracket.

"No wonder I felt like I was riding on a bike of silly putty," he continued. "Oh well, this old Fuji has seen a lot of use over the last ten years—lot of stresses put on this frame. Good thing my tour is just about over. No problem— I'll just pick me up a backpack and finish it on the hoof and with my thumb."

I admired his stoic good cheer. I pictured myself in the same situation rolling on the side of the road, kicking the air, beating my chest, and finally wrapping my bicycle around the nearest telephone pole.

We got back on our cycles and slowly, very slowly, made our way into the city of Berzier. I kept waiting for Mark's Fuji to collapse into a pile of tubes, racks, and packs, but luck was with us and everything held together. We searched out a bicycle shop where Mark was going to attempt to unload his frame and then we shook hands and wished each other the best for the future. I had enjoyed his company for the short day and a half and was sorry he wouldn't be able to continue on with me.

Not long after Mark and I parted ways, my spirits hit the doldrums. I had been riding a high the last week or so: I had conquered Spain—well, sort of; my fantastic crossing of the Pyrenees; exploring historic and enthralling Carcassonne; picking up a little company along the way. I knew it couldn't last. Now, as I headed back toward the coast I battled a stubborn head wind—head winds and low points always seemed to coincide—and I was becoming tired of the daily grind and the constant exertion. I was hot and sweaty. My clothes had not been washed for three or four days. The youth hostel I was looking for appeared to be up an unbelievably steep hill. When I got there I found it overcrowded and not worth the effort. And of course, I was thinking of my own family and the comforts of my own home. All of this I was feeling. I hoped it would pass—it usually did. I had learned from experience that when you head into a nosedive, you have to wait it out; look for the positive in whatever you can. Something good usually came along to set things straight again. That something good was not too far off.

Whenever fellow travelers inquired about my trip and I explained to them the nature and scope of my journey, they would usually let out with some expletive like "Wow!" or "Hey, fantastic!" Well, when I talked to the young Japanese fellow at the hostel in the city of Sète, it was my turn to make with the expletives. This young Japanese adventurer had been walking around the greater part of the world for the last two years and nine months. He began in eastern Australia and walked from Sydney to Perth, crossing the vast and empty Nullibor Plain which is as about "outback" and desolate as you can get in the Land Down Under! Then, hopping to Malaysia, he had trekked all the way from Singapore to southern France, crossing Southeast Asia, India, Pakistan, Iran, Turkey, Greece, Yugoslavia, Italy, and France. On one leg he proudly bore the scars of an unfriendly canine encounter in Turkey, where I had heard some of the dogs would just as soon take off your hand as fetch a bone. Another time a truck swerved into his path on the side of the road and knocked him for a loop, his backpack being the only thing that saved him from serious injury or worse!

"Where to next?" I asked.

"I go to Spain to learn the country," he said in broken English, "and then I do not know."

I took my leave of the youth hostel in Sète, still very much in awe of the accomplishments of the young traveler from Japan, and set my sights for the French city of Nimes. About midway between Sète and Nimes is the city of

Montpelier, which was the site of one of the great medieval schools of medicine, and it was here that a wonderful experience was waiting for me.

In making preparations for my world tour, I had become a member of a worldwide organization known as SERVAS which tries to promote world peace and understanding by encouraging contact between the diverse cultures of our planet. SERVAS consists of host families around the globe who open their homes to travelers from other countries. It is a wonderful opportunity to experience the culture and family life of another country firsthand. Near Montpelier I made my first SERVAS contact.

I placed a call to the home of Francis and Marité Ginestet. It was Marité who answered the phone and she was excited to hear from an American bicyclist. They would be more than happy to have me come and visit their home for one or two days. Marité met me in the small village nearby her home and then guided me a short way out into the country where her small but comfortable house was set in a beautiful and peaceful location looking out on the Massif Central, or the front range of France's central mountains.

When I arrived, it appeared as though a family gathering was in progress. I was introduced to Francis, Marité's husband, and to his brother and his wife and family. We all sat down at a large outdoor table laden with fresh fruits, vegetables, meat, bread, and of course, wine. Marité's English was quite good, but Francis and his relatives were not quite as accomplished, so Marité acted as our interpreter a good part of the time. Even though communication was a little difficult at times, we talked and laughed and joked while we ate and drank and we even made a game out of pointing things out on the table. They would give the French word and I would come back with the English equivalent. In no time at all I felt very comfortable with this nice group of people—just like a member of their family.

"Alan, I wish to show you something very special—the Pont Romain (Roman Bridge). Please, come. We take the auto," said Francis after we had finished our meal. We all piled into their compact car and set out across the evening landscape, ending up at a spot far off the beaten track. This was obviously a site not visited by a lot of tourists during the year and that made it all the more special and really quite amazing! We walked a short way down a path and then clambered down the steep banks of a small river. There, standing isolated and alone in the middle of the stream was a magnificent Roman arch that had formed part of the bridge which centuries ago carried the road across the river. This road had been part of the main route between Italy and Spain at the height of Rome's power. Over this bridge Roman legions would march on their way to the far outposts of the empire, and traders carrying the commerce of the known world would travel safely from town to town. Walking a little way up a hill, we came upon part of the old Roman road that still bore the tracks of countless chariots and carts that had passed this way over two thousand years ago. I was astounded! In awe, I stooped down and slowly ran my hands along the grooves that had been worn into the cobblestone surface by noisy, iron-rimmed wheels—listening, trying to hear the echoes of the past—trying to capture a sense of a different time—a different world—a Roman world.

I spent two days with Francis and Marité and their little son, and they were the kindest of people, treating me as one of their own. Their lifestyle seemed to be so relaxed and simple. All our meals were taken outdoors so as to enjoy the beauty of the land—seemingly the natural thing to do—and to almost feel one with the environment.

"I am a man of the country," explained Francis. "I do not like the city. This is where I wish to live."

I made my farewells to Francis and Marité, thanking them for their great kindness and hospitality, and set out on a crisp, fresh morning, my renewed attitude matching the blue skies. I returned to the site of the Roman bridge because I just had to see it again and also to snap some worthy photos, and then I headed for Nimes, another treasure trove of Roman history, stopping somewhere along the way for what some people might call an unusual lunch: two pieces of French pastry, potato chips, and two beers.

* * *

Nimes, A.D. 105

Corvinus stood proudly on the floor of the cavernous arena before the provincial governor, the hot Mediterranean sun sending rivulets of sweat down his heavily-muscled torso. On either side of him were forty-nine other men, much like himself—strong, proud, brutal, skilled death dealers, professional gladiators. They would all engage in combat later this day; for some of them it would be their last day in this world. In honor of the great military victories of their beloved emperor, Trajan, games and festivities were being staged all throughout the empire. In Rome itself the games had been going on for over one hundred days where close to ten thousand beasts had been slaughtered on the floor of the Flavian Amphitheater (The Colosseum).

At the sound of the trumpets, Corvinus turned in unison with his fellow combatants. They began their slow procession around the floor of the arena, responding to the cheers and cries of the twenty thousand Roman spectators who jostled for position in order to catch a glimpse of their favorite gladiators. Corvinus had fought ten times—and won ten times—in smaller arenas and his reputation had preceded him and it was acknowledged by the multitude. But he had never fought in an arena such as this before. He let his eye wander to the uppermost reaches of the immense amphitheater, second largest in all the empire. What an amazing structure! So colossal, so magnificent—tier upon tier of stone seats that rose to over sixty feet above the ground level and interspersed at regular intervals with exits that led to descending ramps which could empty twenty thousand people in ten minutes.

Of course, the best and most comfortable seats were on the lower level, reserved for the provincial governor, government magistrates, and visiting dignitaries. Behind them could be found seating for the plebeians (middle classes), soldiers, and priests. Women were relegated to the upper levels, segregated from the men, and the poorest of the poor could fight for the standing room at the very top level. Corvinus' reputation would be at stake in this glorious setting today; he fully intended to protect that reputation.

The gladiators completed their slow circuit around the perimeter of the arena. Once more standing in front of the governor, they extended their arms in salute and together uttered their solemn oath,

"Ave Imperator, morituri te salutant." (Hail Emperor—those about to die salute you.)

Retiring to the gladiatorial waiting area—part of the maze of rooms, animal pens, and criminal cells that lay under the massive tiers of stone seats—they began to prepare themselves mentally for the coming ordeal. There could be no more physical training; that was finished. Now their minds and wills had to take over from the grueling physical preparation. Corvinus found a quiet corner where a small window gave him an unobstructed view of the amphitheater floor, and fell into silent reverie.

On the floor of the arena, the first part of the day's program was already under way. Where gladiators had stood five minutes before, now scores of wild beasts roamed, stalked, charged, and fiercely attacked each other. There were tigers from the far eastern provinces, leopards from Asia Minor, lions and elephants from Africa, and wild bulls from the northern borders of the empire. The arena floor soon became a swirling vortex of savage animal cries and bloodied beasts that continued to rip at each other's flesh even until their last breath. The blood added to the savagery of their attacks and fed the mounting excitement of the crowd.

The animals' attention soon became diverted by a new threat—a troupe of Bestiarii silently appeared and carefully approached the crazed animals. These were the beastmen or professional hunters whose special skills allowed them to cut down and ruthlessly butcher the remaining animals with knives and spears and axes. Soon the arena floor was littered with the carcasses of the once ferocious beasts that roamed no more and the mangled remains of one Bestiarii whose agility had deserted him at the most important moment.

Corvinus saw that the first part of the day's festivities was nearly completed and he watched indifferently as slaves spread a new layer of sand over the bloody reminders of the preceding agony. His mind drifted back to his homeland in far away northern Gaul along the banks of the great, swift-running river (the Rhine). He had been a peaceful farmer, a member of a clan belonging to one of the many Gaulic bar-barian tribes that had settled quietly along the borders of the great empire to the south. But the harvest had been bad one year, and he helped lead a raid on one of the Roman frontier outposts in order to secure enough food to insure that his family would survive the brutal northern winter. He had been captured and soon found himself sentenced to serve as an oarsman in one of the Roman galleys that plied the waters of "Mare Nostrum" (Our Sea), the Roman's name for their great inland sea (Mediterranean Sea). It was there, because of his great size and formidable strength, that Corvinus had come to the attention of the manager of a traveling company of gladiators. He became the property of Junius Brutus who provided the best gladiator training possible. Corvinus learned quickly and was soon designated a Hoplomachi, that class of gladiators noted for their great size and strength. Corvinus had lived up to his expectations over the last five years, and he was now on the brink of fame and, yes, even fortune.

He started at an anguished cry that came from the arena floor and directed his gaze out the small window, and what he saw surprised even him. A number of poor, wretched fellow humans were bound hand and foot to posts while packs of starvation-crazed wild dogs and hyenas tore away huge chunks of human flesh. These common criminals had been condemned to the arena floor to furnish the grisly enter-tainment for the second part of the day's program. These Romans certainly craved variety in their thirst for a bloody spectacle, thought Corvinus. Most of the smaller arenas where he had fought so far featured only the gladiatorial combats. He turned his eyes away, for this seemed obscene even to him.

At the eighth hour of the day (about 2:00 p.m.) the trum-pets heralded the start of the long-awaited gladiatorial combats. Magically, the floor of the arena had been trans-formed into a landscape with miniature hills, trees, and even a small lake. First to appear on the newly-created stage of battle were two teams of gladiators, each composed of the different styles of specialized fighters. There were the huge, heavily-muscled Hoplomachi, the lightly-armed Thracians, and the Retiarii, who faced death with only a net and triple-pronged trident. The crowd squirmed with anticipation in the hot Mediterranean sun, for they always loved variety and mismatches were highly thought of. Here they would have their fill.

The sound of metal crashing against metal reverberated throughout the arena as the combat commenced. The gladiators fought in small groups, retreating and attacking over the hills, around the trees, and into and through the shallow lake, showing great ardor in their desire to remain among the living. The crowd became swept up in the bloody panorama before them, cheering enthusiastically those combatants who displayed great skill and ferocity while jeering any who appeared to strike less than hearty blows or seemed to retreat too much. A Thracian sank to his knees under the crushing blows of a massive Hoplomachi. His appeal for mercy to the provincial governor went unheeded as the crowd booed and called derisively. Following the dictates of the bloodthirsty citizens of Rome, the governor extended his arms with thumb downward and in an instant, the Thracian's head was no longer a part of his body.

At the close of the first round of combats, six out of ten gladiators were able to exit the arena floor while slaves, costumed as the god Mercury, used red-hot pokers to reveal any impostors among the four lifeless figures.

Corvinus had not been part of the group combats. But now he stood alone on the arena floor. The crowd grew quiet. From the far end of the amphitheater came three heavily muscled, but smaller gladiators—one Thracian and two Retiarii. Because of Corvinus' proven skill and great size, he would face all three at once in the premiere event of the afternoon. He looked to the sky as if in prayer to the gods to grant him one more victory. As he did so he noticed the great velarium, or huge awning, which almost completely covered the open-air arena had been pulled into position to provide shade for the sun-baked spectators. The shade, though, would be of little value to Corvinus now.

As his three opponents drew near, Corvinus took his position and then attacked with a vengeance. They were caught off guard by the speed and agility of their huge adversary, but they feinted, parried, and struck back with great skill so that no one seemed to be gaining the upper hand. But then a tremendous blow from Corvinus' double-edged sword cleaved through the Thracian's small round shield and severed his arm at the elbow. Out of the corner of his eye Corvinus saw the lightening cast of a Retiarii's net and ducked at the last instant, spinning under and into the now net-less gladiator, simultaneously raining down a skull-crushing blow on the smaller warrior's head. Caught off balance by his tremendous strike, Corvinus saw the spin of the other Retiarii's net, but too late; he was not quick enough to evade its entangling grasp. One step forward and he crashed to the earth in a great cloud of dust. The Retiarii stood over him with his trident poised at Corvinus' throat and looked to the governor for his signal. The face of Corvinus betrayed no emotion as he waited stoically for the delivery of his fate, final thoughts of his homeland playing across his mind. But the arena was now a floating sea of white kerchiefs, signalling the favor of the cheering crowd, and the governor knew that his only decision could be to spare this great fallen warrior who had fought so well. On this day not only would the life of Corvinus be spared, but he would also be granted his freedom and the right to return to his much cherished homeland.

* * *

Nimes, A.D. 1985, August 1

What an amazing sight! Standing on the uppermost level of the Roman arena in Nimes—the best preserved arena in all the world—I tried to imagine the gruesome entertainment that thrilled crowds of two thousand years ago. Far below me was the arena floor where those entertainments took place. But now that very same floor where gladiators fought and died was set up to provide seating for spectators to sit and listen in comfort to some twentieth century musical strains. Quite a turnabout! I inched over to the very edge of the arena roof being careful not to take that last sixty foot drop to the street below. There I noticed blocks of stone that projected out over the outer wall of the arena. In the center of each block was a large round hole which at one time secured the huge poles that supported the velarium—the immense awning that could be drawn over the arena so that Roman spectators could watch pain and death in shade and comfort. It appeared that Houston's Astrodome has nothing over the Roman ruins of Nimes.

About three hours later I again found myself scaling the heights of another formidable Roman engineering marvel. Located about fifteen miles from the city of Nimes, the Pont du Gard is another one of those spectaculars that seems to populate the landscape here in southern France. This bridge which carries the aqueduct across the River Gard supplied water for the Roman citizens of Nimes. It was ordered to be built by the first Roman emperor, Augustus Caesar, and "august" is most certainly an appropriate adjective when applied to this structure. When you first lay eyes on it, just as the aqueduct in Segovia, your mouth tends to be agape and your only thought is, "How in the name of Zeus/Jupiter did they do this almost two thousand years ago?"

The climb to the top of the Pont du Gard is not for the faint-hearted, for once on top there are no guard rails to prevent you from taking the one hundred foot plunge into the River Gard far below. But if you do decide to join the crazies strolling along the top of the eight hundred foot long edifice as I did—well, what a sight! You also are rewarded by seeing how the Romans constructed the very top of the aqueduct where the water was carried. The passage for the water was a rectangular channel about five or six feet high that ran along the very top of the structure and because it has long since ceased carrying water, you can walk its entire length. The channel was covered by massive capstones which protected the water supply, many of which are still in place. As I perched atop the Pont du Gard surveying the breathtaking panorama that stretched in all directions, I pondered the Roman people and the paradox that was their civilization. On the one hand they could build such amazing—and life-giving—structures such as this that astound even the twentieth century eye, and at the same time thrill to the bloody and ghoulish entertainments to be found on the floor of the arena. Can a darker side of human nature be found anywhere? Well, yes—Germany of the 1930s and 1940s was certainly not a beacon of light for the current century and truly outdid the Romans in brutality and inhumanity. It almost seems as though history has been trying to send us a message—human nature, uncontrolled and improperly channeled, can be a frightful thing.

It had been a long and satisfying day which had offered up more than one historical treasure. But the day was not over, for I still had one more surprise awaiting me. I had yet to come face to drooling face with the largest dog in the world.

After pausing for a refreshing swim in the River Gard at the base of the towering aqueduct and trying to be nonchalant about the bare-breasted young lasses who were sunning themselves on the banks of the river, I headed toward Arles, favorite city of Vincent Van Gogh.

The lengthening shadows on this first day of August reminded me that the warm Mediterranean night would soon be upon me and I as yet had no place to stay. Since Arles was still a good cycling distance away and no camping or caravaning parks presented themselves at this hour of need, I decided to knock on the door of a large and comfortable-looking country chateau that might furnish me with a small patch of ground on which to pitch my tent. A slender, French gentleman answered my knock and greeted me with a smile. This eased my fears somewhat as I launched into my explanation in French of what I was doing—one that I had practiced a few times before I approached the door. "Bon jour , Monsieur, Je voyage autour le monde avec mon bicyclette." Since this just about exhausted my French vocabulary once again without a further dictionary search, I resorted to English with a "French accent" and sign language to communicate the idea that I would like to pitch my tent somewhere out of the way on his spacious grounds. Together with his smattering of English and my smattering of French we came to the understanding that it would be a fine thing for me to do just that. With a wave of his arm he indicted that I could pitch my tent wherever I wished, and I thanked him with an enthusiastic "Merci beau coup!"

I surveyed the surrounding, well-manicured estate, which was really quite beautiful, until I decided on the perfect spot on which to pitch my tent. I began to set up my portable accommodations on a section of the grounds with pillow-soft grass in the middle of which was an ornate fountain that sent streams of water cascading into its surrounding pool. It would be nice to be lulled into a well-deserved slumber by the gentle music of the falling streams of water. I glanced in the direction of the chateau and saw that my host was approaching me, but he was not alone. Attached to one arm was a leash, at the other end of which was possibly the largest canine beast to be seen anywhere on this planet. In fact, it would be more correct to say that my poor host was functioning only as a minor brake in slowing down the progress of this "Super Fido" as he surged toward me, eager to investigate this strange thing that had violated his domain. In an instant I was looking eyeball to eyeball with "S. Fido" as he placed his forepaws on my shoulders and slobbered his enthusiastic and friendly greeting. My host wanted to know if I was getting settled in satisfactorily, and when he saw that I was, he summoned up a super human effort and hauled his eager companion off in another direction.

I was hoping that this would be my one and only encounter with man's best and largest friend, but here again I was sadly mistaken. I sat down on the edge of the fountain, ready to enjoy a sumptuous repast of rolls, cheese, ham and fruit which I had purchased earlier that day. By this time my appetite was in high gear and I dug in eagerly. By the time I saw him, it was too late. Out of nowhere came the huge, black beast and without an invitation, he began devouring my precious food in mammoth gulps. I looked on in horror as my dinner became the subject of this outrageous disappearing act. In desperation, I scooped up what little I could salvage and dove head first into my tent, hoping that my unwelcome dinner guest would not follow me in or worse, decide to eat my tent with me in it. The fates were with me and Goliath, his huge tongue lolling from side to side, watched from the outside as I picked up where he left off, the thin screening of my tent the only thing that kept me from becoming this mutt's "gravy train." The following morning my kindly host invited me in for coffee, toast, and jam and I think he was apologizing for his "pup's" over-ambitious appetite. At any rate, I think he understood why all that was edible in front of me on the table seemed to disappear with amazing rapidity!

After bidding farewell to my host, I set out for Arles, glancing nervously over my shoulder to make sure that I wasn't being followed by any large, black shapes. The ride on this morning of my fiftieth day was a true joy! The weather was superb—a crystal-blue sky; a strong tail wind; a road with little traffic guiding me through the vineyards of Provence. I pedaled slowly, trying to make it last. But still, even as I pedaled through this idyllic setting, I thought of fifty days gone by, and so many more to go to complete my journey—could I really last that long?

I at last arrived in Arles, the city that had enchanted the talented but troubled artist, Vincent Van Gogh. Arles has a history that pre-dates Rome. It has a superb location at the apex of the Rhone River delta. It had seen the comings and goings of different barbarian groups, Greeks, and Romans. Because the people of this area sided with Julius Caesar in his civil war with Pompey, Caesar established a colony here for his veterans, naming it *Colonia Julia Paterna Arelate Sextanorum*—quite a mouthful. Since that time , it always held a favored position in the empire. The theater was constructed during the reign of Augustus, and could seat twelve thousand people. The famous arena of Arles is slightly larger than that of Nimes, but not as well preserved. Both arenas at Arles and Nimes were converted into fortresses during the Middle Ages. At Arles, crenellated towers were constructed and dwellings for the poor and shops were built inside—almost a miniature city in itself. There were even two or three churches which catered to the spiritual needs of the huddled masses within. These were all cleared out in the nineteenth century when restoration began. The arena, site of gladiatorial combat and animal hunts, could seat up to twenty-five thousand people. On this day, twenty centuries later, the arena floor was set up for the popular French version of "fighting de bull."

Within a day's ride of Arles is one of the loveliest cities to be found anywhere in southern France, Aix en Provence. (This area of France is called Provence because of the Romans who referred to this region simply as "la Provincia"—the province—being one of the first provinces outside of the Italian Peninsula to be incorporated into the expanding Roman Empire.) After tearing myself away from the morning market on Arles's Boulevard de Lices which featured just about anything you'd want from anchovies to zucchini, I set my sights for Aix and ran into one monumental traffic jam on the way. At first I supposed that somewhere up ahead was a massive pileup with bodies and crinkled autos strewn all over the roadway—not a surprising scenario when calling to mind the Grand Prix mentality that many European drivers seem to possess. But as I weaved my way in and out of the unending line of cars, campers, and vans—feeling quite smug in the process—I concluded that there had been no pileup, but that it was simply the glut of vacation-crazed Europeans clogging the highways in their quest for the sun and fun of the French Riviera.

The enchanting city of Aix was a welcome reward after dodging cars for a good part of the afternoon. I was greeted by broad, tree-lined boulevards; beautiful, ornate fountains shooting torrents of water skyward; narrow, winding streets lined with shops of all sorts opening onto private little squares; and sidewalk cafes from which you could watch the passing parade and sip on a favorite beverage. On Sunday morning all the artisans of Provence converged on the city of Aix and set up their booths on the beautiful Cours Mirabeau, one of Aix's main avenues—and the loveliest! Every kind of handicraft imaginable could be found displayed on this morning beneath the tall, stately trees that formed a natural canopy over the heads of browsers and shoppers who strolled leisurely from booth to booth. It was with great difficulty that I pulled myself away from the marvelous display of crafts and wares, but I was anxious to experience the beauty and excitement of the Riviera coastline, and it was in this direction that I headed.

Once away from the main artery connecting Arles and Aix, the surroundings and weather became a biker's delight.

I wound my way through the peaceful and rolling countryside accompanied by the ever-present sunny skies and another strong tail wind. Late in the day I happened on a peaceful and serene—not to mention free—camping site on the shores of Lake Caceres, and in the morning I awoke to the sight of a mirror-smooth lake, reflections of the surrounding hills within the border of the twisting shoreline. I broke camp early and as I did so, I felt a slight twinge of excitement and anticipation, for this morning I would be setting my course for famed St. Tropez. Ah, yes, St. Tropez—the name seemed to ooze a sun-bronzed sensuality. This is the mecca for many of Europe's jet set, and I was ready and willing to assume my rightful position along with my trusty two-wheeled companion, as a member of this fast-paced society—right alongside the million dollar yachts and a French movie star or two. As I coasted down and out of the small mountain range separating me from this sun-seekers' wonderland, little did I suspect that the hills surrounding St. Tropez for the next twenty-four hours would be a fair approximation of *Dante's Inferno* and I would find myself holding on for dear life as my tent became a plaything for forty-mile-an-hour winds.

* * *

Is it true what they say about all those Riviera beaches? I wasted no time in checking out this tantalizing prospect firsthand upon my arrival in St. Tropez. As I staked out my piece of sand at the first available beach, the bare truth was not hard to uncover. If you adore bare boobs, then this is the place to be. Young boobs, old boobs, middle-aged boobs—they're all here for the world to see. Of course, most Europeans maintain a certain nonchalance about the carefree display of the female human anatomy, while Americans are easily detectable because of the tendency of their eyeballs to hang down around their chins. I must admit to fitting the above description myself; but it's just something you don't see at the beach at Cedar Point, Ohio.

After a couple of somewhat distracted hours trying to give the impression that I was actually sunning myself, I'd had enough, for the rising winds whipped the sand about, coating all with a fine, white gritty film. I soon found myself among the multitude of European vacationers strolling along the boardwalk of St. Tropez's harbor. I meandered through many of the touristy shops whose prices told me that I would just be looking on this day, and I marveled with a small degree of envy at the million dollar yachts that rode leisurely at their moorings. Their owners scampered about, performing their dockside duties, and I couldn't help but wonder about the success behind these obvious, mega-buck-type seafarers.

Forget about the million dollar yachts, for I now came upon a diversion that seemed to be attracting quite a crowd of onlookers. Barely visible in the middle of a growing throng of curious board walkers was a fully rigged and outfitted, shocking pink Harley-Davidson motorcycle with trailer attached. It was bedecked from headlight to rear mud flap with every type of auxiliary light and reflector possible. Emblazoned across the back of this mechanical symphony in pink were the words "The Spirit of America." Sometimes Europeans have the impression that most Americans tend to be rather "showy" and brash. As I pushed my "two-wheeled rig" through a gap in the crowd, I wondered where they would get a crazy idea like that.

Although this seemed to be an afternoon of diversions, I wasn't quite ready for the next one. The thick smoke billowed higher and higher into the sky, mixing with the afternoon sunlight, creating an almost surrealistic panorama. At first it appeared as if a ship might be on fire, but from a better vantage point it became obvious that the mountains in back of St. Tropez were ablaze. Not unlike California, this part of France can become like a tinder box in late summer. I recalled, too, that the last time I had seen or felt a raindrop was high in the Pyrenees, and now the winds seemed to be blowing with a real purpose, fanning the flames which, at times, seemed to explode off the mountainsides. Sun-seekers from all over Europe paused to witness a spectacle they hadn't anticipated.

I hopped on my cycle and began battling the protesting head winds on the way to my campsite. Every so often I would pause to take in the inferno that seemed to dance from crest to crest. From miles away you could see the flames eating away at the forested hills, expensive homes being only so much more fuel for the blaze, not even their price tags enough to turn the searching tongues of fire away. Gusts of wind reaching thirty to forty miles an hour continued to blast away at the mountains, helping to send the flames on their way. Arriving back in my campground, I half expected to see my tent waving at the top of a tree, but there it was—still staked securely to the ground. I wondered what kind of night lay ahead.

I knew that "I wasn't in Kansas anymore," but I hadn't contemplated disappearing with the wind à la Dorothy and Toto, or becoming a main character in *Dante's Inferno*—at least not both in the same night! The intensity of the winds seemed to increase as the night wore on, and I made a determined attempt to snatch a bit of fitful sleep here and there. Most of the time, however, I watched in fascination as the inside support poles of my tent did a crazy pretzel dance around my head. Soon it was necessary for me to become an active participant in the support system for my little domicile. I sat straight up in the tent, extending my arms and clasping on to the fiberglass poles that seemed intent on doubling over with the unrelenting force of the wind. I maintained this extremely restful position for the next couple of hours until a new curiosity presented itself. Searchlights were now illuminating the inside of my restless tent. I chanced a peek outside and saw that the "searchlights" actually belonged to a steady stream of cars that appeared to be flooding into the campground. As I contemplated the prospect of a Mercedes-Benz backing over my little nylon home, I heard a friendly Aussie voice call out, "Goodday', mate!" The voice belonged to the owner of the car that had just pulled up next to my tent.

"Bloody bad windstorm we're 'avin tonight, wouldn't ya say mate?" called out my new neighbor from "Down Under" above the roaring gusts of wind.

"You're right there, friend," I replied, still wondering why my campground was quickly being transformed into a parking lot.

"We were campin' way back up in the hills we were," he continued, seeing the perplexed look on my face. "Believe me, mate, 'ats no place to be right now. Those flames are out o' control and consumin' everything in sight. They 'ad to evacuate us out o' there and so now they're fillin' up all the campgrounds down 'ere where it's safe."

I heaved a small sigh of relief at his use of the word "safe," happy that my tent would not become just one more candle in the wind.

"Say mate, I got me an idea," he offered. "How 'bout I pull me car up real close to your tent and maybe give you a bit o' a windbreak. I been noticin' you're 'avin a bit o' trouble holden' down the fort."

"That sounds like a darn good idea," I said without hesitation, and so it proved to be, for when he pulled his car around in front, my tiny abode ceased its wild contortions. I thanked my new windbreak for his kind gesture and crawled back under the flaps. Soon I was lulled into an uneasy slumber by the howling lullaby outside which seemed a nonstop hymn, "awakening" every now and then to see Dorothy, Toto, and the Wicked Witch of the West spin by in a funnel-like haze.

By morning the savage winds had subsided a wee bit, and it appeared as though the once raging inferno up in the hills had been brought under control. The still stiff breezes seemed to be having a good time with me while I attempted to pack up my tent and break camp, but I finally had the last laugh as I strapped everything securely to my bike. I paused momentarily to watch the armada of aircraft that was now swooping low over the mountains, dropping tons of sea water on the smoldering and blackened hills. As soon as the mammoth aircraft discharged their drenching loads, they lumbered back out to sea to retrieve another fire-quenching cargo. I took one last look at the campground around me, noting that most of the remaining tents seemed to be in some state of partial or total collapse. One couple slept peacefully on as their now flattened tent fluttered noisily about them. Yes, camping out on the Côte d'Azur can really be a breeze!

* * *

The slackening winds allowed me to proceed onward along this renowned section of Europe's Mediterranean coastline. The next couple of days proved to be quite an exceptional physical challenge, for the coast road threads its way up, down, and around a seemingly unending series of rocky inlets and bays, one minute taking you down to sea level and the next minute sending you back up to an elevation of maybe four or five hundred feet. I found myself attacking each challenging climb with a gusto born out of the invigorating sea air and a conditioned body that had seen nearly two months of rigorous cycling. It seemed as if nothing could hold me back. But stop I did at one point, not from being exhausted—though at times I was—or from my legs nearly giving out—though at times they almost did—but because the scenery was so unbelievably grand that I just had to stop to attempt to take it all in. At the summit of each arduous climb I was rewarded by a vista of coastline and sea that seemed more spectacular than the last. Here, I had to turn off onto one of the scenic pull-offs. I set my bike down and rummaged through my packs until I found my journal. Finding a comfortable rock, I sat down and let the warm Mediterranean sunshine and the sweet sea breezes wash over me as I attempted to paint a picture in words of the breathtaking land and seascape before me, for I knew not even a camera could do it justice:

> This is a special place, this Mediterranean coast—a place of unsurpassed beauty. The road snakes along the rocky coastline. Off to the right, "La Mer," the sea—a hundred shades of blues and greens reflecting the rays of the sun as countless diamonds dancing in the waves; tiny sailboats catching the ever-present breezes, their sails in stark contrast to the deep blue carpet surrounding them. Off to the left, high cliffs and headlands that fall away to the sea in rapid descents. And far in the distance, the Alps, thrusting upward majestically to meet the sky—all coming together in a spectacular union of mountains, coast, and sea.

I lingered there for an hour or more, not wanting to leave this delicious spot and trying once again to box this special moment so that I might unwrap it at one of those future times—which I knew must come—when my spirits would sag.

Out of the craggy heights and precipices of the rugged Côte d'Azur and on to the more level coastal terrain leading into glitzy Cannes and Nice—this was truly a land of sun-seekers and sun-worshipers; one white sand beach after another teeming with barely-clad bathers soaking in those golden Mediterranean rays. I was becoming amazingly blasé about the carefree display of the female human anatomy (as much as one can about such things). I could now glide right on by a scene that would most certainly cause a fifty-car pileup on any coast highway in the U.S. of A. With the warm sun of the "Middle Sea" bearing down on me, every now and then my gliding came to an abrupt halt and I became just another one of those barely-clad bathers seeking a cooling dunk in the soothing waters.

One drawback to this fun and sun mecca was finding a space for my weary head at the end of the day. As half of the population of Europe appeared to be searching this playground of the Mediterranean for their proverbial place in the sun, this was not an ideal setting for what you would call secluded camping. One night I pitched my tent on what I thought was a fairly quiet and out-of-the-way section of beach—although a bit rocky. Just as I was dozing off to a well-earned slumber, the wild and wooly strains of the theme song from the old TV series *Bonanza* came galloping over the pebble-strewn beach. Here, ten thousand miles from Virginia City and the Ponderosa, I had set up camp right below a French "Wild West" show. Somehow I drifted off to sleep, but now with visions of Pa, Hoss, and Little Joe dancing in my head.

The following night proved to be even worse. I had spent a good part of the afternoon rubbing elbows with the rich and famous in Cannes, that jet setters' haven which has its streets lined with French francs. An exquisite sunset over the Côte d'Azur made me forget momentarily that I as yet had no place to button up for the night. My enchantment soon degenerated into frustration as I found this part of the French Riviera an endless succession of beach-front communities with nary a place to put my tent. Long after the sun had made its exit from the western horizon, I found myself wandering through an exclusive marina that was temporary home to some of the most magnificent yachts I had as yet feasted my eyes on. I stood gawking, only able to wonder at the lifestyles of the denizens of these floating palaces. At the conclusion of my gawking session, I spied what seemed to be a semi-secluded patch of earth that was surrounded by some bushes and small trees, and it was here that I decided to settle in for the rest of the night—well, almost. At somewhere around 3:00 a.m. I was coaxed out of deep slumber by an exceptionally early sunrise which was really not sunrise at all, but the beams of a flashlight filtering in through the netting of my tent. "Uh, oh," was the only thought that occurred to me.

"Excuse me, Monsieur, What are you doing here?" inquired the voice from behind the flashlight.

"Oh, just trying to sleep," I offered in innocent reply.

"But Monsieur, you may not do that here. You will have to move. You must find some place else to sleep."

"Do you have any suggestions as to where I might spend the rest of the night?" I grunted as I began rolling up my sleeping bag and tearing down the tent.

"Yes, Monsieur. The public beach is not too far from here. I think you may spend the rest of the night there," he said, pointing in the direction of a small peninsula that jutted out into the sea.

After packing up the rest of my belongings under the watchful eye of my early morning wake-up caller, I headed in the direction that he had pointed, trying hard to shake the cobwebs out of my head. Since my eyes were not focusing too well at this strange hour, I rode slowly and was relieved when I came upon the beach without too much difficulty. Longing for just a few hours of uninterrupted sleep, I collapsed in a heap on the soft sand of the shore, not even bothering to put up my tent for the second time. I crawled back into my sleeping bag and quickly picked up where I had left off, trying not to be too concerned about the fact that I was really quite vulnerable on this free and open campsite.

It had been a good stretch of time since I had seen the inside of a cozy, hotel room or slept in a nice, soft bed. Nice was to be my reward for living the past week "in the rough." With the high tourist season in full gear, I worried that I might be left high and dry in my search for a room in this famed city of the Riviera, but a brief search turned up a place to stay that was right in my price range—cheap!— at least by Nice's standards. Actually the hotel was quite clean and comfortable and it was here that I settled in for the next couple of days. I picked up my much cherished mail from home, did a little shopping, and just enjoyed strolling the busy streets and squares that abounded with tourists, stopping now and then at a bustling sidewalk cafe to quaff a beer or two.

* * *

"Where ya' headin' to?"inquired the friendly American cyclist on the coast road that led out of Nice. I had pulled up behind twenty-two year old Dave Stein from the Jersey shore as I was setting out for Monaco and the Italian border.

"I'm heading into Italy along the coast toward Genoa, and then I hope to shoot up north to Milano to catch a glimpse of Leonardo's *Last Supper*," was my reply, hoping that he was heading in the same direction and might want a little company.

"Whadaya' say we team up for a while," he enthused. "I'm kind of headin' in the same direction and it's been awhile since I've had some good ol' American company."

I eagerly accepted the offer and we hitched our train together, although I quickly turned out to be the caboose. As we twisted our way in and out of the small remainder of the rugged French coastline, I saw that Dave really attacked the hills with a vengeance, quickly leaving me in his wake each time we started up another incline. I rationalized to myself: "Well, Al, he is about twelve years younger and look how light he's traveling with only a couple of small rear panniers. Besides, you're more of a plodder anyway." It was true; I identified more with the tortoise and the hare, but there was no denying it—Dave was a real vigorous biker and it didn't seem to phase him much at all.

In spite of our somewhat different cycling styles, Dave proved to be a personable young guy—as I found out whenever I could catch up to him to exchange a few thoughts. Dave was still attending college in New Jersey and had just decided to see a bit of the Old World on his summer break this year. He'd been cycling for about three weeks and still had a couple more to go before his flight home to the States. He was traveling pretty light with only a couple of rear panniers and a handlebar bag and no camping gear—not even a sleeping bag. He related to me that more than once he had ended up in the barn of some kindly French farmer.

"Yea, Al, you should have seen this one family; they kind of adopted me for the night. They couldn't speak a bit of English and my French is nonexistent, but we all made a lot of wild hand gestures and pretty soon they were bringin' me all kinds of food and they made me feel right at home; it was really something!"

Together we polished off the last few miles of French territory, and "polished" is an apropos term to use, for the final revolutions of our cranks in France took us through sparkling Monaco. We didn't pause long here, but carefully threaded our way between the Rolls Royces and limousines and before too long, we were upon the French-Italian border crossing. Before crossing the border, Dave and I glanced back at France and we both smiled. We each had our pleasant memories of France and these we carried with us to meet the challenge of Italy; and a challenge it would be. An experience I was about to have at the border would prove to be a foreshadowing of events to come in my journey down "the boot."

FOUR

Italy—Down the Boot

"Excuse me, Sir. I would like to change my French francs into Italian lire if you please," was my polite request as I stepped up to the exchange bank teller.

"Yes, Signore. I would be happy to. But we've had a very busy morning. If you will just give me a minute," he replied in a slightly harried and weary manner. He began the calculations on my hundred and fifty dollars worth of French francs, and then right in the middle of our business transaction, a call came from across the room.

"Say, Antonio, whatsa' for suppa' today?"—or at least that is what I imagined was being shouted in Italian across the room by one of the fellow tellers.

Whatever was said, it seemed to jar my teller's concentration, and after answering the question, he resumed his ciphering but with a somewhat confused look on his face. He smiled and handed me my Italian lire and as I stepped away, I decided I should do something which I don't often do—count my money. I walked over to the corner of the room—which was a mistake—and began totaling the thousands of lire the teller had given me. It appeared as though I were a rich man, but since the exchange rate was fourteen hundred lire to one U.S. dollar, the appearance was only a grand illusion. Even with thousands of lire now bulging in my pockets, it still seemed as though I was about fifty dollars short. I promptly stepped back up to the teller's window and in a kindly manner asked if it was possible that he had made an error.

"Oh, Signore, that cannot be; I am sure that I gave you the correct change," he answered with a look of surprise. "We are always very careful here. I am sure that I made no mistake."

"But look at the amount of lire that you gave me. Do you see that it is about fifty U.S. dollars short?" I pleaded, realizing that I should never have stepped away from the window when I began to count my money. Now there was no way to prove that I hadn't slipped about fifty dollars worth of lire into my skivvies. "Isn't there any way you can check to see if by some extreme chance you made an error?"

"Yes, Signore, but that will take some time. We are about ready to close business for the morning, and then we will be able to check our totals for the morning's transactions. I'm afraid you will have to wait a little."

I could see that I had no choice. Fifty dollars was fifty dollars. To a shoestring traveler such as I was, that could mean two weeks worth of meals, and more. It wasn't too long before the exchange bank closed up shop for the morning and the tellers began the tedious task of counting the different currencies they had handled on this morning and checking their totals against their paperwork. I watched my teller intently as he counted his last pile and was rewarded by a look of sheepish horror that spread slowly across his features. That could mean only one thing.

"Oh, Signore, I am so sorry. You were very correct. I have fifty U.S. dollars too much. Oh, but this never happens. Please Signore, forgive me; you saw that I was interrupted and I lost my concentration; please forgive...."

"Hey now, it's alright; as long as I get the correct change," I smiled, trying to ease his embarrassment somewhat. I uttered a few more comforting comments and when he seemed assured that I wasn't going to try to have him shot, I rejoined Dave who had been waiting patiently for the last forty-five minutes. I explained what had happened, and he was glad that the error had been corrected in my favor. This was the first blow below the belt that Italy would shoot my way; more would soon follow, but not with the same happy ending.

Dave and I resumed our ride and were disappointed to see that the rugged beauty of the French coastline had given way to the less than spectacular and people-saturated Italian Riviera. We cruised through one crowded seaside resort after another and decided that the whole population of Europe (well, at least Italy) was on holiday at this very time and place. Our prospects for finding a place to bed down for the night seemed to be in inverse proportion to the masses of bodies crowding the beaches. As we pedaled into the evening, each of our inquiries met with a similar response: "No room at the inn!" There didn't even seem to be a postage stamp-size parcel of open ground where we could pitch my tent. Finally, the proprietor of a resort hotel took pity on us and permitted us to stay in the resort's athletic room for thirty thousand lire, or about sixteen dollars. It had been a long day—eighty miles of up-and-down coastline—and we were in no position to be choosy.

The following day Dave and I parted ways. His cycling was a little faster than mine and he had a different route in mind to the city of Milan. I continued on along the coastline at my own determined pace, stopping at midday for a refreshing dunk in the sea. While toweling off, it didn't escape my attention that here on the Italian Riviera, modesty seemed to be more in vogue. While on the French beaches a girl would be out of place if she chose to cover up her upper anatomy, here the two-piece suit was the hard and fast rule— an interesting difference in cultural attitudes though both countries have a strong Catholic influence.

After spending the night at the youth hostel in Genoa, Italy, home of Christopher Columbus, I once again headed inland and set my sights for the city of Milan. The coastal range of mountains provided me with some strenuous morning pumping, but then a long gradual downhill and finally flat land as I emerged onto the broad expanse of the Po River Valley—the breadbasket of the Italian boot. I had not seen any flat terrain for quite a while and it felt good not to have to continuously drop down into my climbing gears. It felt even better to get away from the clutter of the coastline and the rush of people, many of whom abandon their own homes for the entire month of August in order to crowd into this narrow strip of coastline lining the Mediterranean Sea.

As I set up my tent that night on the farm of a fairly well-off Italian, I locked horns again with those same feelings of doubt, uncertainty, and loneliness that had plagued me thus far on my journey. It was nothing major; just the little things that seemed to be building up. I was tired of the hassle of finding a spot to lay my head at the end of each day. . .camp?. . . hostel?. . .pensione? My little MSR stove kept clogging up because I was burning gasoline which is much dirtier than white gas. The spaghetti I fixed for dinner was, in all truth, lousy. I worried that the film I had sent home the previous week would vanish, lost forever in the abyss of the international postal service. The constant grind and exertion were wearing me down, and to cap it off, I had awakened that morning with a sore throat. I needed something good to happen; I had to have a boost from somewhere. Maybe I would find that boost in the city of Milan. Little did I know that the fickle finger of fate was about to land itself squarely in my eye as I entered the city of Leonardo's Last Supper.

* * *

"Hey, does anyone have some cookware I could borrow?" The voice sounded familiar. Lying there on my back in the youth hostel in Milan, I looked at the source of the voice and I thought even the face looked familiar. Sure enough, there was Dave turning to exit the room, not recognizing me, nor I him, because of my relatively upside-down, flat-on-my-back position, but just as surprised—and pleased—at the moment of recognition to see each other again. Dave had just been to the store, so using my cookware he began to whip up a pretty fair meal of vegetables, rice, and cheese. While we cut, pared, and diced, we compared notes on the last couple of days since we had parted company.

While we busied ourselves in the hostel kitchen, we made the acquaintance of Simon, another cyclist from England and quite an interesting chap. Simon was an artist, but not your typical, run-of-the-mill, paint-on-canvas type artist. In fact, his canvases were the sidewalks of the cities that he visited. As a street artist he rode his bicycle from city to city looking for a favorable piece of pavement on which to perform his craft. Once the right "canvas" was found, usually in the town square or piazza where a multitude of people coming and going could admire his drawing, he set to work creating a beautiful copy of one of the great master-pieces from the past—a Leonardo, a Raphael, or maybe a Michelangelo. He had a number of copies of great art works which he showed me that were the models from which he drew. His medium was simply chalk, being a public sidewalk, but his chalk drawings were unlike and far beyond any student sketching and graffiti that found its way onto my classroom chalkboard. As he worked, passers-by could stop and admire his skill, and if they felt moved or appreciative, they might drop a few lire in Simon's hat which was always set out. In fact, Simon must have been quite a fine artist judging from his success so far.

"Simon, how much can you make in a day doing your street art?" I inquired, a little envious of his obvious talents.

"Well, each city is different of course—some more profitable than others. And sometimes the authorities don't exactly have an eye for art," he chuckled. "But to give you an idea, when I was back in Liverpool, I was taking in over a hundred pounds a day."

I was amazed and almost convinced myself that I should take up street art too. But then I quickly remembered that few people would pay to watch some American draw Dick-and-Jane-type stick figures on the sidewalk. Of course, Simon's sketches were only temporary, lasting only as long as the sunny skies. But then that's part of the attraction of street art; anyone can try their hand and if there are no available "canvases" about, just wait until the next rain.

"Where to after this, Simon?" I asked.

"Well, I'm gradually working my way east and I hope to make it to Hong Kong to work as an artist or architect. Wish me luck!" This I certainly did.

Dave and I consumed the food we had prepared with great gusto and for the rest of the evening we sat around and talked of things we had seen so far in our travels and what our plans were for the immediate future. Dave planned to head toward Germany, Simon would be cycling toward Venice, and I intended to stay in Milan to visit the site that was my main reason for coming to this city. The next day would be a special day and one of the highlights of my trip, but it would also become one of the worst days I had experienced thus far.

* * *

Even in its deteriorated condition, you can still sense the genius that created this masterpiece—one of the giants of the Italian Renaissance—a master of perspective and the use of light and shadow to capture the essence of the moment when Christ utters the words, "One of you shall betray me." Leonardo Da Vinci's *Last Supper* is a painting that, even though it has suffered the ravages of man and of time, has stood the test, and ranks as one of the supreme masterpieces of the Italian High Renaissance.

In teaching about Leonardo and his times to my students, I had always found this to be one of the most fascinating and exciting periods of history. And now here I was, standing before the great master's tarnished jewel. However, the painting was partially obstructed by scaffolding which supported some apparently high-tech instruments. In order to understand the reason for the scaffolding and instrumentation, one should know a little of the history of the *Last Supper*—and an interesting and sad history it is.

Leonardo Da Vinci was commissioned by the powerful Duke Ludovico Sforza of Milan to paint the *Last Supper* as a gift to the monks of the Dominican monastery of Santa Maria delle Grazie. It was to be painted on one of the walls of the refectory (dining hall) of the monastery and it was Leonardo's intention to make the friars feel as though they were actually dining with Christ. But it became much more than just a dining scene. Leonardo chose to portray the moment when Christ has just announced that one of his apostles would betray him. What resulted was a fascinating study in human reactions. Christ, isolated and alone, gazes downward in an aura of sadness while the apostles, in groupings of three, beseech their Lord to tell them who the betrayer would be. Although the subject of the Passover supper had been dealt with before by other artists, none had achieved the psychological study that was Leonardo's.

Somewhere in the mid 1490s Leonardo began his preparations for the wall mural. He wandered the streets of Milan searching for the right face with the right features that would be appropriate for the countenance of Christ and for each of his apostles. In his notebooks today we can see many of the preliminary sketches that were the result of his wanderings and keen observations.

Leonardo, the great master, chose not to work in the traditional fresco style where paint is applied to wet plaster and the two actually become one. Using this method, the artist must work quickly before the plaster dries, but this was not Leonardo's style. He could not be hurried in the creation of his masterpiece, and so he had the freshly plastered wall sealed with a lead white primer. When it was dry, he could then take as long as he liked in the portrayal of his subject. This, however, many experts believe to be a fateful decision.

Leonardo painted the *Last Supper* from 1495 to 1497, and the Duke and the monks often became displeased with the slow progress of his work. But there was no rushing the great artist. Contemporary observers who watched Leonardo work reported that on some days they would see Leonardo paint from dawn till dusk, never taking a break or even putting down his paintbrush—and then stand for hours criticizing his work. Other times he would be absent from the refectory for days and then suddenly appear to add one or two brush strokes. Then he would disappear again, off to one of his many other projects or passionate studies.

But at last the painting was done, and it was immediately recognized as one of the greatest art works to be seen anywhere. Sadly, however, it was realized that even within Leonardo's lifetime, the painting was in trouble. Pieces of the great masterpiece were literally flaking off the wall. Had it been his use of the priming method? His experimentation with different oils and resins? A too quick drying of the plaster? Or a dampness of the wall itself? There have been a number of theories proposed, but whatever the reason, it was obvious that the pigments which Leonardo used had not adhered properly to the wall of the refectory. Within a century, the painting was considered ruined, so much so that in 1652, the monks, perhaps thinking all was lost, actually had a small door in the wall enlarged which cut off the feet of Christ. The painting continued to flake and fade from view and probably reached its nadir in the 1790s when Napoleon's soldiers used the dining hall as a stable and a place to store their weapons and powder. Some of the soldiers even desecrated the work by throwing stones at the heads of the apostles.

In an effort to save the painting, the monks, beginning in 1726 and over the next couple of centuries, commissioned six major restorations. Much of the restoration work, however, actually did more harm than good. Some of the artists were incompetent, burying Leonardo's original creation under layers of darkened pigments and anchoring resins. One restorer even repainted the features of a couple of the apostles, adding his own interpretation of what he thought the great master intended to portray. During World War II the *Last Supper* was nearly lost for good when an allied bomb landed close to the refectory and blew away the roof and two of the walls. Because the monks had had the foresight to brace and sandbag the wall containing Leonardo's work, the painting was saved.

Since 1977 the most ambitious and scientific restoration of the *Last Supper* has been under way—really more of an excavation. It is an effort to remove five centuries of dirt, glue, layers of overpainting by well-intentioned but incompetent restorers, and the residues left by the assault of modern air pollution. This effort has employed techniques and tools that are unique to the twentieth century in order to study the painting and the wall of the refectory—sterophotogrammetry, ultrasound, hygrometers, infrared camera, electric sensors, x-ray and ultraviolet techniques.

The chief "archaeologist" responsible for this excavation of the *Last Supper* has been Dr. Pinin Brambilla Barcilon, who has spent much of the last seven years perched on the scaffolding which now partially blocks a view of the painting. Working behind her microscope, she attempts to identify the original pigments of Leonardo's palette, and uses a paintbrush, scalpel, and specially designed solvents, to surgically remove centuries of grime and repainting. It takes Dr. Barcilon one whole week to clean an area only the size of a postage stamp which is why the restoration will probably not be completed until the early 1990s.

But the results are magnificent. Standing before the painting, I could clearly see the demarcation line between the uncleaned, dirty portion and those areas where Dr. Barcilon's work had liberated the bright and bold hues of Leonardo's true *Last Supper*.

After a half hour or so spent in awe in front of this treasure, I busied myself with my Nikon camera, attempting to capture this precious image on film. Because of the low light conditions a tripod would have been helpful, but I was still confident I had some good shots. I left the monastery feeling happy; it had been a morning well spent.

Although Leonardo may not have taken a snack break during his long and uninterrupted painting sessions, I suddenly realized appreciating great art could work up a healthy appetite. Renaissance Milan was no exception to the European influx of fast food establishments, and so I readily found myself at one of these Italian hamburger joints incongruously located across from the beautiful cathedral of Milan. This was to be my next visit, so it was convenient—not to mention my craving for a hamburger and a shake.

I eased into a booth and settled down to enjoy my hamburger, shake and fries, feeling happy and content at having seen Leonardo's masterpiece. This was the boost that I had been hoping for. But unfortunately, the word boost is not far removed from the word bust. I didn't think much about my backpack containing my Nikon camera which I had placed at my feet; I was too absorbed in the field day my plebeian taste buds were having. Midway through my meal I glanced up to find a heavyset Italian watching me. He stole a glance at my feet and then slid quickly out of sight to the other side of the restaurant. Thinking nothing of it, I returned to my meal and finished off the last few morsels of food and dribbles of shake and then once more glanced at my feet. It took a second or two to register, but then the realization hit me like a sledge hammer. Where my backpack had been there was now nothing but empty floor. I was thunderstruck. In helpless frustration and rage I raced up and down the aisles like a crazy man pleading with fellow patrons to tell me if they had seen a man race by with my pack, oblivious to the fact that many of them could probably not understand English. I bolted out the door, hoping to catch sight of a heavyset man making an obvious getaway, but the thief and my backpack were nowhere to be seen—vanished amidst the bustling tourist traffic of Milan.

My feeling of devastation deepened as I reviewed the contents of my pack. Of course it had contained my Nikon FG camera, but that was not all. There was also my one decent pair of long pants that I had brought along for my visit to the cathedral; a collection of postcards from many of the wonderful sites I had seen thus far; and, I sadly realized, the pictures I had just taken of the *Last Supper*. This seemed almost as terrible as the loss of my camera. For some reason, that morning I had stuffed my moneybelt with my passport, travelers' checks, and other important papers in my pants pocket rather than my backpack where I had been keeping it lately. Even that fortunate circumstance was buried under my despair of the moment. One of the main reasons for my trip was to share my experiences with my future students through the many wonderful pictures and slides I hoped to bring back. Now that prospect had seemingly been dashed on the rocks, and could only be remedied by the expensive purchase of another camera—made more expensive by being in Italy.

Feeling outraged, but helpless, I returned to the youth hostel with my face buried in my chest and sank deeper into a state of depression—a state that was certainly out of proportion to the loss of a mere material item such as a camera. But it was a feeling I couldn't shake. It felt as if it had almost been a personal attack. Before long, I found myself desiring revenge on any and all the thieves who inhabited the environs of Milan, Italy, and it was this feeling that sent me back to the scene of the crime the following day. I figured where lightning had struck once, it could certainly strike again, and this time I would be ready. With an icy glare probably common to most hit men before they swing into action, I sat down not far from where I had been seated the day before. Close by I had set the bait for the trap—my obviously unattended handlebar bag all by its lonesome on the floor of the hamburger shop—easy pickins'. In one hand I clutched my bicycle pump which I fully intended to be the sword of justice—and I waited, my eyes riveted to my handlebar bag which sat invitingly on the floor. Amazingly, one table away from where I had been seated twenty-four hours before, a young girl bolted from her seat, that familiar look of panic in her eyes.

"My purse! My purse!" she blurted. "Where's my purse? It was right here on the back of my chair. Did you see anyone take it? Did you see anyone run by with a purse?"

She ran up and down the aisle, imploring everyone, but no one in particular, while I just bit my tongue because I knew it was a replay of the day before when I had been the main actor. Ironically, I had been so intent on watching my own bag that the crime had taken place right under my nose. I looked at my watch and saw that it was almost the identical time of the previous day. Same place, same time, same crime—I couldn't believe it.

With that awesome display of police work on my part, I knew it was time to get out of Milan, before vengeance got the better of me. In fact, I reflected that it was probably for the best that I had not caught the thief, for it would not have been a pretty sight. While sitting there waiting to pounce, I had not even cared if it was the same thief who had taken my backpack; it was fully my intention to make whichever poor piece of scum I apprehended pay not only for my camera, but also for all the other times in my life that I had been ripped off, both at home and abroad. I decided that it would be better to learn from my mistake of carelessness and inattention and leave vengeance to the Lord, as the saying goes.

From Milan I headed southeast toward the city of Parma, but with each revolution of my cranks, I anguished over the loss of my camera and regretted my hasty purchase of a small autofocus; it was a nice little camera, but not appropriate, I felt, for my needs. When I wheeled into Parma that night, I determined that I would catch a train back to Milan and attempt to exchange my little autofocus for a better model. The next day I rode the rails back to the site of my tragedy, almost certain that the camera shop would be closed, as most of the shops were, either because everyone was still on holiday or they didn't open on Monday anyway. In fact, all of Italy seemed to be on some sort of break or holiday; some sections of the city seemed to be almost deserted. But the spirit of Matthew Brady was watching over me, and I found my camera shop to be one of the few shops that was open. After some pleading, wringing of hands, and pulling of hair, they took pity on me and agreed to exchange the autofocus for an Olympus OM-10 plus about twenty thousand extra lire. The Olympus would give me much more photographic capability, so I didn't hesitate to make the swap. From that point, I felt as though I could put the theft behind me, and on the train back to Parma, it seemed as though I was back on track in more ways than one. However, the lesson which I should have learned in Milan about carelessness would not prove to be a lasting one, even before I made it out of Italy.

When I arrived back at the youth hostel in Parma, I discovered that two other touring bicycles were keeping my two-wheeler company, and the next morning as I prepared to mount up, I made the acquaintance of the two owners.

"Hi! My name is Al," I offered, hoping to get a response in English. I was in luck.

"Glad to meet you!" was their friendly reply. "My name is John and this is my fiancee, Marlene. We're from Canada—British Columbia—and we've been touring around northern Italy for a couple of months."

"John is a cook," Marlene explained, "and his interest is Italian cuisine. We've just been taking our time, trying to experience the flavor of the country and to pick up some pointers from Italian chefs. We even spent a couple of weeks at a mountain resort up at Lake Como where John helped out in the kitchen. Gosh, what a beautiful spot it was!"

"Now we're headed toward the south of Italy," John continued. "We plan to catch the boat to Greece down in Bari and spend a few weeks there before we head back home. How long have you been touring for, Al, and where are ya' headed?"

I told them of my travels and experiences up to that point and they were excited by what I had accomplished so far and just as enthused and interested in my future plans. For the time being, however, it appeared as though our immediate direction of travel coincided, and so I popped the question: "Would you two like a little company since we all seem to be heading the same way?"

"Hey, that would be great!" they both enthused.

"John is a strong rider," Marlene added. "But I'm not quite in the same league. If you don't mind a kind of slower pace...."

"That's ok by me, you two," I happily explained. "I'm not far out of the tortoise category myself."

I guessed Marlene's comment about John being a strong rider was not an exaggeration, for although John was a cook by trade, he looked more like a linebacker for the Cleveland Browns. Tall and blond, he was put together in a very solid fashion that belied his cookery background. On the other hand, Marlene seemed to fit in with the native population. Slender with long dark hair, she had an olive complexion and a sunny smile. They were an attractive and friendly couple and I felt good about teaming up with them for however long our paths coincided. We pedaled out of Parma in good spirits, now a threesome.

We passed the day in a comfortable pace across the fertile Po River Valley, Italy's breadbasket, taking in the sights and aromas of the late Italian summer. We traded tales of the road as we pedaled and delighted in each other's company— they perhaps because of somebody new to talk to and me for just anybody to talk to. On approaching the outskirts of Bologna, we all realized that our daylight would not be with us much longer and that our immediate task was to find a spot to pitch our tents for the night. No campgrounds had presented themselves as we coasted into the city, and before too long we were resorting to my technique of knocking on doors, hoping to find a sympathetic Italian family that would allow us to pitch our tents on a small piece of their property. Our first couple of efforts found empty houses and on the third, a young girl came to the door. She gave us a rather bewildered look, not quite knowing what to make of our strange request. When at last she understood the meaning of what we were asking, the flustered young lady explained in very broken English that her parents were not home and that it would be up to her father. Our further inquiries as to when her father might return produced a shake of the head, and at that point we realized that this would not be our haven for the night.

By this time darkness had almost descended and it looked as though we were going to be left high and dry for the night.

"Well guys, it looks like it's going to be a long night," Marlene moaned.

"Now don't give up yet, Marlene," I tried to encourage. "We'll just keep on knocking and sooner or later. . ."

"Bonsurno!" came a call from across the roadway.

The "Bonsurno" came from a friendly-looking Italian man who had been watching us from behind his fence. We pushed our bikes across the road in the semi-darkness and greeted our observer. Using sign language and the few Italian words that we could muster, we once again explained our predicament and when he finally understood the situation, a large smile spread across his features. He looked at us and then at his well-manicured yard, and with a sweep of his arm, he indicated that his yard was our yard.

Weary and feeling as though we had been delivered from the clutches of the night, we began to prepare our makeshift campsite. While we were setting up our tents our genial host appeared holding a large bottle of beer and three glasses. We showered him with "grazie"s (thank yous) and promptly sucked down the suds, agreeing that it was one of the best beers that we had ever tasted. Since our stomachs were suffering from a definite lack of food, I fired up my cookstove—a luxury that John and Marlene were traveling without—and John put his culinary skills to work by creating a tasty pasta and sauce dish that put my attempts at campsite cookery to shame. Before long, however, our friendly Italian emerged from the back of his home carrying a table and three chairs that transformed our campsite into a kitchen and dining area. As we sat down to our feast he materialized once more, this time holding a bottle of chilled wine which we understood came from his own cellar of wine that he made himself. We ate heartily and sipped the wine which like the beer, was probably about the best wine we had ever tasted. And lastly, when our friend saw that we were done with our meal, he invited us to join a small family gathering for some Cappucino and a lot of sign language and wild gesturing. We finally crawled into our sleeping bags, slightly touched by the beer and wine, but warmed more by the tremendous hospitality of this kind Italian man and his family.

The next morning as we were packing up our gear our host came out to see us off. But before we left he invited us one more time to join him at his table to have some morning toast and coffee. Before mounting our bicycles we grasped his hand warmly and tried to convey our gratitude for his taking in three strangers from another country and for treating us as part of the family. As we pedaled out of Bologna I reflected on how this experience contrasted with the theft in Milan. There are good and bad people in every country, city, and village on the face of the globe, and often it is just a matter of pure chance whether you come in contact with the good or the bad. Since Milan I had been harboring some pretty ill feelings toward all of Italy, in spite of the Italian blood coursing through my veins—my grandmother's maiden name was Bertoli. But our night here in Bologna went a long way towards purging those ill feelings and shedding a new light on the hospitality of the Italian people.

Leaving Bologna, we climbed out of the Po River Valley and entered Italy's mountainous interior. Most of the central portion of "the Boot" is dominated by the Apennine Mountains and they are sometimes referred to as the "spine" of Italy since they just about run the north-south length of the country. They are not high mountains, but it is a rugged terrain with a special beauty, and it offers a challenge to any touring cyclist as we soon found out. We spent most of the day huffing and puffing our way up a couple of mountain passes, and as we climbed I thought of the terrible obstacle this terrain proved to be for the Allies during World War II. They spent many months slugging their way up the Italian boot, sustaining a great loss of life and many casualties so they could come a knockin' on Hitler's southern door. Too bad they couldn't enjoy it as we were enjoying it now, in spite of the hefty grades.

The following day we coasted down, out of the Apennines, gliding through the hilly countryside of Tuscany where Leonardo once wandered as a youth, sketching and contemplating the great beauty and mystery of nature. Our route brought us into the valley of the Arno River and to the jewel of the Italian High Renaissance—Florence. It is here that some of the greatest works of art achieved by humankind can be found. Under the guidance and patronage of the powerful Medici family, especially Cosimo I and Lorenzo the Magnificent, Florence became the cultural engine that powered the rebirth of learning and a new interest in painting, sculpture, science, and exploration that spread to all corners of Europe and the new world. That it happened in this spot is logical because Italy, since the fall of Rome, had been a fallow field under which lay the seeds of our Greek and Roman heritage which was at the heart of the Renaissance. These seeds burst forth in the fifteenth and sixteenth centuries, giving us one of the greatest flowerings of cultural activity in the history of Western Civilization.

John, Marlene, and I headed for the campground on the outskirts of Florence and it proved to be a beautiful location up in the hills with an excellent view overlooking the city. It also proved to be one of the largest campgrounds I had ever seen. After we pitched our tents amidst a sea of tents, we prepared to go back into the city for a feast of cultural appreciation. For the day and a half that we planned to stay in Florence we decided to go our separate ways—they had things they wanted especially to see, and I did too—and so we agreed to meet back in the evening to prepare supper.

It was a treat to be off the bike and to just walk through the streets of Florence and to appreciate some of the most wondrous things to be seen. For the remainder of the afternoon I visited the Baptistery and the "Doors of Paradise," the Duomo (the domed cathedral), and the Church of Santa Croce where Galileo and Nicolo Machiavelli are entombed. On the following day my first stop was the Acadamy where I marveled at Michelangelo's *David* that he sculpted out of a huge block of marble that no other artist wanted to touch because it was thought to be a bad quality stone. When they saw what he accomplished they probably could have kicked themselves for not attempting such a great work as Michelangelo had. David seemed so lifelike that at any moment he might step off his pedestal and explain to me how he caught that overgrown brute Goliath flush in the face with his slingshot. From there it was over to the Uffizi Gallery to look at the heart of Renaissance painting—Leonardo, Raphael, Titian, Michelangelo—all masters who left us a heritage that cannot be counted in dollars. My last stop was the Museum of Science which has a great display of Renaissance scientific instruments, many of them coming from the Medici collection. One of the highlights was Galileo's middle finger which is on display—probably the same one he used to wave at the Church Court at the end of his celebrated trial.

Each evening we met back at the campground, satiated on renaissance art, and exchanged notes on what we had seen during the day. We did this over a couple of cool beers supplied by the well-stocked camp store. The heat of central Italy's late summer was fierce, and I had never realized that art appreciation could work up such a huge thirst. After our beer, John raided the camp store once again and I fired up my little stove. John's cooking skills and my stove proved to be a perfect match, for he whipped up some pretty tasty dishes; I could tell he had a great future as an Italian chef! The day was usually concluded with a little gellato—Italian ice cream—that was surely a gift of the Roman gods and one that would make Baskin and Robbins drool with envy.

It had been an enjoyable and enriching day-and-a-half, and the next morning as we continued our push in a southeasterly direction toward the Adriatic coast, I started to think about the posters of Michelangelo's *David* and his *Pieta* that I should have purchased back in Florence. They would look great hanging in my classroom when we studied about the great masters of the Renaissance.

"Hold on, guys!" I yelled out to John and Marlene, bringing our little caravan to a screeching halt. "I really wish now that I had bought those posters that I was telling you about. We're only about ten miles outside of the city, and I figure if I hustle back and pick up the posters, and you two continue on at a leisurely pace, I should catch up to you some time this afternoon."

"That's OK by us, Al. Whatever you want to do. We'll try and take it easy today," John agreed.

"And if we decide to stop somewhere," Marlene added," we'll be sure to leave one of our bikes out by the side of the road; be sure to keep a close eye out though! Good luck!"

That decided, we bade each other farewell, temporarily we hoped, and I hightailed it back to Florence. I made good time and bought my posters without a hitch, and in about an hour and a half I found myself back in the same spot where I had parted with John and Marlene. However, by that time I had already clocked thirty miles on my odometer and my two friends had to be twenty or so miles up the road. From that point I battened down the hatches, gritted my teeth, and cycled like a man with a mission. I stretched myself close to the limit, my cranks spinning as if they had a mind of their own—maybe not "Tour de France" caliber cycling, but definitely not your leisurely Sunday ride.

Late in the afternoon as I pushed hard through a small village, my head buried in my handlebars, I heard a familiar voice call out: "Hey, Al, over here!" It was John and in one hand he held a beer and with the other he waved frantically trying to get my attention as I sped on by, oblivious to the world around me. John and Marlene and two other cyclists, John and Laurie, were relaxing at a sidewalk cafe nursing some cold beer that soon found its way into my sweaty palms. They were the most welcome sight I had seen that day and we greeted each other with huge smiles as if it had been weeks, not hours, since we had seen one another. John and Laurie had also spent most of their summer cycling in Italy and were soon going to be returning home to New York. They were a personable young couple and for the next hour we talked of cycling in Italy and quaffed down another beer or two.

By the time we hopped back on our bicycles, our little group had now grown to five. The lengthening shadows spoke of fleeting daylight, and so we decided to ride another ten miles to the small town of Passignano on the shores of

Lake Trasimeno. Those last miles had a curious tilt to them under the influence of two soothing beers, and it was with a sigh of relief that we all collapsed at our free campsite on the shores of the lake. Total miles for this very long day—one hundred and five—my longest riding day yet!

After we established our little community of tents, it was "last one into the lake is a rotten egg" time. Before too long, the heat, stress, and strain of the hundred plus miles fell victim to the chilly but invigorating waters of Lake Trasimeno. But as we splashed each other with great enthusiasm, my friends were not aware that two thousand and two years before in 217 B.C., these very same waters had run red with blood—the blood of fifteen thousand Roman legionaries who died at the hands of one of the greatest military geniuses of history—Hannibal Barca. The Battle of Lake Trasimeno was one of the worst defeats suffered by the Roman armies during the Second Punic War which lasted from 218 B.C. until 204 B.C. The wily Carthagenian general, Hannibal, ambushed the Roman legions as they traversed the narrow passage between the surrounding hills and the shores of the lake where we now frolicked. The early morning mists on that day long ago swirled about the heads of the Romans so that they could barely see in front of them. As they were drawn deeper into the narrow passageway according to Hannibal's plan, the Carthagenian army, waiting in ambush, swooped down upon the Roman legions and the terrible slaughter began. The fighting was so fierce and the thunder of battle so great on this day, that nobody noticed another thunder—the thunder of an earthquake that rolled across the land at the height of the engagement. The British poet Lord Byron made note of this occurrence in a verse from *Childe Harold:*

> And such the storm of battle on this day,
> And such the frenzy, whose convulsion blinds
> To all save carnage, that, beneath the fray
> An earthquake rolled unheedingly away!
> None felt stern nature rocking at his feet,
> And yawning forth a grave for those who lay
> Upon their bucklers for a winding sheet,
> Such is the absorbing hate when warring nations meet.

There was another site where the Romans suffered a worse defeat, and my journey down the Italian boot would bring me to that solemn place in another ten days. Trying not to sound like a schoolteacher, I explained to my friends that at one point in time this had not been the peaceful spot that it seemed to be now. They seemed surprised and amazed that it could have happened here—this postcard setting that was now treating us to an idyllic sunset over the peaceful hills surrounding Lake Trasimeno.

In the morning John, Marlene, and I said good-bye to John and Laurie, and we headed on toward the Adriatic coast. About midday we began a fairly hefty climb into the upper reaches of this sector of the Apennines. The terrain was rugged but quite beautiful, and as we climbed higher we could feel the hot, sultry air of the interior valleys give way to the cool, invigorating air of the upper elevations. As we rose, our spirits seemed to rise also; it was part of the nature of mountain riding—that sense of freedom and accomplishment from knowing you don't need a motor and two thousand pounds of metal surrounding you to get you up and over a mountainous terrain. And there also was that familiar sense of being one with the environment and seeing things in a unique way—a way that only cyclists and backpackers can know.

Late in the afternoon we reached the mountain pass that would send us scudding down out of the Apennines. Instead of beginning our descent so late in the day, we chose to remain in the fresh mountain air and find a place to camp close by. When we came to a small mountain village that had a pleasant little park, we knew that this was the place to sojourn for the night.

Surrounding the perimeter of the little park were a number of small apartment buildings with balconies which afforded their inhabitants a pleasant overlook. While John and Marlene busied themselves setting up camp, I knocked on one of the apartment's back doors with my water sack in my hand. When a middle-aged Italian lady answered my knock, I produced my best American smile and asked politely "Agua caliente?", hoping that my Spanish was close enough to the Italian words. My message apparently got through for she beamed a broad smile and motioned me to come into her kitchen where her tap produced a heavenly stream of hot water. I thanked her profusely and returned to our campsite with my treasure. John and Marlene had not seen my water bag before, and when I told them of its intended purpose, their eyes lit up. It had been a long day of mountain riding accompanied by the inescapable layers of sweat, and public showers are not a standard feature of small, village parks. Bicycle tourists desire nothing more than to get clean at the end of a strenuous day, and this we now proceeded to do. John climbed a nearby stone wall and perched above Marlene's head with the water bag at the ready. He opened the spigot on the sack and the mini-waterfall commenced.

"Oh Lord, I think I've died and gone to heaven," Marlene purred as the hot water cascaded off her head and shoulders. "Al, that water bag is a gift of the gods! Why, it's even better than...than Oreo cookies!"

The shower was short but sweet, being only a two and a half gallon water sack. We each, in turn, took our place under the stone wall after refills from the friendly apartment dwellers who were now crowding their balconies, laughing and waving at the three squeaky-clean American cyclists.

The next morning, after a good night's sleep—after a clean night's sleep—we finished our descent out of the Apennines. It was an amazingly easy cycle. It was one of those days where the sun shone, the terrain was all downhill, and a friendly tail wind hurried us along—cyclists' paradise. As we hit the coast of the Adriatic Sea, we pointed our front wheels south toward the heel of "the boot." About mid-afternoon we came upon a nice-looking campground, and even though we still had plenty of daylight for riding, we decided that we would "splurge" here for the night. It was a full-service campground with showers, a camp store, and the works, and after raiding the little grocery, Chef John whipped up another Italian feast fit for the Pope himself (even though he's a Pole). However, this Italian feast was going to provide a less-than-welcome surprise for us somewhere in the wee hours of the coming morning.

It hit us all at the same time! I woke up in the darkness with a terrible fullness in the pit of my stomach, as if I had just swallowed ten pounds of pasta. I weaved my way to the camp bathrooms and coming in the opposite direction was Marlene with a sorrowful look adorning her features. She had been camping out in the john reviewing everything she had eaten in the last twenty-four hours.

"Oh, God, I feel terrible," she moaned. "Like the Roman army just marched across my stomach."

"I know," I groaned back. "I think the same army detoured through my tent."

I took Marlene's position of honor at the commode, and then before too long it was John's turn to stare into the white porcelain. In the morning three weak and pale cyclists crawled out of their tents. We knew without speaking that last night's Italian feast was the culprit that had left its calling card. We tried to figure out what it was that we had eaten that made us all feel like we were nigh death's door. The canned mushrooms which had gone into the pasta sauce were high on the suspicion list.

Since the thought of eating breakfast knotted our already ravaged stomachs, we listlessly packed our bicycles and just as listlessly began riding. Luckily, a merciful tail wind pushed us along, but by midday it was clear we would not make it much farther in our sick and weakened condition. We paused by the side of the road and exchanged looks that said none of us had much left.

"We've been in the rough for the last week—camping out every night," I reasoned. "Whadaya' say we look for a room; God knows we could use it tonight—and those clouds up there don't look too friendly either. And it feels like it's getting cooler and..."

"Say no more, Al," John interrupted. "That's the best idea I've heard all day! Let's look."

The thought of being warm and snug for the night gave us the extra energy to make it to the nearest pensione. The owner spoke a little English and informed us that the price would be thirty-seven thousand lire, but we were able to bargain him down to thirty thousand lire, explaining that we were all very close to death. The pasty look on our faces aided us in our tale of sorrow and woe. Upon entering our room we were greeted by two spacious, inviting beds and here we collapsed for the remainder of the day. My whole body felt like a lead weight, and as my head hit the pillow, the rain began to descend in buckets outside our window. In my last moment of consciousness, I thought how wonderfully terrific it was to be exactly where we were—and not out there!

We awoke the next morning feeling rested and somewhat rejuvenated—understandable since we had slept about fifteen straight hours. This would be my last day together with John and Marlene, as the winds of bicycle touring would blow us in different directions. We attempted to make up for our short mileage of the previous day and covered about seventy-five miles along the Adriatic coast, again with the same strong tail wind. The weather on this day, August 28, was almost fall-like, with cool temperatures and dark, blustery skies merging with the unsettled Adriatic off to our left. The heavy seas and angry surf testified to the strength of the wind that was urging us farther south. We spent our final evening together at a relatively deserted campsite and decided it would be wise not to eat too much for dinner, for our tummies were still protesting about the ordeal of the other night. Instead, we set up our tents and just sat and talked for a while, and then turned in early, taking note of the shortened days of the waning summer season here in this Mediterranean land.

I said farewell to my two friends outside of Foggia. They planned to ride on to Bari where they would catch the boat for Greece. This was also my eventual goal, but one of the most fantastic sites of Roman antiquity—Pompeii—lay eighty miles to the west on the Bay of Naples, and this I had to see. In our nine days together we had shared some highs and lows and become close; it was tough to say good-bye. I watched until they rode out of sight, and once again I found myself on my own.

The next few days would prove to be "the best of times and the worst of times"—the best of times because wandering through the ruins of Pompeii was an experience I had been looking forward to since the start of my trip. In this I would not be disappointed. It would be the worst of times because I had to again battle the loneliness bugaboo. John and Marlene's absence underscored the value of riding companions and the moral support they could provide when you found yourself down in the dumps. Add to that the roadside trash and filth that seemed to mar much of southern Italy and another episode of Italian thievery, and I nearly had the recipe for ending my trip.

The worst of times immediately set in that night. I had decided that I would take the bus from Foggia to Naples since bicycling from east to west would actually be backtracking, and I had no desire to cross the same mountain range three times. Unfortunately, however, the next bus did not leave until early the next morning. Normally this fact would not have presented much of a problem, but the pensione rates in this part of Italy were out of my budget-traveler's price range and, try as I might, I could locate no secluded piece of ground on which to pitch my tent. Long after the sun had made its exit from the western sky, I found myself wandering aimlessly the streets of Foggia. Finally, on the outskirts of the city I came upon an abandoned dwelling. Here I spent a few restless hours trying to sleep, but mostly listening to the chilling wind whistle through the broken windows of my desolate shelter and worrying that a band of Italian brigands would make short work of me and my bicycle.

The bus ride across central, southern Italy did little to lift my spirits. The land appeared desolate—almost like a moonscape in some parts—and as I stared out the window, my negative thoughts drove me deeper into depression. By the time the bus reached the outskirts of Naples, I was all ready to hop the next plane back home. But from somewhere came that special reserve of strength and determination that cyclists must tap every so often. Part of that reserve sprang from the knowledge that no matter how terrible things might seem at one point in time, it would pass; there would be better times ahead. And with this hope, I proceeded on to the youth hostel located on the Bay of Naples.

I awoke on my first morning in Naples and things didn't look quite so grim, especially with the anticipation of seeing Pompeii. I caught the train that circumvents the base of towering Mt. Vesuvius, and before too long I found myself standing in the middle of a time capsule.

Pompeii—the name evokes images of Roman antiquity and a way of life forever vanished. But thanks to the eruption of Mt. Vesuvius in the first century A.D. (though rather unlucky for Pompeii's ancient inhabitants), we have the opportunity to walk the streets of a Roman city virtually brought back to life through decades of careful excavation and restoration; it is a window to the past.

Today Pompeii is ruled by the sound and footstep of the tourist, but once it pulsed with life as one of the most important industrial, trade, and port cities of Rome's empire. For centuries the citizens of Pompeii had lived their lives in the shadow of the great mountain, unaware that their mountain was in reality a sleeping volcano on the verge of a catastrophic reawakening. Memories of the last eruption had fallen victim to the passage of time and so the slopes of Vesuvius were blanketed with vineyards, farmhouses, and the sumptuous villas of the wealthy. In the first century A.D. Pompeii was home for twenty thousand inhabitants—merchants, slaves, freedmen, artisans, and aristocrats. The city was organized in the orderly Roman fashion with intersecting streets forming blocks or insulae. It boasted all the amenities of a thriving Roman town—public baths and latrines, numerous street-side taverns and cafes, a forum, a large and small theater, gymnasia, and an amphitheater, or arena, that was built a century before the Colosseum in Rome.

Pompeii's citizens were no strangers to disaster, for in A.D. 62 an earthquake had destroyed much of the city. By A.D. 79 much of Pompeii had been rebuilt and there was still much reconstruction in progress. However, reconstruction, and life itself, would proceed no farther for the citizens of this doomed Roman city.

In the early afternoon hours of 24 August, A.D. 79, most Pompeians had just finished their midday meal and were either preparing to rest or take their leisure at one of the public baths. The peace and calm of their late summer's day was suddenly shattered by the thunderous explosion of Mt. Vesuvius. The mountain had literally blown its top. Above the volcano billowed an ever-expanding cloud of volcanic debris—flames, smoke, ash and red-hot lava stones. Higher and higher the mushrooming cloud reached as it began to spread out over the plain of the River Sarno, unleashing its lethal rain of hot ash, pumice stone, and asphyxiating gases. Soon, the angry cloud of debris turned the light of day into the black of night. The ground rumbled and shook while the sea churned, and bolts of lightning pierced the terrible darkness. To most of Pompeii's inhabitants it must have seemed the end of the world, and for many indeed it was. Thousands died either trying to hide from their impending doom in their own homes or seeking avenues of escape, only to be overtaken by the poisonous gases that permeated the smoking landscape. The rain of death continued unabated for three days, burying Pompeii's newly reconstructed buildings and many of her unlucky residents under a blanket of volcanic ash and pumice stone from fifteen to twenty feet deep—the blanket would be the city's death shroud.

In the meantime, Herculaneum, a smaller village of seaside villas frequented by the patrician class, was suffering a different fate. Initially, the people of Herculaneum may have felt the gods were smiling on them, for angry Vesuvius was spewing its red-hot innards in a southerly direction over Pompeii. But it was a false smile, for disaster was imminent. Approximately twelve hours after the initial eruption, the twenty-mile high column of smoke, ash, and debris collapsed, creating a volcanic surge—similar to a shock wave from a nuclear bomb explosion—that blasted down the slopes of Vesuvius and through Herculaneum at sixty miles per hour. This was followed by a slower moving flow of molten lava and mud that entombed the seaside resort in a cement-like coffin.

The buildings of these two ancient communities would not see the light of day for another eighteen hundred years, for although Vesuvius' fallout extinguished all life, it also acted to preserve Pompeii and Herculaneum as if frozen in time. For eighteen centuries they lay buried and forgotten until their chance discovery in the 1700s. Careful and systematic excavations were begun in the mid 1800s and continue even today, for parts of Pompeii and Herculaneum still lie buried. Some secrets may never be yielded up, since modern-day Herculano rests atop the remains of her ancient ancestor. Even so, these windows to the past have revealed to the modern world an intimate look at the Roman world of the first century A.D.

As I wandered over the ancient stones of Pompeii, I could almost sense the heartbeat of this once-bustling city— the luxurious houses of Pompeii's rich merchants; her many roadside shops; the streets with their stepping stones and grooves left by innumerable carts and chariots; the arena where gladiators drew each other's blood; the public baths where citizens socialized and washed away the cares of their day; the restaurants and food stalls opening onto the streets where the ancient passers-by could stop for a snack or beverage; and, the figures of those Pompeians whose final moments of life were forever frozen in time by the ash which surrounded their bodies—all of this made it easy for me to imagine how it was just before time stood still for the people of Pompeii and Herculaneum.

Early in the evening I caught the train back to Naples feeling satisfied and content. I reflected on all that I had seen as we passed beneath the cone of sleeping Vesuvius; it had been a day well spent. But this interlude of contentment was fleeting, for two things occurred to shatter that. The first thing was that the flash on my smaller second camera ceased working—not a major setback, although I did use it in certain situations when my better camera had the wrong speed film loaded in it. It was just another one of those little things that gets under your skin. The second item was far more up-setting, especially in light of the recent theft of my camera in Milan. On the morning of my third day in Naples, I came out of the youth hostel to inspect my bike which was locked to the bike rack located on a kind of side porch. The area, I had assumed, was fairly secure because you had to pass through the hostel in order to get to the porch, so it was not accessible to anyone just passing by—wrong again! The first thing that attracted my attention was the dangling wire which should have led up to my cycle computer that on the day before, had been mounted on my handle bars. Now there was only the empty bracket and the dangling wire. Once again, I could feel the rage build within me; it welled up like the hot magma of an active volcano—how appropriate. I was ready to explode as Vesuvius had done two thousand years ago. I was now convinced that thieves and scoundrels lurked behind every bush and within every doorway in Italy, and I wanted nothing more than to get my hands around the neck of just one of them. But seeing as how no thief willingly presented himself so that I could do just that, I did nothing but simmer and think about how much I would miss my little cycle computer. I had grown quite attached to it, for on long riding days it helped to pass the hours by punching the various buttons which supplied me with all kinds of interesting details on speed, time, mileage, etc. It was even more maddening to think that the computer would do the thief absolutely no good since he had not taken the other parts of the unit that would make it operable. But ultimately, I knew it was again my carelessness. I should have removed the computer from my bike. It was easily dismountable, but I had just not given it the thought or time. Another lesson learned the hard way.

At that point I'd had enough of Naples, and I knew it was time to head back to the Adriatic coast before any more Neapolitan thieves helped themselves to the rest of my worldly belongings. I caught the same series of buses back to Foggia from where I would continue my journey south toward Bari and my final stop in this country which had served up a smorgasbord of good and bad luck. As we threaded our way through the central mountains, I thought back to the border crossing between France and Italy and how prophetic it had been. When the teller at the exchange bank almost shortchanged me fifty dollars, little did I realize that it was an ill omen of events yet to come.

By the time we arrived back in Foggia, it was early evening and daylight was fleeting. I had no desire to spend another night in an abandoned building as I had done before on the outskirts of the city, so I did my best to inquire about the whereabouts of any nearby campgrounds. My inquiries produced a vague set of directions from a friendly Foggian who thought there might be a campground "over thataway". Obligingly, I rode in the direction of "over thataway", but no campground was to be found. Another inquiry sent me back north in the opposite direction of "over thataway", but still no campground. Finally, with a dark, moonless night upon me, I came upon a lonely road that led me to a beachfront community of trailer sites that appeared to be closed for the season.

I knocked on the door of what I figured to be the camp office and my rapping was promptly answered by a middle-aged Italian man who gave me a curious inspection and a look that seemed to say, "Sorry my friend, but you're about two weeks too late for the vacation season around these parts." I launched into my standard spiel which featured a combination of my limited Italian vocabulary and a few appropriate gestures which I hoped expressed my desperation for a place to throw my tent for the night. By this time it was pitch black out and I knew that riding any farther was out of the question. My performance must have been an award winner, for the man's look of curiosity turned to one of pity, and he indicated that I should pitch my tent in one of the many empty campsites.

This campground was definitely not established with the tent camper in mind, and so I proceeded to find the softest-looking patch of dirt and gravel on which to situate my little blue domicile. While I worked to set up my tent, my camp host and a smaller man with a wiry and grizzled look converged on my campsite and treated me to a shouting match of which I was the focus. Their argument featured much wild gesturing, and what it was about, I could only guess. The smaller man definitely appeared to be less than pleased with my presence in the campground. Happily, he stormed off and my savior shook his head and gave me a half smile, and at last I felt secure that I had a place to sojourn for the night.

With my tent firmly established, I dug into my panniers to find the bread, cheese, and fruit that I had purchased earlier that evening. With these and a life-saving bottle of beer which I bought from the camp manager, I headed down to the beckoning seashore. There, amongst the abandoned cabanas and the stacked tables and chairs which told of a summer season gone by, I sat down on the pier and consumed a much-needed meal. The surf played a gentle tune on the silent sands while I munched and it lulled me into a pensive and somewhat strange mood. The past few days had been difficult ones for me, but yet I felt happy and content sitting there alone on this quiet and abandoned beach. Once again, I thought of what lay ahead. What did Greece hold in store for me? And if Greece treated me kindly, beyond that lay the frightening prospect of bicycle touring in Africa and the Third World. That frightening prospect would soon become a reality.

* * *

Looking out across the plain, I tried hard to hear the clash of sword and shield; to see where Hannibal formed up his troops into his battle line and where the Roman legions formed theirs; where the two armies began their charge, moving like a couple of steamrollers bound for a head-on collision; and where they met—the noise, confusion, the cries of pain and anguish, and the shouts of victory for the great Carthaginian general and his army. Today, Cannae is quiet and serene, the broad plain covered with vineyards and olive groves. The only reminder of the greatest struggle of the Second Punic War between the Carthaginians and the Romans is the crumbling ruin of the Roman fortress and supply depot that overlooks the broad plain where the Battle of Cannae took place.

In 217 B.C. these two great armies met on the plain below where I now stood. It was Hannibal's greatest victory and the Roman's most devastating defeat. In a battle that lasted from five to six hours the Romans lost perhaps as many as fifty thousand men which equals approximately the number of soldiers the United States lost in ten years of fighting the Vietnam War. Hannibal employed his classic double-envelopment. He tricked the Romans into attacking the bulge in the middle of his battle line, and when the bulge collapsed, what to the Romans seemed like an initial victory soon became a hellish nightmare. The Romans were sucked into the middle of the battle line, and Hannibal's cavalry on the wings encircled the doomed Roman army. It soon became a field of death and the ground disappeared under layers of Roman dead. Standing there now, it was hard to imagine such a scene of horror and devastation. Hannibal's battle plan became a model of military strategy and has been studied ever since by students of battlefield tactics. It was even copied by Germany's General Von Schliefen in World War I as a part of his design for the encirclement and defeat of France.

I was disappointed in the site itself, for there was very little information for the visitor about the battle—where it took place exactly; how it was fought; and its terrible consequences. There appeared to be a small museum that was either being renovated or rebuilt, but there were no artifacts from the battle inside or any other information that would give one a clue about the importance of this historical site. Of course, the battle took place only about twenty-two hundred years ago, and it seemed as if the Italian government was just getting around to doing honor and justice to this sacred place.

* * *

On September 7, I wheeled into Bari, my final stop on the Italian Peninsula and my jump-off point for the sail to Greece. It was true that Italy had thrown a few curve balls my way, but it had also taught me some valuable lessons about taking the extra time and care to protect your worldly belongings while on tour. One of the most important lessons to be heeded by all cycle tourists is never give a thief a chance by making that added effort to protect your equipment, for if the opportunity is there, your possessions will soon become history. It makes no difference how worthy or altruistic you feel your intentions are. You could be on a ride for world hunger or you could be Mother Theresa herself, bicycling from mission to mission; the thieves and scoundrels who prey on travelers would steal the bicycle right out from underneath you. They care nothing for your good intentions. Italy had lived up to its reputation for thievery, but I also knew theft is a problem in any large city around the world. And for every thief in Italy, there were scores of decent and honest Italians who treated foreigners such as myself with hospitality and warm hearts.

So as the curtain came down on this episode of my adventure, I thought not of the unfortunate things, but the good things—standing before Leonardo's *Last Supper*, my friendship and shared experiences with John and Marlene, the kind man in Bologna who extended to us his warm hospitality, and the wonder of Pompeii. The good always seems to cancel out the bad, and that is the way it should be. Italy had been no exception to this rule.

FIVE

Greece

Mr. Sun gazed down from a cloudless sky and smiled on the spacious ferryboat that was transporting me and my fellow passengers through the calm waters of the Adriatic Sea and into the azure depths of the Ionian. The invigorating sea breeze whipped warmly about us while gulls dipped and darted playfully in our wake. On the uppermost deck of the ship I lounged in solar bliss with Moshe, an Israeli, his girlfriend, Thia, who was an American, and Till, a young German cyclist. We had all met while boarding the ship in Bari for the 18-hour voyage to Patras, Greece. And now, here we all were, like old friends, camped out in the middle of our gear on the open, sun-drenched deck. We each produced a copious amount of food which we had brought along to tide us over for the journey and set it out in a kind of potluck in which we all shared. While we supped, we spoke of our travels, and Moshe and Thia explained how they earned money as they went, making and selling some sort of East Indian game. That night the upper deck became our open air bedroom and we were lulled to sleep by the fresh air and the steady drone of the ship's engines.

The next day, as we approached the coast of Greece, we glided past the island of Ithaca, the home of the legendary Greek hero, Odysseus. I imagined his beautiful wife, Penelope, gazing out from the upper windows of his palace, looking longingly for the return of her long-absent husband who had been ten years in battle on the plains of Troy. It took him another ten years before he was able to thwart the will of Posiedon and at long last return home to his beloved isle of Ithaca.

Late that afternoon, as our ship nosed into the port of Patras, we were all slightly half-baked and crazed by the sun. We bade each other farewell and fair luck, after which I proceeded to the youth hostel, Till to a campground, and Moshe and Thia to a train bound for Athens. Once again, four lives had briefly intersected, shared some thoughts and experiences, and gone their separate ways.

Just as the French-Italian border crossing where I was almost shortchanged fifty dollars had been an ill omen of things to come in Italy, my first heavenly piece of baklava in Patras would be a harbinger of good tidings that lay ahead in Greece. I had the feeling, even before I pedaled out of Patras, that I was going to enjoy this country. In this I would not be disappointed. I had not been there 24 hours yet, but I already felt quite comfortable. People seemed to be friendly and helpful, and the prices, too, were in the comfort zone. In fact, I was surprised at how inexpensive Greece appeared to be when compared to Italy—no small concern for the shoe-string traveler. And Greek cuisine was also to my liking—after overloading on pasta—with a great variety of dishes to choose from. I really liked the custom in Greek restaurants of being invited back into the kitchen by the chef to see what's cookin', and to have the opportunity to select the dish that catches your eye and nose. Of course, the Greek pastries were right up sweet-tooth alley, which is where I live a good part of the time, and, as I indicated before, the baklava was out of this world.

However, one of the main reasons I looked forward with anticipation to Greece was because it would be my first experience with this culture which has contributed so much to the western world. The Greeks broke ground in so many different areas—government, philosophy, science, theater, art and architecture—and in so doing they laid the foundations for the later cultures of Western Europe and the New World. This also served to remind me that as I continued my eastward journey, each new culture that I experienced was more ancient than the one before it and in many ways influenced those cultures that followed.

One of my first discoveries as I headed south into the Peloponnesus was that Greece has an excellent system of campgrounds. On my first night out of Patras I stayed in a tidy little municipal campground in a perfect spot right on the tranquil shores of the Ionian Sea. I set up my tent not 30 feet from the gently lapping surf and settled back to watch a golden sunset that could have been a gift of only Zeus himself. The orb of the sun turned a fiery crimson as it hung low over the hazy outline of the isle of Zakinthos which was visible far out to sea. While sitting there trying to drink in the beauty of the vista that lay before me, my thoughts drifted 6000 miles to the West to Toledo, Ohio. But this time it wasn't a case of the blues that goes along with being so far away from home; it was, in fact, just the opposite. I must confess to feeling slightly smug about the fact that I was sitting there dangling my toes in the Ionian Sea while at that very moment my fellow teachers and students of the previous year were slaving away in the coal mines of education. However, that feeling of smugness was carried away on the sea breezes when I thought about all that I had gone through up to that point in my travels and the difficult times that surely lay ahead.

Continuing south following the coastal route, I arrived in the seaside town of Pyrgos. There I paused for a badly needed shave and a haircut. The shave I gave myself; the haircut I received from a friendly local barber who did a pretty fair job. With my Greek phrase book I explained I wanted a little off all the way around, and after my haircut I shook the barber's hand warmly and bid him a hearty "efharistow" which brought an even bigger smile to his face. From Pyrgos I headed inland toward a place that would leave a lasting impression on me. It was a place about which I taught my students every year when we studied Greek history, for its name is synonymous with the spirit of the Golden Age of Greece and the ideal of excellence. The name of the place was Olympia.

* * *

The Eternal Afterglow. This metaphor has sometimes been used when speaking of the cultural heritage of ancient

Hellas (Greece). Never was that ancient light of the past more apparent to me than on the day on which I bathed in its golden reflection. This was the day I visited the beautiful valley of Olympia, the site of the most important religious and athletic festivals in all of ancient Greece. It turned out to be one of those days from my year of travel that stands out above all the rest—a day that I won't soon forget. I will let my journal entry for Wednesday, September 11, 1985, describe this memorable experience:

> I can feel the chills as I stand in the *Altis*, or Sacred Grove, listening to the late summer breezes whisper through the olive and cypress trees. I gaze up at the hills that embrace this picturesque valley—the same hills that had gazed down upon centuries of Olympic victors who came here to honor Zeus with their triumphs. This is Olympia, site of the Ancient Olympic Games, the most important games throughout all Greece, not only because of their great prestige, but also because they brought a brief period of peace and unity to the fiercely independent city-states of Hellas. It's easy to see why the Greeks thought this a sacred place. It seems to cast a spell, even today, over the 20th century visitor who wanders through the ruins of these great temples and athletic facilities that speak of the ancient Greeks' belief in the spirit of athletic competition. These games had the power to bring together rival city-states, even during times of war, and make them forget their differences. Instead, the games helped to stress the common bonds that they all shared—their language, their gods, their cultural heritage and their belief in the human spirit. To this end, the Sacred Truce was established at the very beginning of the games in 776 B.C., and it forbade armies or armed soldiers from entering the district of Olympia and nearby Elis. All hostilities throughout the Greek world were to cease for a month (eventually three) so that athletes and spectators could have safe passage

to this holy site. Violators would lose their right to participate in the games, and would be required to pay a fine. So these were much more than just athletic contests; they were a catalyst for peace, an affirmation of something good that could bring an end to conflict, if only temporarily, and help strengthen the bonds that all Greeks shared. And their spirit is carried on today, despite the political chicanery, through the modern Olympiad which still has the power to bring nations together in peace. Its roots can be found where I stand now—in the Sacred Altis!

When the games first began back in 776 B.C. a more apropos designation might have been "The Game," because there was only one event. This event was the stade—or the dash—which was approximately 192 meters long or the distance of the straight-away in the stadium at Olympia. (This, of course, is the origin of the word stadium.) People from all over Greece would travel for days just to witness this one event which lasted no more than 30 seconds. Throughout the long history of the games this remained the premier event. The winner of the stade would have that Olympiad named after him; he would be exempt from paying taxes; and he might receive free meals for the rest of his life. City-states took great pride in their Olympic victors—especially in the stade race—and they would be treated as celebrities and heroes. Sometimes a section of the city wall was torn down in preparation for the triumphal return of the Olympic champion in a four-horse chariot. The greatest honor would be to have a statue of the champion erected in the Sanctuary at Olympia for all to admire and praise.

That one event grew into a religious and athletic festival that lasted for five days, attracting athletes and spectators from all over the Greek world. The games began on day one, much as they do today, with the procession along the Sacred Way and the swearing in of the athletes, their trainers, and the judges. The athletes made their sacred oath before Zeus and swore that they would abide by all the rules of the games and compete fairly. In addition, they also swore that they had trained for ten months in their home city-states and the last month within the district of Elis, which had control over the site of Olympia. On the agenda for the first day also were contests for trumpeters and heralds and a kind of junior olympics for young boys.

The second day saw the staging of the equestrian events—the two- and four-horse chariot races—and the contest which determined the best, all-around athlete, the ancient pentathlon. This included the five events of the dash, discus, javelin, long jump, and wrestling.

The third day was the most magnificent of all, although somewhat bloody and rather unlucky if you happened to be one of the local oxen thereabouts. On the morning of this day a great sacrifice of 100 oxen was offered at the altar of Zeus which stood before his splendid temple in the heart of the Sanctuary of Olympia. This sacrifice took place under the appreciative eye of King Zeus himself who gazed out from the interior of his temple with regal bearing. The seated figure of the most important of the Olympian gods and goddesses was no ordinary statue, for it was one of the Seven Wonders of the Ancient World along with the pyramids, the hanging gardens of Babylon, and four other magnificent structures from antiquity. It was created by one of the most accomplished craftsmen and artists throughout all the ages of history, the great sculptor Phidias, who had also designed and built the beautiful statue of Athena that at one time stood within the Parthenon in Athens. Like the statue of Athena, this forty-foot figure of Zeus was created by using a wooden frame overlaid with sheets of ivory and pure gold, and the throne on which he sat was made of bronze, ebony, ivory, and gold. It is said that if Zeus would have stood up from his seated position, he would have burst through the ceiling of his temple. If we could only put ourselves in the place of a young Greek athlete coming to Olympia to compete for the first time—the first sight of this amazing statue must have had a staggering impact. Historians tell us that the statue was still in place when the games were abolished in 393 A.D. by the Roman emperor, Theodosius, and that sometime around 395, the statue was taken to Constantinople where it may have been destroyed by the great fire of 475.

After the grand sacrifice of 100 oxen in the morning of day three, which probably today could keep McDonald's in business for at least a month, came the premier track events of the ancient games: the stade; the diaulos which was two lengths of the Olympic stadium; and the dolichos, which was the distance of 24 stades, or roughly equivalent to our 5K race of today.

On day four were the man-to-man, blood and guts events such as boxing, wrestling, and a violent contest called the Pancration. This was a combination of boxing and wrestling in which no holds were barred. In this less than delicate sport the athletes could kick and punch anywhere, twist limbs, and break bones. The only thing not allowed was gouging the eyes. This event seems a little bit uncharacteristic of the Greeks, but one that would especially appeal to the bloodthirsty Romans. Also on this day was held the Hoplite Race which was a very impressive event in which the athletes ran in full, bronze armor which could weigh as much as 40 or 50 pounds.

On the final day, the champions received that which all competitors had dreamed of on their journey to the vale of Olympia; not a monetary prize, for that would have been contrary to the spirit of the games, but a garland of wild olives taken from the sacred olive tree that stood close to the temple of Zeus. With this the victors were crowned and it symbolized to all that here was an individual in whom could be found the qualities of virtue, honor, and strength as they had been revealed in the crucible of athletic competition. After the crowning of the victors a huge feast was laid on in their honor and all the delegates of the city-states as well as any dignitaries—be they statesman, poet, or philosopher—were invited to attend. Meanwhile, the common people feasted and celebrated according to their means into the wee hours of the morning before beginning their long journey homeward the following day.

As an indication of the central role the Olympic games played throughout the Greek world, it is worth noting that the Greeks began to use their Olympiads, or the four-year period separating two successive celebrations of the games, as a means of keeping track of time and dating important historical events. Using this system all the events from 776 B.C. to 393 A.D., or a period of 1168 years, could be recorded. For example, the Battle of Thermopylae which is one of the famous battles of the Persian Wars (it was a Little Bighorn type battle in which 300 Spartan hoplite soldiers held off the entire Persian army; all the brave Spartans were killed) is recorded as having taken place in the first year of the 75th Olympiad, or the year 480 B.C. by our reckoning.

I spent most of the day at Olympia wandering through the ruins of the once stately temples and athletic facilities, lingering there until the late hours of the afternoon. Sitting there on the ancient stones, I found it almost impossible to tear myself away from the quiet beauty of the valley and the soothing music of the wind as it rustled through the branches of the surrounding cypress trees.

As I reluctantly headed back to my lodgings in the quaint little village of modern day Olympia, I decided that this day had definitely been a highlight of my travels. As the beer commercial states, "It doesn't get any better than this!" Up to this point, Greece had proved to be a wonderful experience, and I felt happy and content that I had made it this far.

From Olympia I headed farther south into the Peloponnese, following Route #9 which hugs the coastline. It afforded me a wonderful ride that required a minimum of effort, but little did I realize that this would be the last level stretch that I would enjoy in quite a while. However, that realization should have come as no surprise, for a quick glance at a map of Greece will tell you that your legs had better be in shape if you want to cycle this terrain. Aside from that, it was easy to understand how the Greeks developed a deep love and patriotism for their city-states and homeland. Greece is a ruggedly beautiful country with picturesque valleys surrounded by hills and mountains covered with olive, cypress, and pine trees—one valley leading to the next, and the sea never very far away—the sometimes emerald green, sometimes crystal blue waters, lined by miles of deserted beaches and rocky outcroppings. And for some reason, the colors seemed accentuated; the greens, blues and golds seemed deeper—vibrant and alive!

As I rode, I also took note, as I had in Italy, that the days were growing shorter, the shadows longer—fall was in the air, even in this Mediterranean land. It appeared as if the legions of tourists had gone home, leaving Europe to the natives and the hard-core travelers. The pace had slowed down. It was good to be here at this time.

On September 14, I celebrated my three-month anniversary. It was hard to believe that it had been three months since I had pedaled out of Toledo, Ohio—a long time to be on the road, to be constantly moving. And yet, I knew that an even longer span lay ahead. But by now, it almost felt natural—to be on the go, traveling here and traveling there, seeing new things every step of the way.

The southern-most part of the Peloponnese is formed by three peninsulas. The middle peninsula is called the Mani, and it is a rugged, desolate, uniquely beautiful section of this country whose people have maintained a sense of independence down through the centuries. In the southern tip of the Mani can be found the caves of Pirgos Diru. I had heard a few people speak of these caves and read about them in one of my guide books, and by all accounts they sounded as if they would be well worth the time and effort to see. Again, because this was really more of a side excursion and not on my intended route of travel, I rationalized myself into the seat of a bus with my bicycle stored snugly in the undercarriage. After seeing the terrain that we traversed, I was damn glad that my rationalization had won out. On our journey south, we snaked our way up incredibly steep climbs that were followed by precipitous drops—the scenery was spectacular to put it mildly. Next to me on the bus sat a Greek peasant woman wearing a black scarf, her face lined with the years of toil and hard work that are required of the natives of the Mani. Curiously, about every five minutes, the woman broke into a frenzy of making the sign of the cross—five, six, seven times in succession. What is the meaning of this, I thought to myself. Aha! She has figured out that she's sitting next to a heathen, and she's praying to the Almighty for my redemption. Or, maybe she knows something about the bus trip that I don't—like that bridge that was there yesterday, but for some reason is not there today. A glance out of the window at the edge of the cliff and the 1000-foot drop below almost confirmed this option in my mind. But then I noticed that her spasm of crossmaking coincided with our passing of anything of religious significance, be it a church, chapel, or any of the numerous roadside shrines that appeared along the highway. Here in the Mani, in this remote appendage of the Peloponnese, people are deeply religious, and tradition and the old ways persist.

A visit to the caves of Pirgos Diru is well worth the time of any traveler who ventures into this remote part of the Peloponnese. I and my fellow spelunkers were loaded aboard a trusty, rowboat-sized craft which transported us into a magical, labyrinthine world. The underground river on which we set sail wound and twisted its way through caverns and chambers populated by deeply colored stalactites and stalagmites. Sometimes the passageway became so narrow that our boat could barely squeeze through, and other times it broadened into a huge cavern—a miniature lake in this subterranean world. And what does one say to a 400-million-year old stalactite? How about, "Hang in there!"

From Gythio on the east coast of the Mani—a seaside community framed by the imposing headlands of this rugged peninsula—I headed north into the very heart of the Peloponnese. I entered the modern day town of Sparta, and I was somewhat taken aback by the broad, palm tree lined main thoroughfare. This certainly bore no resemblance to its ancient ancestor, the militaristic city-state of Sparta, rival of Athens for dominance in the Greek world. The Spartans did not leave much in the way of ruins—no beautiful temples, theaters, or statues to admire. For while the Athenians and other Greek city-states were molding our western culture, the Spartans' entire preoccupation was warfare and being militarily strong. It was for this reason that young Spartan boys began their military training at the tender age of seven when they were taken from their mothers and placed in a barracks, and they were not allowed to lay down their shields until the ripe old age of 60. This training regimen produced the desired result, for Sparta had the most feared and respected army of hoplite soldiers throughout all the Greek world—really one of the most formidable forces in all of ancient history. Alexander the Great, that intrepid conqueror of the known world, gobbled up just about every piece of real estate he could get his hands on. However, there was one city-state that refused to submit to Alexander—one that he wisely chose not to try to subdue. That's right—Sparta!

Just outside Sparta there was something worth seeing— the medieval fortress city of Mistra which is carved right into a mountainside. It was a fascinating spot and quite a sight to behold. The city was battled over by Franks, Venetians, Byzantines and Turks, and it commands a tremendous view of the valley below. On the very top lies the fortress itself in a seemingly impregnable location.

Headwinds and mountains—this seemed to be the bill of fare that Greece was dishing out to me as I trekked northward toward the Isthmus of Corinth and eventually Athens. It was developing into a real test of my physical stamina—much as Pennsylvania had been. Even so, the hard work paid dividends, for the terrain and scenery were incredible—the high peaks; the barren, rocky slopes, the valleys planted in olive groves and vineyards (apparently the only things that grow in this soil). In my classroom when we studied ancient Greece, I often spoke to my students of the country's rugged landscape which contributed greatly to the isolation and political independence of the Greek polis, or city-state. Well, here was a firsthand experience that would surely help me get that point across to my future students, although sometimes I lost sight of that fact as I alternately cursed the headwinds and strenuous, uphill climbs.

* * *

When traveling in Greece one would expect to come in contact with natives who go by the appellation of Aristotle, Theodopoulos, or Democrites. But one afternoon I had the pleasure of meeting Harry. It was late in the day and there yet remained one challenging climb before I could coast back down to sea level and the campground that awaited me in Nauplion on the Gulf of Argos. All morning had seemed as though it was an uphill and, in fact, it was. But now, as I took five on the roadside on the outskirts of a small village, trying to summon my energies for the final push, I heard the call of a friendly, but insistent voice.

"You—come over here; sit on bench." This was Harry—a sixtyish, portly Greek fellow with a twinkle in his eye. He and the Mrs. and their daughter were sitting on the porch of their small home apparently selling the fruits of their garden.

"Why, thank you very much, Sir," I grinned. "But you see, it's very late in the day, and I'm trying to make the campground in Nauplion."

"You come here and sit—rest a little," was his good-natured but strong response. This I obediently did. "My name is Harry. This my wife and daughter. What your name? Where you from? Where you going?"

I attempted to fill in all the details for Harry and his family of who I was and what exactly I was doing, but somehow they just didn't seem to comprehend why anyone would want to undertake such a journey as I had. After they had had a little time to digest the meaning of what I had said, Harry plunged on with his in-depth interview.

"I visit United States two years ago. I see my brother in Chicago. He has restaurant. Very good restaurant. You know my brother?"

"Well, you see, Harry," I reasoned, "the United States is a very large country, and I have been to Chicago before, but I don't think I've had the pleasure of meeting your brother. Although, if I had, I'm sure I would have liked him!"

Now we moved into the up-close and personal phase of the interrogation.

"You look like nice fellow. You married? You have wife?"

"Well, not yet. Just haven't met the right girl yet," was my explanation. "Besides, how could I take a trip like this if I was tied down?"

"Ah, too bad," was his reply that expressed a good deal of pity. "You need good wife. Settle down. Have family. like me!"

As it was growing ever later in the day, I explained to my sympathetic and concerned hosts that I really had to be on my way. "Before I go, Harry, could I possibly purchase from you one tomato to eat with my dinner tonight?"

A big smile beamed from his face. He chose one of the largest, juiciest tomatoes from his bushel basket and happily declared, "You take—no pay!" And so it seemed to be with most of the Greek people I had met so far—curious, warm, and friendly.

* * *

General Hospital, All My Children, The Days of Our Lives— mention these names to most any citizen of the U.S. of A. and he or she will know immediately that you are speaking of "The Soaps"—that vast wasteland of daytime TV. But what most Americans don't realize is that ancient Greece also had their own little soap opera, and the setting was not a sound stage in Athens, but the real life, behind the scenes shenanigans of the royal court of ancient Mycenae. Mycenae is located about 20 miles north of the Gulf of Argos, and it was the heart of Mycenaean civilization which flourished on the Greek mainland between 1600 and 1100 B.C. This was the Age of Heroes—that inspiring time period about which Homer wrote in his *Iliad* and *Odyssey*. Achilles, Odysseus, Helen of Troy, Hector and Paris, old King Priam—they are all of this age. And, of course, Agamemnon (his name seems to roll off the tongue), leader of the Greek forces in the Trojan War. His palace was located atop the fortified acropolis of Mycenae. When Agamemnon returned home after ten years of warfare on the plains of Troy, he found that his wife, Klytemnestra, had taken a lover. His wife and her lover killed Agamemnon to avenge the death of Iphigene, Agamemnon's daughter, whom he had sacrificed so that the Greek fleet could sail on their mission of death and destruction. In turn, Klytemnestra was killed by her son, Orestes, who was not a happy camper when he found about the fate of his father. Although he had some misgivings about doing in his own mother, revenge was his—and just about everyone else's it seems; and so, "As The Oracle Turns," so ran the troubled House of Atreus, the rulers of ancient Mycenae.

The ruins of the palace fortress high atop the acropolis of Mycenae were amazing and the view from Agamemnon's own throne room out over the vast plain of Argos was spectacular. I spent the good part of a day exploring the remains of the palace, the Royal Grave Circles within the palace walls from which was plucked the famed Death Mask of Agamemnon (not really his), and the awe inspiring beehive royal tombs. I even led a contingent of fearless tourists (I was the only one with a flashlight) into the heart of the Acropolis—90 steps down a spooky, slippery, pitch-black passageway at the bottom of which was one time a secret cistern which assured the palace defenders of a safe water supply. Of course, the cistern had long ago yielded up its last drop, and when we determined this, not wishing to incur the wrath of any inhospitable ghosts, we turned right around and slithered our way back up to daylight.

* * *

One of the wonderful things about Greece is that you are never very far from the next point of interest. The country is a treasure trove of ancient ruins and historical sites, many of these sites within easy cycling distance of each other, especially as you approach the Isthmus of Corinth, that ancient crossroads of the Greek world. On one marathon day I visited three amazing sites of antiquity—Argos (of Jason and the Argonauts fame), Tiryns, and Epidaurus—and still managed to squeeze in 35 miles or so of cycling.

I began my marathon day by stopping at Argos, one of the most important settlements of Mycenaean times. I almost decided to bypass Argos, but I was glad that I didn't. There was hardly a soul but me at the remains of the ancient theater and the Roman baths, and there was no admission charge. Sometimes the less visited spots are as good as or better than the more popular and crowded sites; you feel almost as if the ruins belong to you. You can climb over and through the ancient remains to your heart's content, which I proceeded to do. I was a little surprised that there didn't seem to be anybody around to stop souvenir hunters from pilfering the ruins and maybe adopting their very own ancient pet rock.

The ancient theater was carved out of the bottom of Larissa hill, and the acoustics of this natural amphitheater were amazing. The ancient actors could speak in a slightly louder than normal speaking voice and still be heard plainly in the "upper elevations" of the back rows. The theater was immense; it could seat 20,000 people, more than the more famous theater at Epidaurus. The theater has not been restored at all—in fact, only the central part of the seating is still evident—and, in a way, it was much neater. I really got a kick out of climbing to the top and sitting there, trying to imagine the Greek drama that would have been performed in front of me centuries ago. The Roman baths, just a few paces away from the theater, were also fantastic because they showed clearly the engineering and architectural techniques which the Romans employed in these marvelous facilities. The baths, of course, were built much later during the Roman period, while the theater dates back to the 4th century B.C.

My next stop on this very exceptional day—Tiryns of the mighty cyclopean walls situated in the heart of the Argonian plain. This was the home of the legendary Hercules, and it was from here that he left to perform his famed twelve labors. The walls of this massive fortress are constructed of huge blocks of stone that certainly could only have been placed in position with the help of those lovable monsters of Greek mythology, the one-eyed cyclops; hence the reference, cyclopean walls. Within the exterior walls which in some places reach a width of 18 meters, you will find an amazing feature—vaulted passageways which run the length of the walls and were intended for the safe movement of the fortress' defenders. They were constructed in the grand Mycenaenan style with peaked vaulting and they give you a sense of the ingeniuousness of these master fortress builders.

With time running out, I had yet one more stop to make. It's hard to say that on this day I saved the best for last, but here that oft used phrase may apply. As the late September shadows lengthened and the waning sun transformed the surrounding landscape into a kaleidoscope of golds and greens, I wheeled into the beautiful sanctuary of Asclepius and the famous theater of Epidaurus. Once again, as at Olympia, I immersed myself in the quiet beauty that surrounded me. What an inspiring setting in which to watch the timeless plays of Sophocles, Euripides, and Aristophonies!

The theater of Epidaurus is not quite as large as the one at Argos (it could seat 14,000 people), but it is in a remarkable state of preservation, with a little help from the modern era. The surrounding hills and mountains provided a splendid backdrop for the ancient players and the theater's placement at the base of a hill created an amazing acoustical effect. Sitting in the very top row of the theater close by to one of the many tour groups that were about, I listened to their group leader explain far below in the orchestra about the wonderful natural sound system of the amphitheater. She spoke in a normal speaking voice, yet we could hear her plainly. Then, to emphasize the point, she took out a small coin and dropped it on the circular floor of the amphitheater where she stood, and once again we could hear the sound clearly. This magnificent theater is not only a relic from classical antiquity, but it is also still in use today. Every summer, just as their ancient ancestors, modern theater-goers flock here for the festival of Greek drama. In this unbelievable setting, the enduring Greek tragedies and comedies are performed 23 centuries after they played for the Greeks of another age.

After you thrilled to the sights of Oedipus Rex on stage at the theater of Epidaurus, you could run over to the stadium for your daily workout. This was not only a center of drama, but a great athletic site also. Games were staged here every four years just as at Olympia and Delphi.

One of the most important reasons, however, for visiting the site of Epidaurus was to make a pilgrimage to the holy temple of Asclepius. Asclepius, son of Apollo, was the god of sickness and healing and it was his good graces that you sought if your body was not behaving the way that Zeus intended it to. The sick and not so sick from all over Greece journeyed here and to other sites like it in the hope of finding a cure for what ailed them. From overdue pregnancies to baldness, this was the place to come to find a solution. According to one of the inscribed tablets discovered here describing a number of cures, one poor Greek matron had been pregnant for five years but had not given birth (that was one hell of a big lady). She arrived here—probably in a wheelbarrow—and performed the prescribed rites. On the

Saying goodbye to family and friends, June 14, 1985.

A quiet campsite in Pennsylvania.

Pointing the way across the Pyrenees Mountains.

An ancient Roman road near Montpelier, France bearing the tracks of long-vanished chariots.

John, Marlene, and Al in the Apennine Mountains of Italy

John helping Marlene
to get clean.

ancient Roman
pares for his bath
bath house at
mpeii.

Al standing where
Greek athletes of
the Golden Age
once stood to take
their sacred oath
at ancient Olympia.

Al and Billy (from Chicago) wrestling in the pit at ancient Delphi.

The pyramids at Giza.
Al in foreground,
Paul in the distance.

Egyptian workers mold thousands o bricks for drying i the sun.

A time capsule — an Egyptian village unchanged by the passing of centuries.

cycling in the i-desert conditions he Indian State of asthan in -December.

Alison (at left) is the center of attention on the outskirts of an Indian village.

A sacred cow meanders through traffic in Jaipur, India.

A brush with the Grim Reaper: photo shows where an Indian truck sliced through my rear pannier at a headon speed of 50 mph, missing me and the bike frame by a fraction of an inch.

Taking on the Mohave Desert.

Umbrellas provide moving shade for two hikers in the Mojave Desert on their way to Virginia.

ssing the
ntinental Divide.
ld it be all
nhill to Ohio?

Al and "Ike Godzy" from the TV series *The Waltons* at the entrance to Grand Canyon National Park.

Happy to be home in Ohio, "the heart of it all.".

A welcoming party of family and friends greets me with champagne and balloons in Secor Park on the outskirts of Toledo, Ohio.

Reunited with my family at long last.

also engaged in a world jaunt. Billy and Judy had been traveling for over a year, and their time on the road made my three months seem like a mere weekend excursion. We quickly became friends and eagerly shared our common, uncommon and some downright weird experiences of the road.

During my first week in Athens I religiously made a daily pilgrimage down to the American Express Office in hopes of finding my packages from home waiting to be picked up, and each day I came away with the same discouraging reply: "Sorry, Sir, nothing for you today." It wasn't long before some of the employees began to think that I actually worked there.

After my daily disappointment at the American Express office, I usually would take in one of the many sites of Greek antiquity. One afternoon was spent at the Greek National Museum which contains much of the archaeological treasure spanning the history of Greece and the Aegean world. On another day I explored the ancient agora which was the heart of classical Athens. I meandered over the ancient stones where the feet of Socrates, Plato, and Aristotle once trod. And listening hard, I could almost hear the echoes of long ago conversations that debated and considered the important issues of the day—issues of civic pride and duty; issues of war; issues that contemplated the nature of truth and justice. In this cradle of democracy, the Greeks were progenitors of a philosophy and a form of government that is embraced by all freedom loving peoples around the world today.

And, of course, one day was set aside especially for my ascent to the heights of the Acropolis where the patron goddess Athena once held court within the sanctuary of her beautiful temple. For over twenty-four centuries the Parthenon has stood proudly as a beacon of learning and enlightened thought, although at times, that beacon has shone less brightly than at others. It was the most visible symbol in the plan of Pericles, that great Athenian statesman, to make Athens a school for all of Hellas (Greece). The temple was begun in 447 B.C. under the direction of the most accomplished craftsmen and artists of the day—the architects Ictinus and Callicrates and the great sculptor Phidias—and it was brought to fruition just nine years later in 438 B.C. The building is one of optical illusion. The floor is not level, but rises gently toward a high point in the middle, while the graceful Doric columns bulge toward their midsections. This counteracts the tendency of the eye to see a completely straight column as concave. The columns also lean slightly inward so that if they could be extended upward, they would come together at a point one mile up in the air.

From inside, Athena herself gazed out over the city that bore her name and which she was sworn to protect. Her forty-foot statue was the creation of the master sculptor Phidias. With skin of ivory and a flowing gown of gold, her left arm resting on her battle shield and her right hand supporting the goddess of winged victory, she must have sent chills up and down the spines of all those who stood before her.

Over the many centuries, the Parthenon has mirrored the history of Greece and, unfortunately, been victimized by the winds of war. Depending on the rulers of the day and their religious bent, the Parthenon has served as the sanctuary of the Olympian goddess, a Christian church (both Orthodox and Roman Catholic) and seat of the bishop, an Islamic mosque (under the sultans of the Ottoman empire), and a fortress and arsenal for gunpowder. It is this fact which led to the greatest disaster of all to befall the great temple. In 1687 the Venetians were laying siege to the Acropolis which was under the control of the Turks. Toward the end of the battle when the outcome had already been decided, the Venetians thoughtfully lobbed a shell through the roof of the Parthenon and into the heart of the gunpowder cache. The resulting catastrophic explosion blew off the roof and destroyed a number of the surrounding columns. If it had not been for that incident, the Parthenon would have been delivered to us through the ages much as she had begun. Even so, this beautiful monument now faces a battle with the twentieth and coming twenty-first centuries which threaten to administer the final blows. The air pollution of metropolitan Athens continues to eat away at the noble ruins and even the minute vibrations from the footsteps of the hordes of tourists threaten to weaken the structure. I could see evidence of the ongoing struggle to save her in the scaffolding which completely covered the eastern facade and also the many numbered large and small chunks of marble which lay scattered across the Acropolis, waiting to be placed lovingly back in their original position. Hopefully, the experts will win this battle to save the Parthenon, and so preserve this rich part of our Western Heritage for coming generations.

* * *

During that first week in Athens some important decisions had to be made. How would I get to Africa? Did I really want to go to Africa at all? Should I go by air? Should I schedule passage on a ship heading south? Or should I plan on spending the next nine months right there in Athens, which appeared to be my immediate fate anyhow. I made a visit to one of the so called "bucket shops" which specializes in discounted tickets of all sorts which can get you to anywhere from downtown Los Angeles to the middle of the Gobi Desert. There, I talked to a travel agent who wanted to sell me a travel package that would fly me from Athens to Cairo to Nairobi; back to Cairo, to Bombay, and then Dacca to Bangkok and so on, all the way to Los Angeles. And, of course, I would cycle the portions in-between. Total cost would be around $1700 for all those flight hops, which seemed like a huge chunk of money. And too, I didn't want to tie myself to a set pattern or schedule. Sometimes that eliminates interesting options that would appear on the horizon and also removes some of the spontaneity of world travel. And, so, after much pulling of hair and gnashing of teeth about what I should do, I scheduled a berth on the next ship sailing to Cairo, Egypt. But because the Greek postal system failed to produce my long awaited packages from the home front, I was forced to cancel my reservations and continue my period of waiting.

Week one transformed itself into week two of my Athenian sojourn as I faithfully attended to my vigil at the American Express office. In the meantime my cyclist bunkmates, Billy and Judy, and I rented a car and drove up to Delphi, a trip that proved to be well worthwhile. We visited the sanctuary of Apollo and the home of the Delphic Oracle which made prophecies about every aspect of life in the Greek world. It is situated in a beautiful location at the foot of Mt. Parnassus, and some parts of the site are actually half way up the side of the mountain. This was a fitting spot for one of the most important political and religious centers in all Greece. The Greeks referred to it as the "navel" of the world. In addition to being the home of the Oracle, it was also a site of tremendous athletic significance. The Pythian Games were held here every four years and were second in importance only to the games at Olympia. The games took their name from the Pythia, who was the priestess through whom Apollo himself spoke to those seeking knowledge of future events. All of the important Greek city-states maintained official representation at Delphi for on-the-spot advice about "coming attractions", and even private individuals with enough money could hear the words of the Pythia. Although Apollo did not speak through the Pythia every day—some days he appeared not to be in the mood to speak—the payment of the pelanos (fee) and the sacrifice of a goat could usually loosen his tongue. And when the Pythia did mouth the words of Apollo, they were usually incoherent and so had to be interpreted by the priests. The interpreted message was ambiguous and could be taken by the humble inquirer in whatever way it pleased him. However, a misinterpretation could have less than happy consequences. For example, King Croesus of Lydia who was the Donald Trump of the ancient world, wanted to know if he would be victorious over the Persian Empire. The Oracle responded, "If Croesus crosses the Halys, a great power will be destroyed." Rich ol' Croesus failed to see both sides of the coin, crossed the River Halys separating Persia and Lydia with his great army, and was soundly defeated by the Persian juggernaut. The Oracle was right again!

We spent the afternoon wandering through the ruins, visiting the museum, and just taking in the beauty of this amazing spot. Billy and I posed for a couple of shots in the remarkably well-preserved stadium, re-enacting some events from the ancient pentathlon. I wanted to make sure my students saw how a "real" Greek athlete would have looked in the heat of competition. It was a long day, but a good one, and worth the 250-mile round trip.

At long last my packages from home arrived and I devoured the letters, news clippings, and other remembrances of home that Mom always included. I also received a small slip of paper telling me to go to the parcel post office to pick up a small package. There I discovered that the Greek postal system was going to charge me 25 dollars before they would hand over my replacement solar odometer, being a nice little piece of electronic gadgetry. Two weeks of waiting had considerably shortened my fuse, and I went off with a bang.

"You want to charge me how much? My God, you must be kidding!" I bellowed at the postal clerk. "You must be crazy! Why, that's almost as much as the damned thing cost to begin with. God, I don't believe it. You must think...."

"I'm sorry, Sir," the postal clerk interrupted with a look of uncertainty as to what this crazy American might do. "But that is the charge and you must pay it if you want to receive your package."

Still enraged, I slammed my money down on the counter, grabbed my package and, to underscore my unhappy state, threw my small backpack full force against the office wall using my best fast ball delivery. Momentarily forgetting all the enriching experiences Greece had provided me, I stormed out of the building cursing Apollo, Athena, and even Zeus himself. My little tirade probably did little to enhance the American image that day, but I was starting to get the feeling that not only thieves, but also governments were trying to rip me off.

Being a fairly mellow fellow, and having learned by this time that it doesn't do much good to get bent out of shape over such trivial things, I put the experience behind me. At least now I had my mail and there was nothing holding me in Athens any longer. And so, without any further delay I rebooked reservations on the next ship bound for Egypt and attended to some last minute purchases and preparations before I departed the Balkan Peninsula.

On top of the list of my last minute things to do was to call home. It was so wonderful to hear the voices of my parents and to catch up on all the things that were happening in Toledo—what my nieces and nephews were up to; how things were going out at my school; and how all my friends were anxious to hear news of my trip. I told my parents that Greece had been a wonderful experience, and that all was going well—and, of course, not to worry. But I knew they would and, now that worry would be justified, for Africa and India lay before me. As I spoke to my mother and father, tears welled in my eyes and my voice broke. They were so far away and such dear people, and it seemed like such a long time before I would be able to see them again—if I would ever. As I hung up the receiver and walked away from the phone, the tears began to flow freely, and I felt very much alone.

* * *

After a two-week layoff, I once again mounted my trusty companion and bicycled the short distance from Athens to her seaport of Piraeus to search out the boat that would transport me to the Dark Continent. I located the passenger boarding area, but as boarding would not begin for another hour or so, I surveyed the large rusty ship which rode easily at anchor before me. It was an Italian boat which bore the name plate of the Star of Venice. As I pondered the sea-worthiness of this craft and whether or not it was likely to transport me safely across the Mediterranean, two heavily laden cyclists who would be a large part of the future wheeled up to where I stood. They were a male-female duo and they returned my eager greeting with an apparently American hello.

"Where are you two from?" I asked, anxious to discover all about these two fellow cyclists.

"Well, we're from the United States," the male half of the duo offered. He was blond and slender and had an amazingly full beard adorning his face. "My name is Paul Lierhaus and this is my wife, Alison."

"Hi! Great to meet you, especially another cyclist," Alison chimed in. She was also blond with a pretty face and warm smile. "Never expected we'd meet another cyclist heading in this direction."

"Same here," I beamed back. "My name is Al Thompson and I'm from the States, too—Toledo, Ohio, to be exact.

They looked at each other and broke into wide grins. "Well, as of the last couple of years, we're from Alaska," Paul explained, "but we're originally from Ohio too."

My mouth dropped and then assumed the same wide grin. The three of us stood there flabbergasted and delighted that here we were, thousands of miles from home, waiting for a boat to Africa and discovering that we all hailed from the very same Buckeye State, even living within a hundred miles of each other.

For the next hour, while we waited for boarding to commence, we chewed each other's ears about our backgrounds and how it was that we came to this point. Paul had been an engineer up on the pipeline in Alaska, while Alison was pursuing courses in health and physical therapy. After a couple of years up in Alaska's "ice castle", they decided to pack up shop and head for the lower latitudes. But rather than relocate with a job in the lower 48, they decided to first tour Europe. Alison explained that once in England, they couldn't decide the best way to tour the continent. But since they both loved to eat, it came down to either riding the train and getting fat or cycling and staying healthy. Since they were both athletically inclined, the latter won out. After purchasing their bicycles and all their equipment in London, they set out across Europe, sampling the varied cultures and native cuisines along the way. Instead of taking the southern route through Italy as I had done, they had braved Eastern Europe down through Yugoslavia and ended up here in Greece. Their plan was originally to just tour Europe, but here at the continent's edge, they decided they liked it so much that they'd just keep right on going—Egypt, maybe Kenya and Tanzania, India, Southeast Asia, and on, as long as their enthusiasm and funds held out.

Their itinerary sounded like a close relative of mine, and so here, I figured, was a glimmer of hope that I might not have to face the Third World alone. They were a personable and friendly couple, and we seemed to enjoy each other's company. But even so, I didn't immediately broach the topic of hitching our trains together. I thought that might come about eventually anyway since we were all heading south toward the Land of the Pharoahs and three would be safer than two (from their standpoint) and certainly one (from my standpoint).

It wasn't too long before we were permitted to push our bicycles up into the loading bays, and as our voyage would last for two nights and a day, we were assigned a sleeping berth in a cabin. Once settled in, we met back on deck to watch the Star of Venice ease out of her slip and into the busy harbor or Piraeus. Dusk was falling and a thousand harbor lights were reflected in the darkening seas. While watching their shimmering dance across the gentle swells and drinking in the invigorating sea air, I made my silent good-byes to Europe and reflected on all that I had seen and experienced over the last three months—both the good and the bad. Then, turning to look south toward the Aegean and the broad Mediterranean, I wondered about Africa which lurked somewhere unseen and mysterious below the horizon and what surprises it held in store. And as I pondered these things, out in that vast blackness, another Italian ship approached the African coastline carrying vacationing passengers who were about to endure the most terrifying experience of their lives. Among those passengers were 14 Americans, one of whom would be brutally murdered by four Arab terrorists in less than 48 hours. The name of the ship was the Achille Lauro.

SIX

Egypt — Culture Shock

Our sun drenched crossing of the Mediterranean Sea took about 30 hours and a good portion of those daylight hours were spent soaking in the abundant rays on the upper deck of the Star of Venice. But in spite of my prostrate position of relaxation, I could feel a growing sense of anxiety over the huge land mass which lay just to the south. That anxiety might have escalated to panic had we known of the terrorism and tragedy that was unfolding about 400 miles to the southeast.

At around 1:00 P.M. on Monday afternoon while Alison, Paul, and I munched lunch and lounged on the Star of Venice, the Achille Lauro, an aging Italian cruise ship, was steaming leisurely just off the coast of Egypt while many of her passengers were enjoying an excursion to the Pyramids. Those passengers who had remained on board were enjoying lunch when their peaceful world was shattered by the reports of gunfire. Four Palestinian terrorist had take over the ship and were now forcing all hostages into the dining room. The terrorists quickly separated the 14 Americans, six Britons, and two Austrians (who they mistakenly thought to be Jewish) from the rest of the passengers. For the next three days these unlucky 22 passengers turned hostages would live under the threat of execution. The terrorists threatened to begin shooting hostages if their demands (releasing 50 Palestinian prisoners in Israel and asylum in Syria) were not met; for one of the Americans, Leon Klinghoffer, that threat would become a reality.

In the meantime, while the Achille Lauro steamed toward Syria and Lebanon looking for support from those countries, our ship approached the coast of Egypt. At 6:15 A.M. on Tuesday morning the announcement crackled over the ship's public address system that we were entering the harbor of Alexandria, Egypt. The moment of truth had arrived, and so I rolled out of my bunk to meet Africa. It took us about two hours to proceed through passport control, customs, and about five other checkpoints that want to make sure you're who you say you are. We had no idea at all of the tense drama that was taking place in our part of the Mediterranean, and little did we realize that the lengthy entry process was probably a reaction to the situation of the Achille Lauro. Nor did we know how lucky we had been that the four Palestinians had not chosen a ship called the Star of Venice as their target.

As soon as Alison, Paul and I emerged onto the streets of Alexandria, we knew that we were a long way from home. We had left the West behind and entered another part of the world with a culture very different from our own. Our senses were bombarded by novel sights, sounds, and smells: block upon block of tenement housing complexes; Egyptian men and young boys in their long, flowing galabias and skull caps; beggars looking so destitute it was hard to glance their way; the chanting of the muezzin echoing through the streets calling the devout to prayer; the smell of urine and excrement mingling with exotic odors emanating from the food stalls and bazaars—culture shock was setting in.

Alexandria is a huge city strung out for miles along the coastline, and it was no easy task to get our bearings and to locate a hotel that would be our refuge for the next two nights. Everything was new and different and strange to us and we felt as though we had stepped into another world. Everywhere there seemed to be crumbling buildings and piles of broken bricks and rubble as if someone had decided to tear down parts of the city but forgot to build them back up again. We cycled the debris-strewn streets wide eyed and wary, and as we did, young boys on their one speed bicycles darted in and out, seeing how close they could get to us before we had to hit our brakes. One little brat got very close to Alison and cut her off, causing her to go down in a crash. As he ran from our screams of anger and outrage, we could see a smile and a laugh on his face, obviously very amused by the whole situation. We helped Alison up—only a little shaken up and a minor scrape—and continued our quest for lodgings for the night. At long last we located a hotel for the next two nights which, unfortunately, was situated on the 7th floor. The elevator operator was a grizzled old man dressed in a dirty red and white galabia and a skull cap. He greeted us with a kind of wild eyed look of unbelievability as we pushed our bicycles bedecked with all of our packs and gear up to the doors of his elevator. With a few appropriate grunts and looks of disdain, he indicated that packing all of this junk onto his elevator was not high on his list of things to do. But once he saw that there was no other choice in the face of three determined Americans, he began cramming our bikes and gear into his tiny cubicle with reckless abandon. Before we finished our unloading up on the 7th floor, our pilot shot out his and and uttered a word that would ring in our ears constantly as we traversed the land of Egypt—BAKSHEESH!

After paying him the appropriate amount of baksheesh, we registered at the hotel and were given our rooms which were fairly basic, but at least clean and quiet. Considering the outward appearance of Alexandria, that was a definite plus. Since it had been quite a spell since I had answered nature's call, I made a trip to the communal bathroom on our floor where I found a new and curious twist on taking care of business. It was a western style sit-down john all right, but protruding into the middle of the toilet bowl was a skinny piece of copper tubing bent in the shape of a U. The open end of the copper tube was situated right under the spot where right cheek and left cheek come together. With a look of puzzlement I inspected this curious gismo, and when the lightbulb in my head clicked on, I sat down with a sense of "yuk!" As I had brought no toilet paper with me and there was certainly none in the bathroom, I had no other option. Casting fate to the wind, I reached for the valve and gave it a spin. In doing so, I received probably one of the most uplifting experiences of my life. A little later on when I ran into Paul in the hallway with a big smile on his face, I knew that he too had just made the discovery.

"Hey Al, have you been to the john yet?" he chuckled. "God, what a great sensation!"

For the rest of the afternoon we tried to relax and accustom our minds to the idea that we were now in Egypt—and it was a whole new ballgame. At 3:05 P.M. we had no reason to look at our watches and guess that it was any moment of significance. But it was, for at that moment an American passenger aboard the Achille Lauro—Leon Klinghoffer, a 69 year old Jewish gentleman crippled by a stroke and bound to a wheelchair—was being shot in the head and pushed off the upper deck of the cruise ship. Thus, the four Arab terrorists were now murders.

The following day, Wednesday, still unaware of the international crisis, we spent seeing the sights of Alexandria which really only takes about a day. We visited the Greco-Roman Museum which was quite good; Pompey's Pillar which wasn't even built for Pompey (the rival of Julius Caesar) but for the Emperor Diocletian; and the former Royal Palace of King Farouk until he was deposed in the coup of 1952 by Nasser. The grounds were quite beautiful with acres of tall date palms filled with fruit standing tall against the blue Egyptian sky. The bus ride there and back was an experience in itself, and it introduced us to mass transit in the Third World. A bus designed for maybe thirty to forty souls packed in-between ninety to a hundred in sardine fashion. The only way to find a spot on the bus was to make a hole in a solid wall of humanity, and this the Egyptians did with unbridled enthusiasm and great gusto.

We looked forward to the next day when we would take on Egypt from the cyclist's point of view. I had a great curiosity about what lay beyond the city of Alexandria. What would it be like to cycle across the Nile delta? How would the people of the villages react to us? It seemed hard to believe that here on this spit of lush, green territory, we were on the edge of that vast sea of sand known as the Sahara Desert. Actually the Nile delta is no small spit of land since it is about 150 miles from Alexandria on the coast to Cairo which is situated at the apex of the delta. It would take us two days to cover that distance, and it would be two days of eye opening experiences. And so with these thoughts in mind, I turned in early hoping to get a good night's rest.

The next morning we loaded up early and headed out of the city together. There seemed to be no question of riding as a threesome. It was the natural thing to do. The strangeness of our surroundings had drawn us together, and I felt good about having their company. I hoped that Alison and Paul felt the same way; it seemed to me that they did.

We headed south into the heart of the delta, but within that first hour of cycling, I found that our riding styles might not be the most compatible. Whereas my pace could be described as slow and steady, theirs was fast and steady, and I felt as though I was really pushing to keep up. Add to that the fact that I had not done any real hard riding for the last three weeks, and the result was one bushed bicycler by the time we stopped to buy lunch after riding a straight 50 miles. Even so, I felt fortunate to have met them when I did, and that it was up to me to accommodate my riding style to theirs.

That first 50 miles proved to be a real education. You can read about it and see pictures of it, but until you come face to face with poverty in a Third World country, I think it's hard to have an understanding for what it really is. Not just a small section of a city or a village or an isolated area of the countryside, but everywhere you look you see it. It is always with you as you traverse the broad flat plain that is the Nile delta as we did on this morning. Many of the villages we passed through appeared as a scene from antiquity: houses constructed of mud and sun-dried brick; oxen treading their never-ending paths around a water wheel made of clay jars which emptied their contents into hand dug canals; the women swathed in their black gowns and veils washing the family clothing and pots and pans along the banks of an irrigation canal; the dilapidated and run-down condition of almost every building you see both in the cities and villages. To me this seemed so far removed from life in the United States or any place else I had seen up to this point that sometimes I had to pinch myself as a reminder of where I was.

It goes without saying that we didn't come across too many Burger Kings or McDonald's along the delta's main highway, so we stopped for lunch at a small roadside stand that consisted of a few boards slapped together and which could have passed for a breeding farm for flies. The bill of fare was the ubiquitous felafel—deep fried patties or balls of mashed beans or peas and vegetable paste—and flat pita bread. We initially thought the felafel to be quite tasty, but by the time we left Egypt, the prospect of one more deep fried patty sliding down our throats would make our stomachs do somersaults. For less than a dollar, we filled ourselves up on felafel, bread, tomatoes, and onions—and probably a few flies too—and then attacked the last 30 miles of our ride to Tanta, a large delta city midway between Alexandria and Cairo.

By mid-afternoon exhaustion was upon us, and part of that was due to the condition of the roadway we were traveling. The delta region has only a few main highways which carry the bulk of the traffic—much of that, heavy trucks whose drivers have a love affair with speed and blowing their horns. The surface of the road offered cracks, valleys, and bumps aplenty and required our constant attention lest bicycle and rider disappear in some gaping chasm. In the very near future, I would pay dearly for a moment's inattention, but on this first day of riding in Egypt, all three of us were very focused on negotiating the battle-scarred highway.

By the time we reached Tanta, we were covered with layers of sweat, road grime, and dust that seemed always to hang in the air. Our entrance into the city was a memorable experience. As long as we kept moving we were OK. But as soon as we stopped, people would rush to come and take a look at these strange foreigners on bicycles. When we finally pulled up in front of a modern looking hotel, it was the cause of a small riot. We immediately attracted a crowd of staring faces and young boys shouting, "What you name Meester? How old you Meester? What time is it? Do you have a pencil?" They gathered around us, pressing closer, grabbing at our bikes, until some of the adults would drive them back using a stick and shouting strong admonitions. Momentarily we were granted a reprieve, but soon the noose would tighten again. Above the din, Paul shouted, "You guys stay with the bikes; I'll go in and see if I can get us a room."

Alison and I stood guard over our bicycles and equipment, smiling at each other uneasily amidst the noise and confusion, attempting to thank those elders who seemed to be coming to our aid. After it seemed Paul had been gone too long, I called out to Alison, "I better go in and see what the problem is. You hold the fort."

"Ok, but don't leave me out here too long," she pleaded with a look of wide-eyed anxiety.

On the inside, Paul was negotiating with the hotel manager whose sky-high rates were not even in the ball park—geared more toward rich foreigners and business people with padded expense accounts. We shook our heads and gave him our no-thank-yous, and rejoined Alison in front of the hotel. She seemed to be lost in a sea of dark faces, and we had to push through to her rescue. Word of our arrival spread like wildfire, and now people seemed to be running from every direction to find out what was the cause of the great commotion, just adding to the massing throng surrounding us. The children continued to shout their same questions, while the men thoroughly inspected us and our machines, and the women stared, pointed, and giggled at Alison, for many of them had probably never seen a girl bicyclist before. We seemed to be the vortex of a revolving storm of noise, shouted questions, and confusion.

At last a young, well dressed Egyptian man pushed his way through to our encircled position.

"May I be of assistance?" the young man inquired in excellent English.

"Yes!" we answered in unison.

"We're Americans traveling through your country by bicycle," I explained, "and we're trying to find a place to stay for the night. We inquired at this hotel, but it's much more than we want to pay."

The man informed us that he was a doctor and apologized for the over-zealous curiosity of the people. "You must remember that this is a very rare sight for them. Not many tourists bicycle through Egypt as you are doing. But please, follow me. I know of a hotel in another part of the city that I think will be more appropriate for your budget."

The good doctor hopped into his compact car while we pushed our way out of the mass of humanity that still engulfed us. We threaded our way through the cluttered streets and alleys of Tanta doing our best to keep his small, white car in sight. Our mini caravan came to a halt in front of a hotel that was much more in keeping with our pocketbooks. But yet, it was clean and comfortable and seemed to be in a slightly quieter section of the city. We pulled out our wallets to offer a monetary thank you to this kind man who had literally saved us from the Egyptian mob, but he refused to take our money and expressed his happiness at being able to help and also his hopes that we would enjoy his country. He left us with his card and then said good-bye. We felt very good and fortunate to have made the Egyptian fellow's acquaintance.

We registered at the hotel, paying about 15 Egyptian pounds for one room for the three of us. I was worried that it might be imposing on Alison and Paul, but they seemed to think it was a good idea, especially while we were on the road. It helped to save on money, and three commiserating at the end of an exhausting and stressful day is always more fun than just two commiserating.

Each of us was desperate to remove our outer skin of sweat and grime, but before we could begin, the sound of crunching metal brought us running to the balcony which overlooked the street below. An Egyptian style fender bender had taken place right below where we stood. The two drivers jumped out of their cars and began a shouting and arm waving match while onlookers and passers-by came running to join in the fray. Before long everyone was shouting and screaming in Arabic, waving their arms, and jumping up and down, and in the background car horns blared incessantly as the drivers swerved to avoid hitting the already crumpled autos, each other, and any unwary pedestrians. Alison, Paul, and I looked at each other, smiled, chuckled and then broke into a fit of hysterical laughter over the scene of Egyptian pandemonium that we seemed to be presiding over.

That evening we ventured onto the streets of Tanta, attracting stares and looks of wonderment from the dark faces as we threaded our way through the crowded alleys and passageways. Once again we had another filling meal of felafel, pita bread, and vegetables for less than a dollar for the three of us. It was becoming apparent that Egypt, as tough as it might prove to be on our souls and spirit, would at least not break our pocketbooks.

On our way out of Tanta the following morning, we stopped momentarily to get our bearings. This was a mistake, for as soon as we came to a halt, a platoon of Egyptian children caught sight of us and took off on an all-out charge in our direction, yelling and screaming at the top of their little lungs. We stood hard on our pedals and wasted no time in putting distance between us and the hell-bent thundering herd. The familiar cries of "What you name Meester? How old you Meester?" faded behind us and we continued our quest for the road that would lead us out of the city. When we found that road on the southern outskirts of Tanta, it provided us with a huge dose of Third World reality. Such a degree of poverty I had not yet seen. The crater-filled dirt road was lined with hovels constructed of scraps of wood, cardboard, metal, and about anything else the destitute inhabitants could make use of. Those appeared to be the lucky ones, for some didn't even have a hovel to call home. Many sat or reclined on rugs or blankets surrounded by a few worldly belongings in the middle of the dirt and mud. As we rode into those poor people's world and right out of it, I wondered what kind of a momentary impression we had made on them.

We eventually reached the road we wanted to take us south to Cairo which was different from the previous day's route on the main highway and a more enjoyable ride. This was a well paved secondary road that carried much less traffic, and it gave us a good opportunity to view the fertile lands of the Nile delta. It seemed to be a mixture of Ancient Egypt and the 20th century. In one field a farmer could be seen tilling his soil with a wooden plow harnessed to a team of oxen while in the adjoining field could be heard the steady "chug, chug, chug" of a John Deere tractor. Or a water buffalo might be treading his never ending, circular path to raise water with the use of a water wheel, while not too far away a gasoline engine pump was raising the water and sending it gushing into the thirsty fields. This is Egypt—a land of contrasts.

We covered the eighty or so miles from Tanta to Cairo with relative ease compared to the grind of the previous day's ninety miler on the crevice and bump-infested main highway. Lunch was taken on the banks of one of the many canals that crisscross the delta. We spread out the food we had purchased along the way on a plastic ground cloth and proceeded to munch and swat the flies, munch and swat flies, munch and swat flies. We seemed to be burning up as many calories as we were consuming attempting to keep the black pests off our food and us.

While eating and exercising our arms, an Egyptian man emerged from a nearby dwelling that perched on the bank of the canal. He placed his prayer rug before him and knelt down in a reverent posture facing toward the East and Islam's Holy City of Mecca. He began his daily prayer ritual and assumed a variety of prayerful positions as he recited verses from the Holy Koran. The world of Islam seemed strange to us. Everywhere, it could be seen and heard—from the many mosques with their graceful minarets to the call of the muezzin which echoed from loudspeakers through the villages and along the roadways, summoning the faithful to prayer five times throughout the day. We were riding through a different world—one with a vastly different culture from that of the West.

Our entry into Africa's largest city of eight to nine million people was easier than we expected, though once again sobering. On the outskirts of Cairo we rode through some terrible slums which spoke of the condition of poverty of many of this nation's 55 million inhabitants. The slums seemed to stretch on for miles, but we eventually crossed over the main channel of the Nile and into the heart of the city where we located a hotel that was like the Hilton compared to our accommodations of the previous night. We had spacious rooms that were clean and well kept and it felt good to settle in somewhere for the next couple of days after all the new and strange things that we had seen, felt, and heard.

While I busied myself with unpacking panniers and stowing away camping gear, I heard a gentle tapping on my door which I promptly answered, thinking it would be Alison or Paul checking up to see if all was copesetic. I was surprised to find standing there instead a young Egyptian man who was employed by the hotel as one of the cleaning staff. He inquired in broken English if I liked my room, and then after a brief pause, proceeded to proposition me, pointing to a considerable bulge in his pants with an expectant look in his eye. I gave him a stern shake of my head and indicated that he was now ready to exit my room. As if all this was routine, he turned on his heel and disappeared through the door. Later, when I met Paul coming down the hallway, we quickly compared notes and discovered that it *was* routine, for he had tried to hit on Paul too. That night I · made sure my door was securely locked lest I wake up to find some hairy Egyptian snuggling up next to me in bed.

The next day, forsaking our bicycles, we hopped a bus for a visitation to the only remaining Wonder of the Seven Wonders of the Ancient World—the Great Pyramid of Cheops. The bus had been our second choice for transportation out to the pyramid complex at Giza. Our attempts to flag down a cab for the round trip had met with no success, and when we found out the reason for the scarcity of cabs, it was a little unsettling. By this time we had become aware of the Achille Lauro crisis and the subsequent diversion by the U.S. Air Force of the Egyptair jet which was carrying the four terrorists to asylum in Libya. To our dismay we discovered that all of the cabs were involved in transporting people to an anti-American demonstration at the University. And so, trying to look very European rather than American, we boarded our bus and before too long the massive forms of the largest stone structures ever constructed came into view even though we were still quite a distance away. Our bus began its climb up out of the Nile valley and onto the desert plateau and then we were there. You can look at a thousand pictures of something like the pyramids, but until you stand in their shadow, you can't fully appreciate the tremendous accomplishment of the ancient Egyptians. We spent the rest of the afternoon wandering around the three immense monuments and their ever vigilant guardian, the Sphinx, trying to absorb the awesome grandeur of this most famous necropolis. Because cameras are not allowed inside the Great Pyramid, I waited outside holding all our photo equipment while Alison and Paul made the rigorous climb into the heart of Cheops' (Khufu was his true Egyptian name) "eternal house." And then it was my turn. First, through the narrow ascending passageway and then into the amazing Grand Gallery where stones weighing as much as 50 tons hang overhead; and finally into the King's Chamber in the very heart of the pyramid. Here, the great king Khufu, one of the most powerful pharaohs of Egypt's Fourth Dynasty, once lay in eternal repose for what he probably had anticipated would be "millions and millions of years." But alas, even the imposing pyramids proved no match for centuries of wily tomb robbers, and now only the great Lord of the underworld, Osiris, can say where Khufu's restless spirit dwells.

Besides seeing the Pyramids for the first time we were also getting our first look at the Sahara Desert, and it was every bit as awe inspiring as the Great Pyramid itself—a vast sea of sand stretching endlessly away to the western horizon. As the sun began its downward journey to commence what the Egyptians believed was the sun god Re's passage through the netherworld, the whole setting took on a golden hue. But this seemed to last only for a short while, for soon twilight, and then darkness, was upon us. It all happened so quickly here on the edge of the desert. And then, with a canopy of twinkling stars overhead, we took our seats for the much praised sound and light show and watched and listened as the pyramids and Sphinx were illuminated in shades of red, green, and blue, while a narrator told of their long and amazing history.

The only thing marring our visit to the pyramid complex this day was the army of self appointed guides, postcard hawkers, and camel jockeys who were all over us like flies trying to get us to part with our Egyptian pounds and piasters. Some were so insistent that we literally had to scream in their faces to leave us alone. But then, we were fast discovering that as Westerners, we were easy marks for any Egyptian who had anything to sell. In their eyes we were all wealthy American millionaires, and when compared to the poverty that surrounded us, we in fact were. On the streets of Cairo it seemed as if every doorway held some shadowy figure wanting to change our money on the black market—which was considerably better than the government rate of exchange. And one evening, Alison, Paul, and I were apparently befriended by an Egyptian gentleman who invited us to his place for "tea and conversation." We found ourselves in a perfume parlor sampling all sorts of exotic scents for sale, and in the spirit of international trade, we purchased one or two just so we could gracefully make our exit. From that point on we were wary of anyone who approached us with an offer of "tea and conversation." It was somewhat distressing, because we wanted to be as open as possible to this very different culture, but all too often it seemed a friendly advance masked an ulterior motive.

The following day, Sunday, October 13, we spent almost entirely within the vast galleries of the Egyptian Museum. This experience too can only be laced with superlatives. How else can you describe the treasures of King Tutankhamen which occupy a whole floor of the museum? By staring into the eyes of the boy king's golden burial mask, you are staring into the heart of this ancient culture. His steady and confident gaze seems to stir in you a sense of magnificence and wonder. In fact, there was so much to see within the walls of the museum that we became saturated with Egyptology and had to call it quits for the day.

While in Cairo we also began checking into visas for Kenya and India. Back in Athens I had pretty much crossed Kenya off my itinerary. I had discovered that traveling overland from southern Egypt to Kenya through the Sudan was out of the question given the desert and the civil war in the South. The more practical course appeared to be to train back to Cairo and then catch a flight down to East Africa. But the expense of an additional flight and the image of me and my bicycle ending up skewered on the horn of some wild rhinoceros made proceeding on to India seem the more sensible thing to do. Alison and Paul, however, had a keen desire to see the big game reserves of East Africa, and they also wanted to visit some relatives who were missionaries on the shores of Lake Victoria in Tanzania. I was now giving some serious thought to going with them and keeping our threesome intact. The image of the rhino notwithstanding, the prospect of seeing Africa's big game was indeed exciting. More importantly, we had been together now for a week, and although there were some rough spots—our riding pace being quite different—we liked each other. Our strange surroundings had made us pull together and rely on one another. A kind of bond had been forged and I didn't know if I wanted to break that bond.

"Why don't you go ahead and get your visa for Kenya anyhow," suggested Alison during one of our conversations about the future. "At least you'll have it, and after we cycle down to Luxor and catch the train back to Cairo, then you can decide if you want to buy a plane ticket to Kenya and hang with us."

What Alison said made sense. It gave me the option of postponing my ultimate decision and I also would have time to think about Kenya. After returning from Luxor by train, having my visas for both India and Kenya would give me the luxury of choosing Kenya with Alison and Paul or India on my own. The byword here was "Keep your options open."

On our last day in Egypt's capital we visited the Citadel. It is a fortress that was built by Saladin, the great Islamic leader of the 12th century who fought against Richard the Lionhearted during the Third Crusade. Within the Citadel is the beautiful Muhammad Ali Mosque. While there we listened in on a group discussion that was being led by two representatives of the Islamic faith—a young man and a woman. They were answering questions from a European tour group about Islamic beliefs and how they affected different aspects of their daily lives. The two did not see eye to eye.

"According to the Koran, a woman's responsibility is in the home," explained the young man. "It is her duty to provide a comfortable and loving environment for her children and husband. It is unfortunate that more and more women are having to work out of economic necessity."

Next, it was the woman's turn, and she sounded just the opposite of the type of woman described in the Koran.

"Working outside the home allows a woman to better herself," she said, "and it also allows her to help the family acquire the things to help make life more comfortable. And life around the home could be more comfortable if more Islamic men would help with the daily living chores. Many men do not help in any way around the home and pass this attitude on to the young boys."

Later they spoke of the economy and the many problems Egypt faces.

"It may surprise you to hear that unemployment is not a problem in our country," the man said. "The government provides many low paying jobs for the people if they want to work. One thing that helps many of the very poor is that many of the foodstuffs are subsidized by the government. A major problem for our economy is that many skilled people leave Egypt to work in other countries. We don't work enough in our own country. One-fifth of our population is working outside of Egypt—over 7000 people."

We found the young man's comments about unemployment a little hard to believe considering the degree of poverty we had seen thus far in Egypt. Even so, their discussion was interesting and we felt that it gave us a little of an insight into Islamic thought.

* * *

If someone had told me on the morning we left Cairo that I would end the day bruised and bleeding, I might have stayed in bed. In fact, I probably should have stayed in bed because all through the night before, I began to pay my dues for drinking Egyptian water and the change in food. I was carrying a water purification pump and we each had pills and drops to add to our water, but cycling in Egypt's desert environment required consuming copious amounts of H_2O, and it was impossible to treat it all—especially when the foods we ate were washed in untreated water. We three knew it was only a matter of time, and now my time was here—the Pharaoh's curse had struck! Along with that, I began to feel alternately chilled and feverish. As I wore a path between my bedroom and the WC (bathroom/water closet), I began to wonder if I would be able to leave with Alison and Paul in the morning. However, by sunrise I felt somewhat better, and I was determined that I would ride regardless and not hold Alison and Paul back.

Our objective this day was Beni Suef, about 80 miles south of Cairo. We wouldn't make it. We wheeled out of Cairo through the crowded streets, the sands of the Sahara always hanging in the air, giving the city a dusty and dirty appearance. I new Beni Suef was a full day's ride, but Paul suggested we stop at Saqqara to see the famous Step Pyramid which was one of the first to be constructed—even older than the Great Pyramid of Cheops. We all wanted to see it, but in the back of my mind was that long ride ahead over bad roads. History won out over bodily comfort, and we headed to Saqqara on the edge of the desert plateau and spent about an hour-and-a-half at this wonderful site of antiquity.

The great Step Pyramid is the oldest of all the pyramids and one of the first monuments in the world to be constructed of hewn stone. The Step Pyramid was built for Zoser, a pharaoh of the Third Dynasty (around 2700 B.C.). The architect is considered to be one of the greatest and most mysterious men of early Egyptian history. His name was Imhotep and he is thought to have been a genius not only in building, but also in medicine and astronomy. His name alone attained a magical significance, and he eventually achieved the status of a god. It is believed that somewhere beneath the sands of Saqqara lies his undiscovered tomb.

Close to the Step Pyramid was a smaller pyramid, the Pyramid of Unas, the last pharaoh of the Fifth Dynasty. The outsides were crumbling, but inside and underneath was something truly wonderful. We entered the pyramid and proceeded down a short, steep tunnel that took us to the burial chamber. There we found the oldest known hieroglyphic tomb texts. They were amazing! It was almost as if the hieroglyphs had been cut into the stone yesterday—they were so clean and crisp—and the pyramid dates to 2360 B.C.

Since it was getting late we moved on. But off in the distance to the south, shimmering across the desert sands, we could see the pyramids of Dashur—especially the famous Bent Pyramid.

"Why don't we stop at the pyramids at Dashur," said Paul. "They're on our way south and it would be a shame to pass them up.

"I don't know, Paul," I cautioned. "It's getting late in the morning and we still have 70 miles to Beni Suef."

But I knew he was right. We would probably only pass this way once and it would be foolish to pass up the opportunity to see these great sites. As it turned out, our efforts to reach the site were thwarted by a military roadblock. The area is militarily sensitive since there is an Egyptian military base nearby, and travel by foreigners is sometimes restricted.

Timewise, I knew we were in trouble now. We stopped for a quick lunch and as we pulled back onto the highway, we had about three hours of daylight left and around 50 miles to go. We began to push it, but a stubborn sidewind made the pedaling pure work. I was in the lead concentrating on trying to keep a good pace, dodging potholes and weaving in and out of poor sections of the Egyptian highway. By the time I saw it, it was too late. My bike shot over the huge bump in the road, both wheels leaving the surface of the highway and one of my front panniers coming off with the jolt upward. As my bike came down the front wheel landed on the pannier and the next thing I knew, bike and rider were skidding along the pavement in a cloud of roadside gravel and sand. I was stunned! In a daze, I picked myself up, afraid of what I might find broken both on me and the bicycle. It could have been much worse. My knees and arms were scraped a bit and the palm of my hand began to swell because I had used that to break my fall. I looked at my riding gloves and huge gouges were torn out of the leather. If not for the gloves, my hand would have been a good approximation of ground beef. The handlebars of the bike were twisted, the back brake lever bent a little and the pannier torn slightly, but other than that the bike was OK.

Bruised and bleeding, I hopped back on my bike and we continued on, but we knew we'd never make Beni Suef without some kind of help. That help was not too long in arriving in the form of a pickup truck that came speeding by

and then screeched to a halt in response to our waves. The
driver and his two companions piled out of the truck and
scurried back to where we were standing.

"Beni Suef?" Paul asked, pointing down the road.

"Beni Suef?" I repeated, wanting to make sure they understood we were hoping for a lift.

"Beni Suef," the driver acknowledged with a smile.

We then pointed at our bikes and at the empty bed of
the truck.

"Beni Suef?" we repeated once more.

The driver grinned once again and held up two hands
plus one more indicating, we assumed, that he would like
15 pounds for his services. We gave our heads a shake and
held up 10 fingers indicating in response that 15 pounds was
out of the question and 10 would be our limit. After a brief
hesitation and consideration that he might miss out on some
easy money, the driver nodded yes and we hauled our bikes
and equipment up into the bed of the pickup truck. We
climbed in with our bikes and sprawled amidst our panniers
and gear and began bouncing down the highway, happy that
we had been able to flag down a ride. Little did we suspect,
however, that we were being taken for a ride in more ways
than one.

After about twenty minutes of being jostled around the
bed of the pickup truck with our bikes and equipment, we
came to a halt in what seemed to be a sizable town. The
driver and his two friends began to hurriedly unload our
bicycles and gear as we looked for some indication that we
were in the right place.

"Beni Suef? Beni Suef?" I demanded.

"Yes, Beni Suef," grinned the driver, and as quickly as
that, he and his friends piled into the truck and were gone.

It had not taken long for a crowd of people to gather
around us and we looked pleadingly at them in hopes that
they would confirm that we were in Beni Suef.

"Could anyone please tell us if this is Beni Suef?" Alison
inquired. The townspeople looked blankly at each other until
one man stepped forward.

"Wasta," he said.

Alison and Paul and I looked at each other and smiled through clenched teeth. We knew that we had just been swindled by our three "friends" and left in a real predicament. Darkness was almost upon us and riding any further would be out of the question.

"Could you tell us if Wasta has a hotel where we might stay for the night?" Paul asked, directing his question to the man who had spoken up before.

The man paused, trying to digest the flurry of English words Paul had thrown his way, and then conferred with a fellow townsperson.

"Wasta, no hotels. Hotels in Beni Suef. Beni Suef 40 kilometers," the man finally volunteered.

For the next ten minutes we talked over our options which seemed few and far between while the townspeople spoke rapidly in Arabic. Sensing that we were in trouble and might not have a place to stay for the night, the man once again stepped forward.

"Please, follow me," he grinned.

He led us inside a building across the road, showed us to a room with a table and few chairs, and indicated that we should sit down.

"Please, here wait for important man."

We sat for about 45 minutes during which time complete darkness had fallen and a steady stream of townspeople popped their heads into the small room to get a look at the three foreigners and their amazing machines. We smiled and nodded to all those who looked in and could only guess at what was going to happen next. As I sat I tried to clean the blood from the scrapes on my legs and arms and tenderly probed my swollen palm which was turning various shades of black and blue. Just as we were beginning to suspect that we might spend the rest of the night in this room, a man in western style dress—most of the others around us were dressed in the traditional galabias—arrived in a pickup truck and strode into the room. He was a man of some importance for the others made way for him and their greetings indicated this was not an ordinary townsperson.

"Welcome to our country," he began in rather good English.

"My name is Ezat. I am the assistant to the mayor. I am also a Coptic Christian." This last comment he made with an obvious sense of pride in his Christian background.

We told Ezat of our plight and he became genuinely concerned about our safety and well-being. When we related the part of our story about the three crooked young men in the pickup truck he frowned and shook his head.

"I'm very sorry for the behavior of these three men," he apologized. "This is a very bad way to treat guests in our country. But now, you will meet the major of Wasta, and he will be able to decide what to do."

We followed Ezat outside and there, across the road, was the mayor sitting comfortably with a cup of tea and smoking a cigarette. We were officially introduced and instructed to occupy the three chairs that had been placed on either side of him. He was a tall man also in western style dress and he projected an air of culture and intelligence.

"I would like to welcome you to Egypt," he began in excellent English. "I'm very sorry for your bad fortune. I think we may be able to help you. But if you don't mind, I would like to ask you some questions. How are you finding our country so far?"

We told him of our travels and tried to be honest about the good and bad experiences that Egypt was providing us.

"We have been somewhat surprised by the degree of poverty of many of the people," Alison offered.

"Yes, it is true; we have a very poor country," the mayor explained. "Egypt has never recovered from the disastrous wars with Israel. Those terrible conflicts devastated our economy. Also, many of our farmers are not working as much as they should. Some of our villages are now having television and the people would rather sit and watch the TV set than work in the fields."

Our conversation with the mayor lasted almost an hour and a half and covered a variety of topics, including his own impressions of the United States which he has visited several times. When we broached the topic of the Achille Lauro hijacking and President Reagan's subsequent decision to divert the Egyptian jet in order to apprehend the hijackers, the mayor furrowed his brow and expressed his great concern over the actions of the President.

"Our two countries have built a very strong relationship over the years, but now I am very much afraid that President Reagan has jeopardized that relationship with his decision," he said with a sad voice. We still didn't know all the facts surrounding the international incident, so the only thing that we felt we could do was to apologize for the United States and express our hope that the situation would be worked out and our two countries would continue to be friends.

While Alison and Paul continued the conversation with the mayor, I went with Ezat in his pickup to the police station to register with the police and allow them to look over our passports. When we arrived back, the mayor informed us that some of the people had been preparing food for us and that we should follow Ezat back to the room where we had been waiting before. There we sat down to an especially tasty meal of corned beef, potatoes, eggs, and bread which filled up the considerable hollows in our tummies. But now it was almost 9:00 and, covered with a layer of road grime and dirt, exhausted from the day's long ride (and me, scraped and bruised from my accident), we still didn't know if we would have a place to bed down for the night. Shortly after we finished our meal, however, Ezat had an announcement to make.

"Since our town has no hotels, I would be honored to have you stay with me and my wife for the night. And now, we may load up your bicycles and equipment in my truck, and I will take you to my home."

We had trouble finding words to express our gratitude to Ezat, but the smile he had on his face indicated that he knew how we felt. When we opened the door to his cozy apartment, a small woman with a ready smile greeted us. Ezat's wife seemed a little flustered by the arrival of three unexpected guests, but she moved like a little dynamo as she rearranged things in an attempt to make a little more space so that we could all fit in. She took an immediate liking to Alison and seemed thrilled to have us as her guests for the night. The kindness of Ezat and his wife was overwhelming; they treated us as royal guests in their small home. We stayed up talking with them and some of their neighbors who came to visit until midnight. By that time my eyelids were about down to my cheeks, and it was with a true sense of exhaustion and relief that I crawled beneath my covers and closed the book on a truly exceptional day.

In the morning I woke up stiff and sore, but somewhat rested and relaxed. Ezat and his wife provided us with a delicious breakfast that somehow managed to get our engines revving once again. After expressing our heartfelt gratitude to these two kind people, we bade them farewell and were dropped back at the town administration building where we again had an audience with the mayor for over an hour. In our second discussion we found out that the mayor had jurisdiction over not only his own city of Wasta, but also the surrounding villages which incorporates an area of a few hundred thousand people. He told us of the impending visit of President Mubarak to his district—the first ever for the President—in order to inspect some of the agricultural projects that were being undertaken in this area. We finally made our good-byes to the mayor, very impressed—and thankful—that this important government official had taken a personal interest in our situation and safety.

It was almost 11:00 before we climbed back on our bicycles to finish the ride to Beni Suef. We made a brief visit to the local pyramid and were about ready to head south once again.

"How would you two feel about taking a more roundabout route to Beni Suef?" Paul suggested. "Instead of getting back on that busy valley highway with all those damned trucks and potholes, why don't we take the desert highway out to the Fayum Oasis and from there take the road to Beni Suef?"

The map showed a thick line that would take us south into the desert for about 30 miles until we reached the Fayum Oasis, and then another thick line that led back into Beni Suef. It was a longer route, but off of the clogged main artery.

"I don't know, Paul," I responded in a worried voice. "Are we sure we actually want to ride out into the desert? Beside, I was hoping to make it a short to ride Beni Suef, find a hotel, and then take the rest of the day for some R and R."

But after a little more discussion, we all agreed the road surface would be better and there would be less traffic on the way to the Fayum and the road that then went from Fayum to Beni Suef. Before we could even begin, however, I had to pull to the side of the road.

"You two go on up ahead," I half groaned. "I think I picked up some more of the Pharaoh's curse in that last pyramid."

And so, with my stomach and intestines in knots, I squatted there in the middle of the desert sands and tried to squirt out what I could. Then, rejoining Alison and Paul, we headed into the Sahara Desert, the vast expanse of sand and dunes spreading endlessly before us. My doubts about our alternate route were justified, for we rode into a direct head-wind that evaporated the sweat as soon as it reached our skin. I could almost sense the liquid content being sucked out of my already dehydrated and weakened body from the diarrhea. Water seemed incapable of quenching my thirst and I was afraid to drink too much from my water bottles because I didn't know for sure how long we would be in the desert. After what seemed like an interminable stretch of pedaling, the oasis appeared and danced on the horizon like a mirage— which we fervently prayed it wasn't. But for miles the road seemed to skirt the oasis, keeping us in the hot desert sands. At last we arrived at the city of Fayum, but by that time I could feel a tingling in my hands and feet and even a bit of a chill—sure signs of a heat stroke. We converged with a vengeance on a vendor who was selling semi-cold bottles of Pepsi-Cola and immediately downed three bottles apiece, which sent my stomach into an even greater state of turmoil. Somewhat in a daze, we sat down to a lunch of chicken, salad, and bread which did not sit well at all with the Pepsi sloshing around in my tummy. But the brief rest helped me to regain a little of my strength for the remainder of our ride to our long sought destination. Mercifully, the road from the Fayum back to the valley follows a canal that connects the oasis with the Nile, so it was not necessary to battle the desert and the headwinds on the way back. Still, by the time we reached Beni Suef, I was in pretty sad shape. We wasted no time in locating a hotel room for the night, and it wasn't long before the three beds in our room were occupied by three motionless, dead to the world heaps of humanity.

Somewhere in the middle of the night, floating on the mists of a kind of half slumber, I lifted up my head to see a white blur hurdle across the end of my bed. It was Alison making a mad dash for the toilet. It was evident that her number was up for the Pharaoh's curse because she repeated the process quite a few times throughout the rest of the night. In the morning neither Alison nor I felt all that great and Paul had also had a short bout with the trots. We decided to move on anyhow and set a course that would take us off the main road onto some of the valley backroads. It wasn't long, however, before we were lost and shouting at each other about which way we should head. None of us was in a very good mood on this morning with our stomachs and intestines performing various contortions. To make matters worse, we battled another nasty headwind that sapped the energy from our weakened bodies. And last but not least, on top of my bumps and bruises from the accident and my queasy stomach, I had to contend with the worst case of heartburn I have ever experienced in my life. Every time I swallowed it felt as if a blow torch ignited in my stomach and burned up the entire length of my esophagus and throat.

Be 1:00 P.M. we were still 50 miles from our destination for the night, El Minya, and Alison was sinking fast with Paul and me not too far behind.

"Well, guys, it's almost 1:00 and we're still 50 miles from El Minya; and this wind is just killing us. We could try to find a train station and ride the rails into El Minya," I reasoned. "I just don't think we're gonna make it at this pace."

"God, I'm all for that!" chimed Alison. "Let's do it."

With the way each of us was feeling it didn't take long to reach a unanimous decision, and so we made tracks to the nearest train station and threw ourselves and the bikes on the train for the ride to El Minya. But our arrival at the train station caused a commotion, as it did in all the towns and villages we passed through. Once again, a crowd of young children gathered around us, all staring, laughing, giggling, pointing at this or that piece of equipment on our bikes or us. Their monotonous questions rang in our ears: "What you name? How old you? What time is it?" Some older Egyptians attempted to come to our aid by driving the kids back with sticks, but it didn't last for long since they were right back at it again as soon as the adults stepped back. Even while riding we usually brought most activity along the roadside to a halt. Almost every Egyptian, young or old, seemed to know the same two or three words: "Hello Meesta! How you Meesta!" By this time, it had really begun to grate on our nerves, and we no longer tried to acknowledge everyone's salutation as we had in the beginning of our journey south.

As we worked our way up the Nile Valley toward Luxor and ancient Thebes, I had been attempting to shoot a lot of photos not only of the great temples and sites of antiquity, but also scenes of everyday life that would help me to make Egypt come alive for my future students. These included timeless mud walled villages, ancient irrigation techniques, and the comical and aloof camels with which we shared the road. On our ride to the relatively modern city of Assiout, I pulled to the side of the road in order to snap a picture of a shadoof, an ancient water raising tool that works on the same principle as a teeter-totter. While rummaging through my panniers for my camera, three young Egyptian men robed in their soiled galabias who were a hundred yards or so down the road caught sight of the strangest thing they had probably seen in quite a while—me—and headed in my direction at a trot. My attempts to snap off a quick one and make a swift getaway were foiled by the fact that I had neglected to put in a new roll of film. Against my better judgment I sat down and began to put a new roll of film in my camera. In no time at all, it seemed, the Egyptians were at my side giving me and my bicycle a thorough inspection. As I fumbled with my camera, one of the Egyptians began poking me in the shoulder and mimicking a photographer, communicating I suspected that it would be just a fine idea for me to take a picture of him and his buddies. His two buddies in the meantime had jumped on the shadoof and were swinging to and fro, having a good ol' time, preening all the while for the camera while buddy number one continued to poke me in the shoulder. I just nodded and smiled while I worked on my uncooperative camera, and then a huge truck thundered past kicking up dirt and sand which rained down on the inside of my Olympus OM-10. Buddy number one kept working on my shoulder while buddies two and three were still making like chimpanzees on the shadoof.

"Good God!" I shouted and stuffed my still unloaded camera and film into a pannier and then stood on my pedals in an effort to put distance between me and the three stooges. Tom, Dick, and Hosni took off running after me still waving and shouting, but it wasn't long before their screams of "Hello Meesta" faded away behind me.

This keystone cops scenario was offset by a more sinister and upsetting one the following day as we made the short ride from Assiout to Sohag, a predominantly Christian city. In one of the towns that we passed through, a group of boys followed us on their one speed bicycles as they often did. To them it was a great game to see if they could keep up, then pass us, then drop back, and then repeat the whole process all over again. As long as they kept their distance, we usually didn't mind, but sometimes a would-be daredevil would cut us off either intentionally or unintentionally, and then we would hit our afterburners and leave them in the dust. This group, however, was fairly well behaved and eventually tired of being our official escort—all except one boy who stuck close to Alison. He seemed like a friendly sort and continued on with us to the outskirts of the town. Paul and I were a slight distance ahead when from behind us came a scream of shock and outrage. When we reached Alison she was in tears.

"That little brat!" she blurted. "I thought he was just trying to be friendly. He waited until just the right moment when he could get close enough and then grabbed me in the boob."

In the distance we could see the little scumbag hightailing it back to his village. We debated about chasing him down so that we could give him a kick in just the spot that would cure him of his perverted urges for a good long time, but he was already quite a distance away. We did our best to console Alison and then finished our ride to Sohag in an angry state of mind. This was the first time that something like this had happened—to our dismay it would not be the last. Up to this point in our journey through Egypt we had been less than impressed by the behavior and attitude of the children—especially that of young Egyptian males. The following day would provide us with our worst experience with the youth of Egypt.

We wheeled into Sohag in the early afternoon and quickly located some lodgings for the night. However, what we initially thought to be a hotel turned out to be some kind of agricultural men's club. The man in charge seemed to have no qualms about renting us a room for the night, and so we settled in for a much needed rest. The day before had been about an 85 miler, and even though we had only covered about 40 miles today, we all felt pretty drained and each of us was suffering from some degree of the Pharaoh's curse. The Pharaoh's curse notwithstanding, our appetites were still pretty keen and to our surprise the men's club had a dining hall where they served us an excellent meal of chicken, rice, and beans. Alison and Paul turned in early and I wandered down to the lounge where some young men were watching Richard Harris and Vanessa Redgrave in the movie *Camelot*. It was curious, but as I sat there watching King Arthur and Lady Guinevere amidst the splendor of their magical kingdom, I found myself growing almost melancholy and homesick. Here in the far away desert sands of Egypt, anything reminiscent of the western world seemed to spark memories and longings for a world that did not appear quite so strange and foreign.

Each day seemed to offer up new experiences that were designed to test our resolve and fortitude, and this day would be no different. About 30 miles south of Sohag, we stopped at a truly wonderful ancient site—the Temple of Abydos. It was constructed by the Pharaoh Seti I and his son Rameses II (the Great) who also had the colossal statues at Abu Simbal erected in his honor. The temple was built in honor of Osiris, god of the underworld and so it was one of the most important religious sites in Upper Egypt. Inside, the temple walls are covered with amazing reliefs that deal with the worship of Osiris by Seti and Rameses. Many of the reliefs still have vibrant colors and are indeed beautiful. Also inside on one of the walls can be seen the famous List of Kings that enabled archaeologists to determine the sequence of Egypt's rulers over the long span of its history.

It was hard to tear ourselves away from the spellbinding atmosphere of Abydos, but by the time we did it was already midday and our next destination, the city of Qena, was still 60 miles distant. Because we knew that we wouldn't make our goal before nightfall, we headed to the local railway station and began a three-hour wait that became a real challenge to our patience. As always we attracted a considerable crowd of young and curious onlookers, but this group proved to be bolder and more irritating. They would not leave us or our bikes alone, grabbing at this or that piece of our equipment and making what seemed to be mocking comments in our direction. We had to restrain ourselves from booting one little insufferable brat in his small Egyptian derriere. Even the older Egyptians thought this little terror to be quite amusing and did nothing to quash his ill-mannered behavior.

We were relieved when the train finally arrived, but our problems were by no means over. For the first 45 minutes of our ride all went smoothly, but then at one of the stops an unruly group of from 50 to 75 schoolboys poured into our compartment. They were the most obnoxious group we had yet encountered. They refused to respect our privacy, crowding in on us, asking the same silly questions, poking and grabbing at our bicycles, ignoring the admonitions of the guards who would push them away from us—and then they would come right back to pick up where they left off. Sitting there surrounded by these loud and menacing youths, I could feel my face turn red and my blood begin to boil, and I felt as if I was on the verge of exploding into a verbal assault on these antagonistic kids. Luckily, we, and possibly they, were saved by the train which arrived at their stop, and they poured off as quickly and nosily as they had poured on, leaving us in peace and quiet. However, when we arrived at Qena and began to unload our bicycles, I saw that where my bicycle pump had been, there was now an empty spot. Alison's pump and Paul's water bottle had also been stolen by these wonderful Egyptian lads. Our bikes had been on the same car with us, but the crowd of youths had been between us and our machines which made it impossible to keep them in our direct line of sight. We were outraged, but once again felt helpless about being able to do anything about the theft. It would be impossible to replace our pumps here in Egypt, so it was fortunate that Paul's pump had not been lifted—at least for Alison and Paul. They had Presta valves on their tubes and Presta pumps while I had the standard American Schraeder tubes and pump; the two are not compatible. Because I'd had a slow leak in my rear tire, it was flat by the time we arrived at Qena, but now I had nothing to inflate it with. We tried one of Paul's spare Presta tubes with my Schraeder rim and it seemed to work OK. But I knew I would be in a real bind if I decided to go my own way, and I couldn't depend on Paul's spare tubes forever. Fortunately, the Schraeder valves work with any air compressor that inflates automobile tires, but in the Third World one cannot count on finding an air compressor on every corner. This would prove to be a major headache for me in the coming months until I eventually was able to replace my stolen pump with an adequate one in New Zealand.

On Tuesday, October 22 we arrived in the city of Luxor, the endpoint of our journey south *up* the Nile River Valley. Earlier in the day we had stopped at the Temple of Dendera, one of the best preserved of all Egyptian temples. It was constructed approximately a thousand years after the Temple of Abydos during the reign of the Ptolemies who ruled this part of Alexander the Great's empire after its disintegration (sometime after 323 B.C.). Dendera was dedicated to Hathor, the cow goddess, goddess of women, and to the Greeks, goddess of love and beauty in some way related to Aphrodite. We wandered through the dark, cool recesses of the temple's interior and threaded our way between the 24 immense Hathor-headed columns and then climbed the still intact stairways to the temple's roof where we were amazed to find graffiti left by the soldiers of Napoleon Bonaparte.

From the Temple of Dendera it was only a short ride into Luxor. Luxor, being one of the great tourist sites in Egypt, has a bountiful crop of hotels geared to all price ranges, and we had little problem in locating some lodgings for the next couple of days. There was much to see here in Luxor and across the river at ancient Thebes, and we intended to begin the next day with the main event—the Valley of The Kings and the famous tomb of the boy king.

It is a small tomb by comparison—only a couple of rooms—an ante-chamber, the burial chamber itself and a couple of adjoining rooms. Not really too impressive, until you realize that this is it—the one tomb that was delivered to us through the ages—the only one to escape the ravages of the tomb robbers—the tomb of the boy king, King Tut. His mummified body encased in one of his golden coffins is still here in the burial chamber where he was laid to rest 3,500 years ago. The discovery of his tomb in 1922 by Howard Carter electrified the world and gave us a rare look at how the Egyptian god-kings were prepared to leave this world and enter the next. The burial shrine itself qualifies as one of the most spectacular finds in the history of archaeology. King Tut's mummy, covered by his beautiful golden burial mask, was entombed in three mummiform coffins bearing the likeness of the king, one fitting inside the other, the innermost coffin over 1200 pounds of solid gold. A large stone sarcophagus held the three coffins and the sarcophagus in turn was surrounded by four gilded shrines, each fitting inside the next larger one like chinese boxes. The shrine took up the entire space of the burial chamber so that there was only two feet of space between the wall of the outermost shrine and the wall of the chamber.

There's an interesting footnote to Carter's actual entry of the burial chamber. In the book which he wrote about his ten-year excavation of the tomb, Carter describes how it required many weeks to record, catalog, and remove the multitude of artifacts found in the ante-chamber before he could breach the entrance way to the King's burial chamber. But Thomas Hoving of the New York Metropolitan Museum and one of the men responsible for bringing the King Tut exhibit to the United States relates in his book, *Tutankhamen, The Untold Story*, that Howard Carter was not telling the truth. He tells how Carter, Lord Carnarvron (his benefactor and sponsor), Carnarvron's daughter, and one other archaeologist secretly entered the burial chamber the very first night and examined the exterior of the burial shrine in dumbfounded amazement, and then concealed the evidence of their entrance into the chamber. Apparently, Carter's excitement and curiosity outweighed the requirement that officials of the Egyptian government be present for the opening of a royal tomb.

Most of the 5000 artifacts taken from King Tut's tomb are, of course, on display in the Egyptian Museum in Cairo. One of these artifacts is a beautiful alabaster cup. On it is an inscription that expresses with ancient eloquence the enduring optimism of the Egyptians and their hope for the young king's joy and contentment in his eternal life: "May you spend millions and millions of years, you who love Thebes, sitting with your face to the north wind, your two eyes beholding happiness."

We emerged from the tomb of Tutankhamen into the Valley of the Kings, the desolate, out-of-the-way desert site that the Pharaohs of the New Kingdom chose for their burials so as to be safe from the hands of centuries of greedy tomb robbers. We visited a number of the other 60 or so tombs which were even more astounding because of their depth, size, and amazing wall reliefs that were alive with beautiful colors—some of them looking as though they were just painted yesterday. We spent a good part of the day wandering from tomb to tomb, each one seemingly more spectacular than the one before it. But we could tell that Alison was really hurting as she dragged herself along the walk ways of the valley.

"Fellas, my stomach is really doing flip-flops," she grimaced. "And I feel like I've always got the squirts, but not much comes out. I think I've about had it for the day."

Both Paul and I knew the feeling well and so we headed back to the ferryboat that would transport us across the Nile River and to our lodgings in Luxor. On the second day of our Luxor sojourn Alison felt pretty weak and washed out, so she decided to let Paul and me go it alone for the day while she holed up in the hotel room and tried to regain some of her strength. We visited the temples of Luxor and Karnak and both were grand sights. The amazing temple of Karnak was dedicated to Amun, one of the most powerful gods of the Egyptian pantheon, and it was the largest temple anywhere in the ancient world. These fantastic structures, though victimized by centuries of time, leave a lasting impression on the 20th century visitor; it's hard to imagine the effect they would have had on the Egyptian peasant of 3500 years ago. By the time we returned to the hotel Alison felt a little perkier, so we treated ourselves to a western style meal at one of the luxury tourist hotels (ours definitely didn't fall into that category). We'd had our fill of fried felafel—just the thought of it turned our stomachs queasy now—and we craved anything that our tummies would gratefully recognize as American cuisine. I was quite sure that I had died and gone to heaven as I bit into my deluxe hamburger. And the comfort and cleanliness of the hotel's restaurant and lobby insulated us for just a short time from the dirt and poverty through which we had ridden over the last two weeks. That was something that we all relished right at that time.

The next morning we boarded the train for the 13-hour journey back to Cairo. During the long ride north, I had the opportunity to reflect on some of our experiences in this ancient land. It had been a mixed bag. The recorded history of Egypt spans a 5000-year period and here were planted the seeds of our own western civilization. The monuments that the ancient Egyptians left us are second to none and they have given us an insight into the vitality and richness of the lives of the ancients. To see these had been a truly wonderful experience. And many of the Egyptians with whom we came in contact had been so very kind and eager to help. The helpfulness of the kind doctor in Tanta and the hospitality of Ezat and his wife will always bring a warm glow to our memories. But modern Egypt is a country beset by many problems. It seems ironic that this should be so in a land that contributed so much to our western culture. None of us realized how poor or "third world" Egypt is. Many of the towns and villages we passed through seemed not to have changed much over the centuries and are still constructed of sun-dried mud brick. Many of the dwellings appeared to be half falling down and numerous other buildings constructed of more modern materials stood half completed with no apparent work in progress.

Our western backgrounds made the dirt and filth difficult to deal with. Standards of sanitation are far below that of the West and result in chronic illness and disease for many of the poor and destitute. It is true that Egypt is a desert land and much of the dirt that seems to cover everything is the result of airborne desert sands and debris, but it appeared that very little effort was being made to keep pace with the accumulation of dirt and garbage.

Overpopulation is another difficult problem. There are over 50 million people packed into the narrow strip of arable land—only about 3% of the total land—that depends on the Nile for its fertility. The same land area had to support only three to four million people 3,000 years ago. Egypt is also suffering from the loss of some of its best talent. It's estimated that one-fifth of the population is working outside of the country; and these are some of the most capable individuals. It is possible that many feel they have no choice if they want to get ahead because wages are so low. A future biology teacher we talked to on one of our train hops said his monthly salary would be just 45 pounds, and another young Egyptian we talked to said if he wanted to make enough to have his own apartment, he would have to leave the country which is what he was planning to do. Related to this, the mayor of Wasta said in our discussion with him that many leave the country, make a sizable amount of money and then come back and "sit" and do not continue to work as they did outside of Egypt. Also, the country is still very much a traditional Islamic, male-dominated society that continues to ignore the valuable talent source of its female population. And the behavior of young Egyptian males really shocked us. Many—at least the ones we had contact with—seemed to lack a sense of common decency and respect for authority, not to mention a lack of consideration for foreign guests. Some of these values and attitudes hopefully are changing, but it appeared to us that Egypt has a long road to haul.

During our ride south I had been silently debating with myself what my future plans should be. I felt a great sense of relief when I finally made my decision. On Saturday,

October 25, I bought a ticket with Alison and Paul for Nairobi, Kenya. Even though the cost of the flight was pretty steep, I didn't want to break up our trio. Our mutual encouragement had helped us all to get through the rough times of Egypt. I didn't want to lose that. Our flight was early Monday morning at 12:30 A.M., and so on Sunday afternoon we loaded up our bicycles for the 15-mile ride out to the international airport at Heliopolis. We had an endless 10-hour wait until our departure, but as flight time approached we rolled our bikes up to the check-in counter and were greeted with some news that we didn't want to hear.

"I'm sorry, but your bicycles must be in boxes," announced the clerk with a worried expression.

"That's really impossible," Paul urgently explained. "There is nowhere we know of in Cairo that we can get boxes and the only way we could get out here to the airport was to ride our bicycles."

"You see, we're on a world bicycle ride," I added, "and it's very difficult to find boxes for our bikes—we tried yesterday in Cairo—and then to find transport for them to the airport. This is the only way we can work it."

"Won't you please help us and make an exception?" pleaded Alison.

The clerk looked at our three desperate faces and then smiled. "Please wait; I will summon my supervisor."

The supervisor arrived on the scene and a huddle ensued involving the clerk, his supervisor, and a couple of other Egypt Air officials.

"Yes, we will take your bicycles without boxes," the supervisor turned to us and announced.

We breathed a huge sigh of relief and thankfully handed our bicycles over to the baggage handler, but as we did we also slipped a ten-pound Egyptian note into his hand that we hoped would ensure a little extra loving care for our fragile machines. The handler flashed a big smile and rolled our babies away to, we hoped, a safe spot in the baggage compartment.

Primed and ready to board our flight, our bubble was deflated once more when they told us there would be a delay until 6:30 in the morning. Fortunately, however, they took good care of us; we and our fellow passengers were carted off to a modern, spic and span clean hotel for a few hours sleep—a little godsend that we were thankful for since we had been waiting at the airport since early afternoon. We even were treated to a free buffet dinner before we retired. At 6:30 A.M., with no further surprises in store, we boarded our Egypt Air winged chariot for the flight to equatorial Africa.

* * *

Our plane touched down at the airport in Nairobi, Kenya and we were amazed at the transformation from Saharan Africa to sub-Sahara Africa. After Egypt, Kenya seemed to be like the Garden of Eden. We had grown weary of the ceaseless Egyptian sun, beating down mercilessly from a cloudless sky and the arid landscape that loomed menacingly beyond the valley of the Nile. But here just south of the equator it was surprisingly cool and it was a joy to see billowing clouds once more. Nairobi, located in the central highlands of Kenya at an elevation of around 5000 feet, has a much cooler climate than steamy Mombasa on the coastline.

We bicycled out of the airport perimeter and onto the plains of East Africa and could clearly see Nairobi about 15 miles distant rising up out of the African savanna like an Emerald City. Grasslands stretched away as far as the eye could see—such a stark contrast to the desert environment of Egypt—and I half expected a lion, tiger, or bear (Oh My! —well, maybe not a bear) to come pounding after us for a midafternoon snack. This prospect was not entirely out of the realm of possibility since there is a national game reserve not too far from the outskirts of Nairobi. We arrived in the heart of the city and were taken aback by what we saw. It was almost like stepping back into the western world. Modern, stylish buildings, clean streets and boulevards, and parks with greenery and blossoming flowers were everywhere to be seen. It was wonderful to be able to walk the streets without kicking up layers of sand. Bustling shops and restaurants tailored to the western appetite abounded, holding forth the promise that meal times would be more of a pleasure than a challenge.

We located some peculiar but pleasant lodgings—a series of rooms that were situated around an open-air court—and then set out to feed our faces on hamburgers and french fries. But it was necessary to fish our jackets from the bottoms of our packs for the evening temperatures were downright chilly. As we walked we were even more amazed when a light drizzle filtered down from the overcast skies above. That was something I hadn't experienced since high in the Pyrenees Mountains of Spain and France.

On Wednesday, October 30, I celebrated my 36th birthday. It was the first birthday of my life that I did not share with my family back in Toledo, Ohio. I missed them a great deal and, of course, this day made it even more so. My surrogate family, Alison and Paul, took me out to dinner and we had an excellent Chinese meal. I think they sensed I was feeling a little bit down and they did a wonderful job of filling in for my family back home.

Kenya is not a country that is particularly suited to cycling, especially through the large game parks which abound with all manner of wild beasts, unless, of course, one happens to be an especially fast cyclist. There are only a few main roads that connect the major cities, and we would soon find out that a line which appeared on our map as a secondary highway could be a well paved road, a deep rutted jeep track or nothing more than a cow path. On our second day in Nairobi, we rented a four-wheel drive vehicle and purchased supplies for a week-long safari to some of Kenya's great game reserves. We also looked into our visas for Tanzania and found a storage company that would store our bikes while we were gone. Early the next morning, outfitted for our safari and cameras loaded for bear—er, uh, make that lion—we set off on a journey that would feature some of the grandest sights that I would see during my year of travel.

* * *

Even in the African darkness, you can tell it is there, it's huge mass outlined against a starlit sky. You can sense an overwhelming presence, a kind of spirit, almost a thing alive—indeed it once was. As darkness releases its hold, the subtle shades of a new dawn bring it into focus, as in a developing photograph. The first rays of the sun not yet seen are captured by its snowcapped peak. A burst of sunlight on the horizon and there it stands in quiet majesty—Mt. Kilimanjaro, rising up 19,000 feet out of the East African plains. Amboeseli to the North, Tsavo to the East, and the Serenghetti far to the West. An unforgettable sight, Africa's tallest peak and worthy of the honor.

This is just one of the many spectacular vistas that we encountered during the first week of November as we toured three of Kenya's national parks in our four-wheel drive Land Rover. We bumped and bounced our way over some of the most unblelievable roads through Mehru, Amboeseli, and Tsavo National Parks and in so doing saw the variety of big and small game that Kenya is noted for: elephants, giraffe, lions, cheetah, wildebeest, gazelle, rhinoceros, hippopotamus, zebra, and many more. We free camped in totally deserted campgrounds or stayed in bandas which are very basic shelters that furnish a roof over your heads, beds, mosquito netting, a picnic table for meals, and a toilet—really quite comfortable, and cheap.

On our first night in Mehru National Park—our first park we visited—the sun had long disappeared from the sky by the time we entered the outer perimeter of the reserve. We felt as if we had been swallowed up by the dark African night as we bounced along the park road in search of our first campsite. Three massive shapes loomed about of the intense darkness off to our right and it took us a minute or two to realize that these were wild elephants feeding on the trees adjacent to the road we were traveling. Wild elephants, no barriers, not 50 years away—it took a while to sink in. This was no Busch Gardens. There were no fences. The wild herds were free to move in and out of the park as their instincts and search for food dictated—and, of course, the predators that followed the herds; the lions, cheetahs, and wild dogs that might just mistake Alison, Paul and me for three rather bizarre looking wildebeests. That night we pitched our tents under a sky bursting with starlight—such a celestial display I think I have never seen—and prepared our dinner under the bright beams of the Land Rover's headlights.

On another night in Tsavo Park we pitched our tents in a totally deserted campground within sight of a herd of water buffalo that appeared to be peacefully grazing. The large, black African Cape buffalo with the menacing curved horns would definitely not win the congeniality contest among Africa's wild beasts. In fact, it has a downright mean reputation and it is not unknown to take a potshot with its horns at a passing vehicle. However, this herd seemed to be minding its own business, so we proceeded with our tent pitching duties. Somewhere in the middle of the night I was roused from a half slumber by a sound that was not human. I froze in mid-breath and listened intently. There it was again—an unmistakable grunt that sounded as if it was coming from right outside my tent. Every hair on my body seemed to stand on end and I thought my heart would pop right out of my chest. I lay there for what felt like an eternity waiting for four hooves and big, black, horny head to come crashing through my little nylon envelope, but only the rustling of the night breezes broke the silence. Ever so slowly I unzipped the flap of my tent and gingerly poked my head outside, expecting to come face-to-face with Mr. Cape Buffalo, but a 360° survey revealed nothing. Whatever it was had come and gone and had thankfully left no calling card. In the morning I asked Alison and Paul if they had heard anything strange during the night.

"Nope, not a thing – slept like babies. How 'bout you, Al?" grinned Alison.

"Oh yeah, great – just like a baby."

* * *

East Africa proved to be a feast for the eyes. The countryside ranged from broad rolling plains to bush and grasslands to lush forested regions, but no matter what the terrain, we could always sense the vastness of the African continent. Not only the land and the animals, but also the Masai people were a fascinating part of our safari. Dressed in their brightly colored garments and bedecked in a huge quantity of jewelry, they still live in their traditional villages and tend their flocks and fields much as they have done for centuries.

The end of the week brought us back to Nairobi and a major decision on my part. Although Alison, Paul and I got along well together, I was beginning to feel the urge to be back on my own again where I could make my own un-encumbered decisions. On our week-long safari some frictions between us had become apparent. While bicycling we maintained our independence—sometimes we'd cycle individually or in a twosome or threesome—but couped up all week together in the land rover was a different story. Occasionally I would lapse into a long period of silence—a tendency of mine when something is bothering me—over some trivial thing such as feeling that I wasn't getting to do my share of the driving (driving was actually a real treat after having pushed two wheels for the last five months). And generally, I had a sense that I wasn't following my own nose and that I was on someone else's tour. I tried to remind myself, however, that we had been through a lot together in the short time that we had known each other and that we had been there for one another when one of us was down or feeling low, mentally or physically. We had hitched our wagons together, and there had to be some give and take on both ends, but I couldn't shake the feeling that it was time to be back on my own, at least for a while.

I told Alison and Paul that I wouldn't be going with them to Tanzania where they were going to visit with some relatives. Instead, I would fly on to India and think about tackling the subcontinent on my own. Almost as soon as I made my decision I had the bad sense that it was the wrong one. I expressed my feelings about the situation to Alison and Paul and told them that when I got to Bombay I would see how things were and might just wait for them there. They understood how I felt, and we agreed that they would check the American Express office as soon as they arrived in Bombay for any messages that I might leave them.

In the meantime I purchased my plane ticket for India and then one morning said my good-byes to my friends. I missed them before they were even gone, and I worried that

I was making a foolish decision by not sticking with them, especially with India on the horizon. We actually had to make our good-byes two mornings in a row, for their bus had broken down on the outskirts of the city. When to my surprise I found them back at the hotel that same night. I had a secret hope that they had changed their minds and wanted to head on to India. But the following morning they caught another, more mechanically sound bus south toward Tanzania, and they were gone.

I had about a day and half to shoot before my flight, and so I took the opportunity to explore a little more of Nairobi. The initial enthusiasm of my favorable first impressions had worn a bit thin. Beneath the surface of this modern metropolis, you could see some of the problems of a developing Third World nation. Disease is still a constant danger to much of the population. I had never seen so many people in one city limping along with poles, crutches, and braces or just pulling themselves along the pavement. Many had disfigured or underdeveloped limbs. Polio has really taken its toll in this part of the world. Many of these unfortunates had become beggars who could be found on every street corner. Not just polio victims, but pathetic looking people with every type of disfigurement—no legs, no legs and one arm, hands with just crusty stubs for fingers (victims of leprosy), and a mother with one or two small children caked with dirt clinging to her skirt. It seemed an outrage that these people were not provided for in some way by the government, especially when one takes into consideration the amount of money that is sucked up by the military establishments of so many Third World countries. One afternoon, overcome by my guilt at being a relatively wealthy, well taken care of American, I made a batch of peanut butter and jelly sandwiches and distributed them to some of these pathetic looking souls—a small and futile gesture, but one I felt I had to make.

Nairobi is a modern and relatively clean city with an apparently thriving small business sector, but it seemed that virtually every shop I entered was owned not by an African, but by an Asian—a Pakistani or an Indian. According to a Nairobian that Alison talked to, the Africans mostly end up as the employees of the Asians, and this is a source of a good deal of tension between the two communities. We had also been warned that crime was a problem and that it was not safe to walk in some sections of the city after dark—even some areas close to the central part of the city. This I kept in mind if I found myself out and about in the later stages of the afternoon and into the evening.

One of the last things I did while in Nairobi was to visit one of the schools and talk with the headmaster who was a nun. The school was Catholic, but still a government-run school. Unfortunately, the students were involved in testing the entire week, but the headmaster showed me around the building and filled me in on some of the problems of Kenya's educational systems. She said they had recently changed to the system of grades traditional in the United States—that is, 8-4-4; eight elementary, four secondary, and four higher education. Previously it had been a 7-6-3 setup. It seemed to be working well and it gave those in the lower grades an extra year of schooling since only about 20% of the students received a secondary education. Many children even in Nairobi still received no education at all. She estimated 10,000 children in the area were not in school. She also mentioned the fact that Kenya has the highest population growth rate in the world which contributes to the problem because there are just not enough schools. She did say, however, that tremendous strides had been made since independence was achieved in 1963.

My flight to the Indian subcontinent was a "red eye," so late in the afternoon of November 14th, I packed up my gear and rode the 15 miles back out to Nairobi's international airport. I felt strange and alone as I pedaled those few miles. The last five weeks had been tough ones. Africa had opened my eyes to many new, amazing, fascinating, and disturbing images. But I had faced those images with two friends, and now they were gone. Now, I was on my own, and I felt apprehensive and very much afraid about what lay ahead.

SEVEN

India — Survival! Just Barely

"I will never leave this country alive!" This was the only thought that kept running through my worried head as I sat gripping with more than normal ardor the armrests of the Air India jet that sailed high above the Arabian Sea toward the Indian subcontinent. How would I ever face India alone? All the things I had read and heard about this strange land— the poverty, the teeming masses, the exotic culture, the rugged terrain and, not least of all, the absence of anything remotely resembling a McDonald's or Burger King (not true, however). I should never have split with Alison and Paul. I had only said good-bye to them two days before, and already I missed their company tremendously. I should have gone with them to Tanzania, spent a couple of relaxing weeks on the shore of Lake Victoria with their relatives, and then we all could have faced this thing together. I had let my independent spirit get the better of me, and now here I was, preparing to go it solo through "Hindustan." What the future held I had not the least idea. What would happen to me? Would I ever be seen or heard of again, or would I be swallowed up by this huge land as a whale swallows a minnow? Had I known what India held in store for me, I might have waltzed up to the cockpit and politely asked the pilot if he could please turn this thing around and drop me off back at Nairobi—a parachute would be just fine!

The crackle of the plane's intercom signaled that a message was forthcoming—first in Hindi, I supposed, and then in English: "Ladies and gentlemen, we are now preparing for our descent into Bombay. Please buckle your seat belts; we should be landing in about fifteen minutes."

Oh God, this was it! This was the beginning of my end! I glanced warily out the window and beneath me I could see a vast expanse of lights which carpeted the darkened landscape. It looked like the lights of any large, metropolitan city as seen from an approaching plane getting ready to make a landing, but I knew this was not any other city like a Detroit, Michigan or a Los Angeles, California or a Kansas City, Missouri—this was Bombay, India, smack dab in the "under belly" of Asia. Yes, this time I was really "not in Kansas anymore." It was 4:00 A.M., 10½ hours ahead of Toledo, Ohio time—and I wished now more than ever that I could be in Toledo, Ohio!

The wheels touched down into a fairly smooth landing and I felt slightly encouraged. I half expected the plane to do a hop, skip and a jump up to some thatched-roof hut with a beaten dirt floor where a maintenance crew all dressed like Mahatma Ghandi would be waiting to service the Air India jet. But to my surprise the terminal looked quite large and modern, and the fact that the pilot could put me nicely down on the runway and not slide into the middle of some rice paddy was somehow symbolic that maybe I could handle India after all. It made perfect sense. Still, as everyone scurried for their carry-on luggage in preparation for exiting the plane, I couldn't make my legs move nor force myself into action. The plane's interior seemed so familiar and secure; maybe it would be better for me to stay seated right where I was until... But then I remembered my bike, and that I had better be there to meet it when they brought it in. I was sure that it would be brought out of the luggage area looking like a double pretzel, or that my front wheel—maybe even both wheels—would be missing. My confidence in the Air India pilot didn't transfer to the Indian baggage handlers, for baggage handlers all over the world are a testy lot who sit around devising sinister techniques for butchering all bicycles that they are forced to handle.

Once inside the terminal, I was greeted by a sea of dark faces. There were a few "western whities" here and there, but I felt like I stood out like a lighthouse. I'd experienced the same sensations in Egypt and Kenya, but now there were no Alison and Paul to look at and say, "Well, what do we do now?" I was relieved to see that signs were in both Hindi—which to me looked like scribbling from outer space—and English; I silently thanked the British for not allowing the sun to set completely on this part of their empire. To my shock and surprise, my bicycle was sitting off to the side unattended, but apparently in one, whole functioning piece, and I also located my packs and other gear without a hitch. Things were going smoothly so far, but this was an illusion as I would soon find out.

I set to work repositioning everything on my bicycle, since it is very difficult to ride when your handlebars are turned ninety degrees and your pedals are pointed toward the inside (these are usually futile precautions that one must take when preparing a bicycle to fly).

I soon attracted a number of silent partners in my present task who watched in fascination as I screwed this in and jimmied that around. This was the first of many "shows" that I would put on for crowds of silent, staring Indians, and the novelty of being a standout celebrity would soon wear off as it had in Egypt.

A dark skinned gentleman in a white, Nehru cap stepped forward and volunteered a question in that strange brand of Indian English which sounds pretty peculiar to American ears.

"To where will you be traveling in our country on your bicycle?"

"Well, I hope first to bicycle from Bombay to Delhi and then maybe up to Katmandu," I answered politely, hoping that he might be able to help me with a little basic information.

A look of quiet surprise adorned his features. "That is certainly being a long way to travel by bicycle. You will be needing much strength. We are having a beautiful country and I hope you will be enjoying it."

"That is very kind of you," I thanked him. "Could you possibly tell me if it is very far from the airport into the heart of Bombay?"

He didn't reply at first, but instead gave his head a curious, little shake that was neither an up-down yes nor a side-to-side no. It was rather a somewhere-in-between head shake that could have been either yes or no. It was more like those crazy little toy dogs that wag their heads at you from the back windows of cars in the U.S. I was soon to discover that this was an Indian cultural trait—one that would drive me buggy after a while, for I could never determine whether it meant yes or no. (By the time I left India, I developed a pretty fair head shake myself.) Since I still did not have my answer, I repeated the question, this time asking how far.

"It is being about forty kilometers to the city of Bombay," was his verbal reply this time. "It is being a very large city. I wish that you are finding where you want to be going."

By this time I had just about tightened every nut and bolt on my cycle, and I knew that I was stalling for time. The airport had taken over from the Air India jet as my security blanket, and I didn't want to throw off the covers. But by this time, morning had gained a firm foothold, so I bucked up my courage and pushed my way through the mass of dark faces who all seemed to be waiting for relatives or friends and who all seemed to be staring at me—not seemed, *were*. I passed through the airport terminal doors and steeled myself for the subcontinent.

* * *

They say nothing can quite prepare you for India—no matter how much you read or what you know in advance. I found this to be shockingly true on my ride from the airport into the center of Bombay. Once out of the airport perimeter, I headed out onto a main highway where a sign pointed the way to the city—this was one of the few signs I would encounter that would tell me I was on the right track. It was on this highway that Third World poverty hit me flush in the face. True, Egypt had been an extremely poor country and a rude awakening to our Western sense, but even Egypt hadn't prepared me for what I was to see now. The first sights to greet my eyes are hard to describe, but ones that will always stay with me. Along the right side of this main thoroughfare extending as far as my eye could see were row upon row of the most squalid looking hovels constructed out of old boards, scrap metal, cardboard, or whatever the inhabitants could get their hands on. There seemingly was no water, no electricity, no sanitation. These were not just a few shacks where an unlucky few existed, but a virtual city that was home for thousands. In a field across the road hundreds of men and young boys squatted to relieve themselves as the early morning mists rose up and swirled around them. One young boy perched himself on a bridge which spanned a canal that ran parallel to the road. He hung his small brown behind over the edge of the structure and emptied his bowels into the water below while not too far away people waded into the shallow depths for an early morning bath or to clean pots and pans. Farther along large drainage pipes not yet installed were converted into homes for a "lucky few." The open ends of the pipe were covered with large pieces of cloth or sheets in an attempt to secure a small degree of privacy and to keep out the morning chill.

In my preparation for India, I'd read that in this country of close to a billion people, change was something that occurred at a snail's pace. My first encounter here seemed to bear this out, for this was 1985, and in 1971 John Keay wrote in his book *Into India* the following words of Bombay: "Driving in from the airport you pass miles of shanty town where land in the process of reclamation is covered with tumble-down shacks before it is even drained. And even the drainage pipes before they are sunk in the marshy soil provide accommodation for a few hundred more families. Life in a pipe, the open ends blocked with sacking or rush matting, the floor leveled in places with mud and planks..." Later I discovered that this was not an isolated section of Bombay, but that all over the outskirts of the city were hundreds of these shanty colonies where hundreds of thousands lived in similar conditions. I also learned that these were not all unemployed people, but that many of the shanty town residents had jobs—some of them fairly decent paying by Indian standards—but that this was all they could afford for their living arrangements.

I forged ahead, finding it hard to believe that I was actually crazy enough to be cycling where I was on my own, and still not believing what I was seeing. I suddenly feared that if anything happened to me right now, I, my bicycle, and all my belongings might never be seen or heard of again. I gripped the handlebars tightly and rode on in grim determination, feeling more alone than I ever had before.

Thankfully I passed through India's unsettling and depressing welcome to its foreign visitors and pedaled into an area punctuated by canals and water projects of one sort or another. Bombay is a city born of the sea. When the British arrived in 1665 after having received the site as part of a dowry gift from the Portuguese, Bombay was just a series of seven low-lying, malarial islands. Now, after three centuries of ambitious land-reclamation projects, it is a huge peninsula that juts southward out into the warm waters of the Arabian Sea, connected to the vast subcontinent by a series of road and rail arteries. Here is the home for eight to nine million of India's 900 million inhabitants.

It was this peninsula that was drawing me farther south toward the heart of the city, but the only sign I had seen that told me I was heading in the correct direction had been back at the airport. While my one eye kept a sharp lookout for any sign that might ease my fears of being hopelessly lost already, my other eye kept watch for bumps, potholes and lurking roadway chasms—my first introduction to India's notorious highways.

A motorcyclist now pulled up along side me, smiled, and motioned that I should pull off to the side of the road, which I promptly did, hoping that he might speak English and provide me with some badly needed directions.

"Hello, my name is Deepak," he volunteered in a friendly and easily understandable English. "Where are you from and where are you riding to on your bicycle?"

His friendly attitude helped to ease my apprehension, and I told him the nature of my trip.

"I hope to bicycle across your country," I explained, "but right now I am worried that I may not even make it into Bombay where I hope to stay for a few days. Am I headed in the right direction?"

"Yes, you must be staying on this main road and it will eventually take you to the center of the city," he replied. "Would you like to come to my home for a brief rest and coffee? There I can be giving you better directions."

I eagerly accepted Deepak's hospitality, anxious to make any kind of friendly contact that might prove helpful. I followed him through a maze of small side streets lined with three and four-story apartment blocks. Deepak's home was a small, crowded, but comfortable apartment where he lived with the other members of his good-size family. Over a cup of hot Indian coffee he explained that he worked for Air India and that he had just finished the night shift and had been on his way home when he saw me cycling along.

"I am very happy that you are seeing my country by bicycle," he enthused. "More people are choosing to bicycle in India. Myself, I hope to one day motorcycle across your country with my friend, but before we can do this we must have sponsors. It is being very expensive to do something such as that, and this would be the only way we could afford such a journey."

I told him that I hoped one day his dream would come true and if it did, that he would be very welcome to stay with me in Toledo, Ohio as long as he liked. Deepak then drew me a rough map of how to find my way to the center of Bombay and gave me the name of his friend, Milind, whom I was to contact once I found a place to stay in Bombay. He told me that later in the week I should try to contact him and let him know where I was staying; maybe we would be able to meet again before I left the city for the hinterlands.

I shook Deepak's hand warmly and thanked him for his generous hospitality and helpful information and set out once again, feeling now that at least I had someone I could contact should I get in a real jam.

A "real jam"—that's what I seemed to be riding into now. In fact, the Bombay Peninsula appeared to be acting as a funnel, packing more and more people into an ever diminishing neck of land. The streets became narrower and more crowded with cars, cabbies, motorcycles, bicycles and bicycle rickshaws, buses, and pedestrians all competing for a space to move and jockey for position. I weaved my way in and out of this shifting gauntlet, my eyes searching frantically for the well-hidden street signs which in no way seemed to correspond to the map of Bombay I had picked up back at the airport. To make concentration even more of a challenge, new sights, sounds, and smells bombarded me from every direction as my senses were shifting into overload. Periodically, when I stopped to take a peek at my map, all activity on the bustling streets would come to a halt and 200 pairs of dark, curious eyes would swing in my direction. I would have time for a quick glance at the map before the curious eyes began to envelop me, and then I would make my escape from the slowly-closing human pincers.

But before too long, the thoroughfares broadened once again and the buildings became more stately. At last I had arrived in the heart of the city, passing by the huge Victoria Terminus—Bombay's central railway station—and the mammoth, golden domed Prince Albert Museum, and ending up at the imposing Gateway to India, a majestic commemorative arch that celebrates the royal visit of King George V in 1911. It stands in regal splendor on the well known quay, Apollo Bunder. It was here that generations of English officials and civil servants serving the British Raj caught their first sight of this mysterious land which was their "Jewel in the Crown," and it was here that I finally stopped to catch my breath and ponder what my next step would be.

It was now about midday and the huge quay of Apollo Bunder was alive with activity. Indians and westerners alike strolled through and around the immense triumphal arch, possibly in search of a cool sea breeze grudgingly yielded up by Bombay's tropical climate or maybe a noontime snack from one of the many stalls hawking foods and other treats. Not only the quay, but Bombay harbor too was a bustling beehive with boats of all sizes and shapes riding the sea swells.

Before too long, a middle-aged gentleman approached me and smiled a large toothy grin.

"May I be of assistance to you," he began, "and who are you and where are you being from?"

"Well, I'm not sure," I returned. "I've just arrived here in Bombay from the airport—by bicycle as you can see—and I'm looking for a place to stay for a few days."

He seemed pleased that he could be at the disposal of a western bicyclist such as myself and appeared to think for a minute. "I think I know of a place where you might be staying. Please, to follow me. It is not far."

I fell in behind my new-found guide back out onto the busy Shahid Bhagatsingh Road, threading my way along the pedestrian-clogged sidewalks, still attracting stares, but not quite as many in this section of the city that obviously sees more westerners. He disappeared into a building but soon reappeared flashing another toothy grin.

"Please, follow me," he said confidently. "You can be staying here, but we must carry your bicycle up a few floors."

Together we wrestled my bicycle and equipment into a narrow stairway and up to what was apparently a third floor hotel that in all likelihood cannot be found on Frommer's list of places to hole up in in Bombay. To say this was a hotel of rooms would miss the mark; rather, it seemed to be a series of ceilingless, partitioned walls with doors. The tiny cubicles featured a bed, a small dresser, and a chair, and thankfully an overhead fan to swish the sultry, humid air around one's head.

We stuffed my bicycle equipment into one of these cubbyholes sardine fashion, and when I turned with an expression of uncertainty to my assistant, a look of triumph spread across his features. I thanked him for all his help and when he made no move to leave, it dawned on me that his assistance had a price. I forked over a few rupees and this time he was gone as quickly as he had appeared, probably in search of another westerner in need of a room.

Home sweet home, I thought to myself as I took measure of my new surroundings. I could just about stand in the middle of my cubbyhole and with my arms outstretched, touch either wall. And with my bicycle keeping me company, the cozy factor was quite high. Actually, I felt a great relief to be somewhere, anywhere, that could furnish me sanctuary from the flood of exotic sights, sounds, and aromas of India that were washing over me and the curious eyes that seemed unable to comprehend this mini invasion of western culture.

The first order of business was to dispose of my outer skin of sweat and Indian-road grime which had not taken long to accumulate on my ride from the airport. This was accomplished a lá sponge bath furnished by a small trickle of water reluctantly yielded up by the hotel's plumbing system. Showers and water pressure were obviously not standard features of my "five-star" accommodations; nor was a continuous supply of electricity. Before my sponge bath had concluded, I was plunged into a murky, semi-darkness which suggested a reason for the many candles I had seen lying about upon my arrival. I would soon discover that electrical power is a somewhat whimsical entity, not only in Bombay, but all across the Indian subcontinent. Small village or large city, day or night, power outages would prove to be even more dependable than the supply of electricity itself.

On the heels of my initiation to India's out-to-lunch electrical system and water supply, I was about to open another chapter in my continuing saga of "Tales of the Toilet." As I worked my way around the globe, each country seemed to offer a new and challenging way of disposing of one's bodily wastes. This is a topic not covered in large measure by most of the travel guides, but one that is certainly dear to the heart, or seat, of all budget travelers such as myself. Since I had not been residing at many of Arthur Frommer's recommended hotels, this aspect of my journey had become a true voyage of discovery. The typical Asian-style trench toilet requires a little practice and even a little athletic skill before you acquire the knack of squatting in just the right position so that you can make your deposit on or close to the bull's-eye. Positionings for your feet are thought-fully placed on either side of the porcelain trench to aid you in this task. A poor aim could result in some very unpleasant consequences which was, I assumed, the reason for the near-by, unsavory-looking, long-handled brush. Even if you qualified as a marksman, the brush was still necessary, for a good flush seldom did the complete job for which it was intended and required a helping hand. Another real danger faced by the novice user is the frightful prospect of plunging

seat first into the terrible chasm below—an extremely possible scenario after a long day of cycling when your legs
become like silly putty and offer you little support as you
assume the ol' Asian squat. This was almost my fate, but
with my lightning-quick reflexes, I was able to regain my
balance and save myself from disappearing into Bombay's
sewer system. At least Africa had offered me the luxury of
sitting down!

At last I collapsed on my bed in a state of stressed exhaustion. As the blades of the ceiling fan swished
sluggishly about my head, I reflected on all that my eyes
had seen on this first morning in Asia and how utterly alone
I felt. A kind of fitful slumber gradually enveloped me, but
just before I was snatched from the jaws of reality, I decided
that I would prefer not to face this country alone and that I
would wait for Alison and Paul to arrive from Kenya.
Hopefully they would keep to their schedule and only stay
a few days with their relatives in Tanzania before heading
back to Nairobi where they planned to catch their flight to
Bombay. The question was: Would we make connections
once they arrived?

* * *

For the next couple of weeks I did a lot of treading water,
and more than once I thought I would drown in Bombay's
filth and poverty. It is a city where thousands of destitute
and homeless live wherever they can stake out a little space
for themselves. Many exist in ramshackle shanty colonies
that pockmark the Bombay Peninsula and provide little in
the way of water, electricity, and sanitation. Some families
claim only a small piece of sidewalk pavement on which
to place a few utensils for the preparation of their daily
meals, not lucky enough to have anything even remotely
resembling a roof over their heads. At night I could look
out the window of my hotel room and be greeted by a
scene that would be terribly alien to Main Street, U.S.A.
Like a giant slumber party, all along Bhagatsingh Road,
Bombay's poor settled down on the pavement for a warm
and steamy November night's rest on small portable cots
or simply a piece of cloth—a busy thoroughfare transformed
readily into a communal bedroom.

Wandering the streets on India's second largest city those first few days, I was often taken aback by the grotesque disfigurements and terrible afflictions of many of Bombay's beggars. One poor soul with no arms or shoulders sat pathetically on his rug in the middle of the sidewalk with an alms cup slung around his neck, bowing his thanks every time a few rupees would find their way into his neck-bound container. Another young man lay sprawled in pain on the pavement suffering from a hideous case of elephantiasis; his left leg, literally cracked and oozing fluids, was three times the size of his right leg. And then there were the children dressed in rags who tugged on your hand or shirt sleeve with one arm while the other arm cradled a smaller sibling caked in filth, hoping an obviously wealthy westerner might bestow on them a little baksheesh. Even the knowledge that parents often times intentionally make their children look so destitute to play on the pity of the tourists failed to lessen the twanging of the heart strings, and even more, the rising sense of guilt at being a citizen from one of the wealthiest countries in the world. Along with this rising sense of guilt was the simple question: Why? A question that I am sure is asked by many westerners who journey to this land. Why did people have to suffer so? Why did they have to live in such conditions of poverty and need? Why was I one of the world's lucky "few" to enjoy the fruits of such a comfortable and easy life in a Nirvana like the United States of America? Why so much for some of God's children and virtually nothing for the others?

Juxtaposed to Bombay's squalor were all the trappings of a city striving to rise out of the Third World. High-rise apartments reach skyward out of the exclusive Malabar Hill district, providing an expensive and lofty haven for the privileged classes. Sleek automobiles transport those same classes through teeming streets and boulevards seemingly unmindful of the human misery around them. Bright and garish billboards peddle a wide variety of products, most of them unaffordable by the city's masses. Many of those products were manufactured right here in Bombay, for this city is the bustling manufacturing and trade capital of India. Privilege and lack of, poverty and wealth, affluence and subsistence living—the contrasts are striking. Over the next month and a half I would try to come to an understanding of a country—a world—such as this, but without success.

In addition to waiting for Alison and Paul to arrive from Africa, as I was more and more determined to do, I was also expecting a box from my mother and father that would contain a much-needed pump to replace my stolen one, a new tire or two plus tubes, and cherished words of encouragement and news from home. However, I was to find out that the postal service is much like everything else in India—an apparent disaster. Just about every day of the two weeks I was in Bombay I trooped down to the American Express office hoping to find my package waiting for me.

And every day I came away frustrated and steamed over a postal system that seemed to be a huge boondoggle of red tape and paperwork—a system that I was certain was intentionally depriving me of my precious care package. The kindly Indian clerk at American Express came to know me by name and always expressed great sympathy as he saw my hopeful face come through the door. The package would never arrive and I would be forced to leave Bombay and set out across the subcontinent without a pump. Fortunately the valves on my tubes were Schraeder valves and would fit any ordinary air compressor. In India, though, I would not find an air compressor on every corner.

While trekking about Bombay's maze of streets, I took note of something that was a little puzzling. Each day I would see dhoti-clad workers (a dhoti is a kind of universal Indian garment that can be worn drawn up around the legs as a pair of shorts or let down in skirt fashion) pushing large flatbed carts up and down the highways and byways of the central city. The carts contained a multitude of small cylindrical canisters, each with some type of number or marking on the top. To me they looked much like paint canisters and at the time I thought that somebody was engaged in a heck of a lot of interior decorating. Eventually I discovered that this had nothing at all to do with some mammoth painting project, but it was instead a huge "meals-on-wheels" operation run for the city's legions of office workers. Most of these mid-level employees travel quite a distance from their homes on the outskirts of Bombay into the city's business district where their jobs are located. To purchase a hot lunch every day would be quite expensive for them, so for a nominal cost a hot lunch from home is transported into the city. A team of workers, or dabawallas, collects the canisters of hot Indian food (hot in more ways than one) from the homes, and they pass them to another group of dabawallas waiting at the trains, and then on to another group who deliver the lunches personally to each of the office employees. Every day hundreds of thousands of hot lunches are transported to the right person without a hitch using a system understood completely only by the dabawallas, many of whom are illiterate.

About midway through my first week in Bombay I changed my accommodations to the Red Shield House of the Salvation Army. In addition to aiding the needy, the Red Shield House here in Bombay also seemed to function as a traveler's hostel providing comfortable and spacious dormitory-style sleeping arrangements for shoestring wanderers such as myself, not to mention the blessing of mild, western-style cooking; my stomach had been rebelling at the abrupt initiation to the hot and spicy Indian cuisine.

One afternoon I sat down with the director of the Red Shield House, an American woman who had spent a good deal of time in Bombay and Calcutta. We talked of some of the problems she faced in her efforts here. She said that she received very little help and cooperation from the Indian government and that it was possible that she would soon be replaced by an Indian director. The government did not appreciate the efforts of people like her and Mother Theresa in Calcutta who drew attention to India's overwhelming problems of poverty, starvation, and overpopulation. They wanted to deal with their problems in their own way. However, from what I had seen so far, it appeared their own way was to do very little at all. She spoke with a weary tone in her voice—the voice of one who had dealt with problems that dishearten the spirit and trouble the soul. But she intended to stay as long as she could.

Only a half block away from the Red Shield House was that testament to British colonialism, the Taj Mahal Intercontinental Hotel. In its heyday it served as a haven for India's British masters, a small island of British propriety standing incongruously amid the sprawling confusion of lower Bombay Peninsula. Here I spent a number of my hours in the sumptuous, air-conditioned lobby trying to insulate myself from the strange and depressing world outside. Being an American, it was not difficult to blend in with the largely western clientele, even to the point of taking advantage of the cooling waters of the Taj's swimming pool on those hot and steamy afternoons. I would feel guilty every time I again emerged into the real India, but guilt was something I was learning to live with.

I found out quickly that the color of my skin and my "western good looks" identified me as an easy target for just about anyone and everyone who had something to buy or sell in Bombay.

"Want to buy a watch, mister?"

"Want to sell a watch, mister?"

"Buy a radio, mister? I give you good price."

"How much your bike?"

"Want to change money, mister? I give you good rate!"

Some of these persistent entrepreneurs would shove their wares in your face and refuse to give up until you literally had to swat them away like flies. One evening as I went in search of food that would not incinerate the lining of my mouth and stomach, an older, wiry-looking gentleman with graying hair, mustache, and rather thick bifocal glasses approached me. Uh oh, here it comes again, I thought. But he was friendly and wanted to know who I was and what I was about.

"Could we be stopping somewhere to have something to drink together?" my new-found acquaintance inquired. "I would like to ask you some questions about your country."

I thought twice about this offer, not wishing to end up unconscious in some back alley of Bombay, but he looked harmless enough and so I agreed.

"I know a place; please to follow me," he beamed upon my agreement.

As we walked he explained that he was an assistant instructor at the University in Bombay but that he only earned about 900 rupees a month—about $80 U.S. "You Americans are a very rich people," he gently chided me.

"See, here in my country, someone like me can only be making these very small wages while someone like you can be traveling around the world."

I didn't know quite how to respond, for what he was saying was certainly the truth. In his own good-natured way, he was managing to lead me on a real guilt trip.

He stopped and peered at me through his thick lenses. "Do you know that I have lived in Bombay all my life and could never afford to be traveling to your country," he said after a brief pause. "But wait, you must excuse me for a minute."

He ran over to the wall of a building that reeked of urine—something my nostrils were becoming used to—and made his own contribution to the pungent aroma emanating from that spot. He returned with a half smile on his face and explained. "You see, even a college professor such as me has to relieve himself in this way."

We finally arrived at a small restaurant and sat down over a glass of beer. Here I found out the reason for his befriending me and the subsequent guilt trip on which I was being taken. I was not so much a way to satisfy his curiosity about the wealthy and capitalistic U.S. of A., but rather I represented a free meal ticket. Half-way through our beer and in between comments castigating President Reagan and America's wealth, he suggested we get something to eat and again good-naturedly intimated that I should pay for it, since I came from such an abundant country. Not wishing to create any international tension, I suggested he order whatever he liked. The food appeared quickly and then disappeared even more quickly as he munched and chomped with great gusto. Not with a little relief I finally said good-bye to my self-invited dinner guest, glad that I wouldn't have to spring for any more guilt-induced perks. But this encounter was to have an unexpected Part II.

About midway through my second week in Bombay as I made my daily rounds of the city trying to locate my "care package from home" as well as any news of Alison and Paul, a familiar voice intoned a familiar question: "Excuse me young man, where are you being from and would you like to go somewhere so that we can have a drink together? I would like to ask you some questions about your country."

I immediately recognized my hungry assistant professor from the week before, but curiously, he didn't recognize me—the thick bifocal lenses I supposed—and so he proceeded with his pitch about how nice it would be if we could have a drink together so that he could learn about my country. Since I knew where this second unexpected encounter was leading—another free meal—and I had no desire to sit down with my subtly critical friend, I begged off, explaining that I didn't have time because I was waiting for someone.

When he realized I wasn't going to fall for his specious Bombay hospitality and that he wouldn't be treated to another free meal, his subtle criticism turned instantly into a vehement attack on me and the United States of America and everything it stood for. His arms gesticulated wildly about and his shrill, high-pitched voice was soon blaming me for everything from World War Two and the atom bomb to the rapid depletion of the world's resources. As my own anger began to rise, I reminded my friend, now turned attacker, that he had not said such mean and rotten things the week before when I was paying for his free meal ticket. Suddenly a spark of recognition flickered in his eyes, but instead of retreating from his vicious verbal assault, his attitude became even more menacing once he realized he had been caught in his little charade of hospitality. At last, I'd had enough of his blaming me and America for every ill in the world and I finally told this hateful little man to drop dead and leave me alone once and for all. With that he turned on his heel and stormed away, probably in search of another poor westerner whom he could invite for a drink so that he could "learn about his country."

A much more pleasant encounter took place during my first week. As Deepak (the friendly motorcyclist I had met on my ride from the airport) suggested, I contacted his friend Milind who worked as a reporter for one of the Bombay newspapers. Like Deepak, Milind spoke excellent English and he was glad that I contacted him. He invited me to join him and Deepak for lunch at his press club and I willingly took him up on his invitation. What I hadn't expected when I presented myself at Milind's office was a harrowing ride through the streets of Bombay on the back of his motorcycle. Even though I had my own motorcycle at home, it was quite different not being in control, not to mention the Bombay traffic which is not for the faint of heart. We joined the stream of ubiquitous and ever-honking cabbies, zipping in and out of traffic—and sometimes it seemed over—until we at last arrived at the press club. Luckily my stomach returned to its original position just in time for lunch. While we ate they had many questions for me about the United States as I had for them about their own city and country. I asked my two friends about the problems of the thousands of homeless on Bombay's streets.

"A number of years ago," Milind explained, "the government attempted to move the homeless off the streets of the city and place them at sites where they would be provided with shelter and work. However, many of them filtered back to the city, preferring life on the streets to the organized regimen of the settlement communities. Eventually the government just gave up on its efforts."

Deepak and Milind were great hosts and I even found myself enjoying the Indian food—considerably less hot and spicy for my benefit. They made many helpful suggestions as I talked of my ride across India, indicating places that I definitely should see if I could and some areas that I definitely should avoid because it was not safe to travel— especially for someone on a bicycle. In turn, I talked of the United States and places they might like to visit if their dream of a motorcycle trip across America came true. Milind and Deepak dropped me back at my hotel and we bade each other farewell, exchanging our heartfelt best wishes. It had been a pleasant afternoon.

* * *

Hollywood Interlude

I could see the hate in his eyes as I approached him with my heavy black baton. Rivulets of blood trickled down his face and arms that were chained to either side of a rough-hewn wooden cross. His body told of days of punishment and torture. I drew my baton back and swung the first blow, finding my mark on his already bloodied hand...and then again, and again, and again. I could feel the frenzy of excitement build within me as I saw his agony. At last, the leader of this scum we had interned at this prison was being made an example of, and I was the messenger of his suffering.... Later that same day the commandant of the camp flew in by helicopter and I had the honor of greeting him with a snappy salute and conducting him out of the prison courtyard. Our peace, however, was soon disturbed by a prisoner uprising. The prison yard was a bloody battleground littered by human forms—some lying motionless and others writhing in agony. Prisoners and guards struggled in hand-to-hand combat. Smoke and tear gas filled the air, tearing at our lungs. Although many of my fellow officers and prison guards had already been butchered by these heathen hordes, I was lucky enough to make it to the helicopter. The pilot lifted off at my command as three rounds simultaneously pierced the bubble of our chopper. Airborne, we swung low back and forth over the prison compound as I unleashed grenade after grenade on the heads of the freed inmates. But it was too late. The prison camp was lost and now under the control of the once incarcerated savages.....

No, this was not the latest episode of *Miami Vice* or a scene from *Escape From Alcatraz*, but it was nothing less than my Indian film debut in the hoped-for smash hit *Karma*. Some stars are discovered while sitting on a stool at the local soda fountain or drug store, but this star was discovered at the Salvation Army Red Shield House in Bombay, India. Bombay is known as the Hollywood of India and every so often the people from the film studios come to the Red Shield House looking for extras for the multitude of films that are churned out by the Indian film industry—more than most other countries combined. On this day I boarded the studio bus bound for Film City with visions of my name up in lights on marquees from Bombay to Calcutta. Accompanying me was Amos, a tall, friendly chap from England who was on his last day in India before his return home. We figured this might turn out to be an experience to remember; in this we were not mistaken.

After arriving at the studio, we were ushered into the dressing rooms and were given our costumes. One half of our group of about forty extras were given prison guard uniforms and the other half officer uniforms. I was an ...er...uh...officer. Next we were taken to the set which was that of a prison yard. In the middle of the set was the very famous Indian film star Juikishen Schroff chained to a wooden cross and about ready to receive some horrible punishment. The next scene required an officer, and the next thing I knew I was before the cameras administering unspeakable torture to the movie's hero. I summoned up all my acting skills as I pretended to beat the bloodied hero senseless with my plastic baton, but the director discovered a flaw in my performance and interrupted the scene in the middle.

"Please, don't smile when you beat him," was his directorial comment.

I promptly corrected my performance and from there on the scene went smoothly. I must have really impressed them with my acting ability, for the director and his assistants continued choosing me for small parts the rest of the day. For my final scene the director instructed me to climb into the helicopter which I obediently did, not wishing to be a difficult "star." I wasn't worried, since I figured they just wanted a few shots of an officer sitting in the chopper, waiting to take off. But then, to my abject horror, the engine coughed to life, increased its speed, and soon carried me off into the Indian Blue Yonder. Now I normally don't entertain a fear of flying, but I must admit that there was some small degree of concern on my part that this airborne machine would be like most other mechanical gadgets in India— nonfunctional, or functional just part of the time. All I could think of was the *Twilight Zone* movie disaster where the helicopter crashed killing the American film star, Vic Morrow, and two children. As we swung back and forth over the prison yard below, it occurred to me (in-between Hail Marys—or rather Hail Vishnus) that this was indeed a strange experience—to be flying around in a helicopter over a prison yard in rebellion on the outskirts of Bombay, India.

All in a day's work, I reasoned, when you're on world tour. As the skids of our winged—or rather our non-winged—chariot touched terra firma, I uncrossed my fingers and toes, heaved a clearly audible sigh of relief, and thanked Lord Shiva for granting my wish and not sending me prematurely to my next life without having finished this one. I figured I had made a considerable impact on the director and his staff as a result of my histrionics, for as they handed me my day's wages—one hundred rupees—they asked me to come back the following day to play the role of a doctor. And, ah, yes, I would like to thank the Academy for....

* * *

My hope for Alison and Paul's arrival dwindled with each passing day. I had checked with Air India and there was no indication that they had made any reservations on any of the incoming flights within the next day or two. I made up my mind that if they had not arrived by the end of my second week in Bombay, then I would forge on alone without them. This teeming city of millions was slowly dragging me down and I had to get out.

In the meantime, I celebrated the holiday of Thanksgiving—an American tradition that seemed almost obscene in the context of where I was. How could you celebrate America's Horn of Plenty in a land of such deprivation? This feeling took on added meaning as I walked through the poverty and squalor of Bombay. It was not all poverty and squalor. There were the modern buildings and beautifully kept gardens, but they existed side-by-side with the families who slept on the streets and sidewalks and the beggars who populated each corner with their deformed and diseased bodies. On this Thanksgiving Day I saw a sight that especially drove this point home—something that was even shocking for Bombay where there was plenty of food available. He was just sitting there in the middle of the pavement; a young fellow, but not much more than a shadow, a ghost; a skeleton covered with loose skin; hollow eyes, sunken cheeks, and covered with sores. I'd seen his type a number of times, but only in pictures of the survivors of World War II concentration camps or those that were coming out of East

Africa. People passed by him as if he were not there; something to be ignored; to not be seen. In fact, the only attention he seemed to be drawing was from one well-fed Indian who was trying to shoo him away from the front of his place of business. As he floundered around on the pavement and then hobbled away to a new spot, I ran to the nearest banana stand and bought a bunch of bananas to give him. As I handed him the fruit, he thanked me with those hollow eyes and then began to gingerly peel the first banana. But I didn't stay to watch him eat—I couldn't. I felt very depressed and alone—especially when my thoughts drifted 10,000 miles away to my family sitting down around the Thanksgiving table piled high with turkey, mashed potatoes, and dressing. I wanted very much to be with them at that moment. Yes, this was a Thanksgiving like none other I had ever known.

* * *

"Howdy stranger," came a voice from the mists as I slipped in and out of a fitful midday nap at the Red Shield House. The voice came from above and behind me as I was lying flat on my back at the time, and it sounded very familiar. Sure enough, there was Paul staring back at me from behind his sunglasses and that thick, full beard of his and a huge smile on his face. His huge smile was matched by my huge smile, for I was, to put it mildly, ecstatic to see him. Alison was storing their gear in their room and when I first saw her the only thing I could do was give her a big hug. It felt so grand to see two friendly and familiar faces. It had been only two weeks since we had parted, but it seemed like two years.

We immediately began trading stories of our experiences over the last fourteen days. I spoke with the "wise experience" of a veteran inhabitant of Bombay as I told them of all that I had seen, and they had a great laugh over my recent movie stardom. They had visited with their relatives, who were missionaries, for a week or so on the shores of Lake Victoria in Tanzania, and then managed to get on an Air Kenya flight the evening before and had just arrived this morning. Amazingly, they checked into the Red Shield House without knowing I was there. When they saw my bicycle in the storage room in the basement, they knew this was the place where they would find an old friend. We were now a threesome again and to my great relief, I would not be facing India alone.

* * *

The first day of December was surely the strangest December 1 I had ever spent. Usually December brings thoughts of Christmas and anticipation of holiday cheer. Instead, we were sweating our tails off in ninety-degree heat as we finally pedaled out of Bombay. I was not sorry to leave after two weeks in this city of nine million people, the majority of whom seemed to live a marginal existence in a state of perpetual poverty.

In spite of the draining heat and humidity, it felt good to move again. It had been almost a month since we had done any actual hard riding, and so I realized that I might be in for a little reconditioning. We used up half the morning just trying to navigate our way out of Bombay, since English road signs were few and far between and those local inhabitants we asked directions from usually responded with that curious little head shake which could mean yes, no, or a definite maybe. By midday the heat began to bear down on us with a vengeance, but we took comfort in the knowledge that our destination, the town of Lonavala was only twenty miles away. What we did not know was that an incredibly steep climb lay dead ahead. It didn't take long for our initial enthusiasm about riding once again to be tempered by the pain our bodies were suffering due to the re-initiation to constant physical exertion, and when we pulled into view of the Western Ghats, our hearts sank as we saw the killer grade that we would have to ascend. The Western Ghats are a chain of mountains and ridges that stretch along the western coast of the Indian subcontinent. They are not high mountains, but they have steep grades and precipitous climbs that made it almost impossible to cycle. Even so, we gave it a Herculean effort, straining, grunting, and sweating until we could no longer turn our cranks. We dismounted and continued to push our heavily laden machines up this grade that would make even Sir Edmund Hillary think twice, until we won back to a more rideable angle. By the time it leveled out toward the top, however, my legs were like jelly, my head throbbed, and my body felt as though it was turning into one large cramp from the loss of salt.

Mercifully, as we ascended to the upper reaches of the Ghats, we left behind the hot, sultry air of Bombay's coastal plain and emerged into cooler climes that helped to reinvigorate somewhat our spent bodies. Even so, sixty-five miles of India had passed beneath our wheels; it felt as though it had been a hundred sixty-five. We were ready to stop. However, we had to remind ourselves that this was not the United States and we were not likely to find a Days Inn or a Motel 6 around the next corner. Camping was also out—at least for Alison and Paul, for they had lost their tent in Tanzania when it bounced off a truck on which they had hitched a ride. (They immediately turned around to retrieve the tent, but it had mysteriously disappeared by the time they sped back to the spot where they thought it had fallen.)

However, once we crested the Ghats, it wasn't too long before we came to the old British hill station of Lonavalla. It was to cool retreats such as this that officials of the British Raj would come to escape the stifling summer temperatures of the Deccan Plateau which lies to the east, as well as the squalor, noise, and confusion of India's teeming cities and villages. Because this was a bit of a resort location, there seemed to be a number of places where we could find accommodations for the night. We selected an Indian version of a roadside motel, and by Asian standards it was fairly clean; there was even a small restaurant attached. As we had done in Egypt, we decided to share one room for the three of us while we were actually on the road. It helped to save on costs—though in India that would be of no major concern since a room could usually be had for the "outrageous" sum of forty or fifty rupees, or three or four dollars. But more importantly, it provided a sense of security and a ready source of commiseration (much like that experienced by the British in their cantonments, I imagine) after a day of pedaling through this strange and mysterious culture. This was especially important from my standpoint since Alison and

Paul had each other and I was the odd man out. I hope that they felt the same as I and that I wasn't imposing on their privacy. At least they had not given any indication that this was a problem. In fact, they seemed to enjoy the company of a third person.

After removing the considerable layers of sweat and road grime by what could be described best as a bucket bath, we ventured over to the small eating establishment in hopes of finding something to fill our hollow tummies. As we entered, a waiter greeted us and gestured us to a table where we received a card with an impressive list of food selections from which to choose. We scrutinized the menu, hoping against hope to find a Big Mac or a Whopper with fries listed, or at least some item that would not send our stomachs into a state of panic. The waiter returned and looked at us expectantly.

"Please, may I be taking your order now?" he asked in broken English.

Paul was the first to order. "I would like to have two lamb sandwiches and a large glass of milk."

The waiter responded with a look of sorrow and the now familiar head shake. "So sorry, these foods are finished."

"Well then," Paul continued undaunted, "I will have the chicken sandwich and two hard-boiled eggs."

Again, the look of sorrow. "Oh, but this is also finished," was his apologetic reply.

Paul continued on down the list, naming three or four more items which all seemed to be "finished," meaning the Indian cupboard was bare. Finally he hit on a spicy rice dish which apparently was in ample supply, and then Alison and I also went through the same process, hopefully naming a number of items found on the menu, but which all somehow seemed to be "finished" too. We eventually ended up with the same rice dish as Paul's that set our mouths afire, and to round out our repast we ordered a plate of lettuce and tomatoes that we tried to doctor up with some fresh lemon and salt.

Our first meal outside of westernized Bombay taught us a lesson that we would relearn time and again on our ride across India: When ordering food in an Indian eatery, especially those away from the larger cities, do not request of the waiter, "I will have" or "I would like," but rather ask, "Do you have any of this today?" We would soon discover that very seldom did menus actually have all the food that was listed. Instead, most menus seemed to be a wish list and not a true picture of what was in the kitchen.

The next morning, with our stiff muscles and aching bodies, we hopped back on our cycles and rode the fifty miles to Pune. This day's fifty miles seemed much longer than the sixty-five miles of the day before. A major reason for this was the less then satisfactory roads on which we were bouncing along. It didn't take long to discover that once away from the populated areas, the road conditions went the way of the submarine—nowhere but down. The secondary roads onto which we ventured proved to be a bone-jarring experience. There were decent stretches that only rattled our teeth a little, but these were invariably followed by sections of the roadway that were torn up or in the process of being resurfaced. Since there was no mechanized road equipment to be seen, all of the resurfacing was being done by manual labor, which of course, is one of India's greatest resources. Dhoti-clad, dark-skinned men and young boys, as well as women garbed in brightly-colored saris, trod slowly along the roadway under the warm December sun balancing huge wicker baskets of crushed stone atop their heads. They methodically deposited their bulky, head-supported cargoes of stone along the roadbed and then retraced their steps in order to fetch their next load. Progress seemed to be at a snail's pace, but again I had to tell myself that this was road construction Indian style, and we were not likely to find a sign—as we might have back home—proclaiming, "I-75 Construction—Your Tax Dollars At Work." Unfortunately, riding on the newly-laid stone was much the same as riding in a stone quarry, and at times we were forced to simply dismount and walk until we came to a more rideable section. Even those parts that had apparently been resurfaced proved to be a challenge with bumps and chasms aplenty that took a toll on our bodies and made the miles seem endless.

In Pune we found refuge at a small hotel—the price of our room under three dollars. Amid the sprawling clutter of this industrial city of one million we recouped our forces for the next day's onslaught on our senses. Pune had been a hotbed of independence sentiment and activity during the 1940s as India prepared to drive a stake into the heart of the British claim that the "sun never set on her empire." In fact, on the way out of the city on the following morning, we passed by the Agha Khan Palace where the Great Soul, Mahatma Gandhi, had been secluded—really imprisoned—by the British. We wondered from outside the gate at the beautiful and well-manicured grounds, and Paul even tried to find a way in that might give us a closer look, but to no avail.

Our ride to Pune had actually taken us in a southeasterly direction, but now we began to loop back to the north, heading toward the cities of Amadnegar and Aurangebad where the impressive cave temples of Ellora and Ajanta were located. As we rode, we became captivated by the beauty of the Indian countryside which reminded me somewhat of some of our western states. In fact, once out of the cities, it would be difficult to tell the difference; one could be riding through Nebraska, South Dakota, or Utah. But that illusion is quickly dashed when confronted with a caravan of Hindu pilgrims carrying banners and ringing bells, dressed in their colorful garb on their way to some shrine or temple dedicated to Lord Shiva.

In spite of the interesting terrain and always novel sights, I was really finding it difficult to get back with the program—the daily grind of knocking out sixty, seventy-five, or ninety miles. At the end of each day I felt so washed out—downright exhausted. Alison and Paul too seemed to be below par, for they were both pretty strong riders so that I usually ended up in the role of caboose. Contributing to the stress and exhaustion factor was the unique experience of Third World bicycle touring, so different from a tour in the United States or Europe—strange food, customs, belief systems, and the curious, dark-eyed stares always cast in our direction. Bicycling in India, as it had been in Egypt, was much like riding in a fishbowl. Even in Egypt, the people had seemed a little more accustomed to the sight of Westerners—understandable, since the one main highway that runs the length of the Nile Valley carries the bulk of the traffic, both native and tourist. But for most Indians, the sight of three white-skinned Americans wheeling their space age, 18-speed bicycles loaded to the gills with packs and camping gear through their remote village would be no stranger than if three Martians landed in a flying saucer atop a mud hut. For that reason we were guaranteed a celebrity status wherever we stopped:

It's mid-morning and following our routine that we've established we decide to seek a little refreshment in a not-so-small Indian village. We arrive at the center of the village and all activity comes to a halt, for all eyes within gazing distance are on us.

"I'll grab some oranges, Alison you go for the bananas, and Al see if you can scarf up some peanuts," suggests Paul. It does not take long, for the village bazaar is populated with carts stacked high with fresh fruit, vegetables, peanuts, hard-boiled eggs, and of course, spices.

As we regroup, the curious eyes have begun to converge around us. First five, then ten, soon twenty, and now forty dark, questioning faces surround us and stand in awe-struck fascination as they silently watch us refuel our stomachs.

Slowly the circle around us tightens and Alison mumbles, "Ah, guys, I think it's time for us to make our break." Heeding her suggestion, we slowly but forcefully push our way out of the collapsing noose and thread our way over to a nearby Indian restaurant that affords us a small degree of privacy. We sit in the back of the restaurant and order three Thumbs Up colas (Coca-cola was booted out of India by Indira Gandhi for refusing to reveal their secret formula). The owner of the restaurant, recognizing our need for a little solitude, makes a valiant effort with a broom at shooing away our growing Indian fan club which is now massing in the front of the restaurant, still following intently our every move. Finally I pop up and return their gazes, stare for stare, grab my camera, and snap their picture, hoping that my strange behavior will somehow spook the natives. Nope, doesn't work. We finish our beverages, sufficiently refueled, and guide our machines back out onto the busy main thoroughfare. We pedal off, still under the scrutiny of those same eyes, and slowly melt into the milling bustle of the village traffic. As we emerge once again into the countryside of rural India, we suspect this scene will be repeated for us many times, but that some of these Indians have seen a sight today that they may not experience again in this life or incarnation.

This scenario was not unique to our stops in Indian villages and towns. Even when we "took five" in what was apparently the middle of nowhere, we might soon be joined by three or four silent, staring companions. One time when we stopped for a roadside break a couple of young Indians we had passed a half mile back and moving in the opposite direction did an about face and hightailed it to the spot where we were relaxing just so they could have a closer inspection. And another time we pulled up short of a village, choosing not to go in so as not to cause a commotion. Instead, half of the village came streaming out to meet us, and we soon found ourselves in the middle of our familiar three-ring circus.

We sojourned for a night in Aurangebad, a city of one hundred eighty thousand souls. Aurangebad was named for Aurangzeb, one of six great Moghul emperors who ruled from 1527 to 1707. Aurangzeb was the son of the builder of the magnificent Taj Mahal, but as we would find out on our visit to this symbol of India three weeks hence, they didn't have the ideal father-son relationship.

It was here in Aurangebad that I celebrated my unofficial halfway point. It was December 5, and it had been a hundred and seventy-five days since I had said good-bye to my family and friends on the banks of the Maumee River in downtown Toledo, Ohio. According to my plan, I hoped to roll into

Toledo from the west somewhere around June 1, and so this was an important milestone in my travels. I thought of the exhilarating highs and the depressing lows that the first half of my journey had thrown my way, and I wondered what adventures lay ahead. Had I the ability to see into the future, I might have opted at this point for a flight home, for somewhere not too far down the road lay an encounter with the Grim Reaper and the pitfall of serious injury. But at my midway point, I was proud and happy with what I had accomplished so far.

The following day we caught a standing-room-only bus to take us the eighteen or so miles to one of the most fascinating sites of the Deccan plateau, the Buddhist, Hindu, and Jain caves of Ellora. The caves date back to a period lasting from the sixth to the tenth centuries and they are classified as either monasteries (especially the Buddhist caves) or temples. The caves were literally scooped out of the mountainside from the top down so that scaffolding was not necessary. The most spectacular is the Kailasa which is Hindu and estimated to be twice the size of the Parthenon. The builders had to remove up to two hundred thousand tons of stone as they carved their beautiful temple out of solid rock. It was dedicated to Lord Shiva as many of the Hindu temples hereabouts are. The thirty-four caves of Ellora are noted for their sculptures and many of their figures appear in less than modest pose. A local guidebook describes one figure as a "semi-nude dryad with a slender waist, pouting lips and abundant mammalian equipment...." In other words, she has huge boobs.

On the way back from the Ellora Caves we stopped at Dauhlatabad Fort which was an amazing fortress complex constructed by the Sultan of Delhi in the fourteenth century. He intended this to be his new capital, and so he thoughtfully marched the entire population of Delhi eleven hundred miles south to this location to populate his new city, of course losing many along the way. After seventeen years he decided maybe this wasn't such a good location after all and turned his people right around and marched them back to Delhi.

The following day we set our course for another complex of caves that was also hewn from solid rock—the Ajanta

Caves. I began the day feeling fine—at least as fine as India allows one to feel while cycling across her vast expanses on a rice, banana, and peanut diet. But by mid-afternoon I felt stiff and aching all over, much more so than the usual aches and pains that make themselves felt after fifty or sixty miles on the road. I knew something was not right with my body and my mind began to race. I reviewed all the exotic diseases that inhabit this land and I was positive I had contracted one or more of them. Was it hepatitis, polio, cholera, yellow fever, malaria, or some unknown malady for which there was absolutely no cure?

I pulled to the side of the road and downed a huge dose of Excedrin and then offered a prayer to Lord Shiva as well as the Buddha. By the time we reached our destination for the night at a wayside lodging called the Holiday Resort Camp, I felt a little better. But as we prepared to turn in for the night, my fever was back full force and my body protested against any kind of touch or movement. I swallowed another sizable helping of aspirin and somewhere in the middle of the night broke into a steady sweat that cooled the fires which felt as if they were consuming my body.

By the morning I felt weak and washed out, but just able enough to ride. When we arrived at the site of the Ajanta Caves, however, we discovered that it required a bit of a climb.

"You guys go on ahead without me," I squeaked to Alison and Paul. "I don't think I can make it up to the caves. I'll just stay here and guard the bikes while you two do the exploring for me."

We agreed that this was the best plan, and by the time Alison and Paul returned I had regained enough of my strength to finish the thirty-five miles to the city of Jalgaon. The next day's ride from Jalgaon to Duhle was also mercifully a short one, but our experiences there were most depressing and upsetting. One of the first sights of Duhle to greet our eyes was a young boy relieving his bowels right on the sidewalk in front of us. He was not a baby, but a youngster of five or six years of age. It was true that we were enjoying the beauty of the Indian landscape, but the dirt, the filth, the noise, the odors of urine and excrement that were a fact of life in the overcrowded villages and cities were really getting to us.

Next, a young man on a bicycle, seeing that we were in need of assistance in finding a place to stay for the night, led us to a hotel where we took a room over the noisy street below. We offered our helpful guide a tip for his much appreciated service, but he refused the money, and that really impressed us. However, it turned out he wanted something much more than just money. I was up in our room finding a place for all our packs and gear while Paul was outside guarding the bikes, surrounded by the ever-present circle of curious onlookers. Suddenly from the stairway, I heard a shriek and a cry as if from a wounded animal. We converged on the source of the sounds of distress—I from the top and Paul from the bottom—and found Alison in tears and shaking uncontrollably. Between sobs and gasps for air, she told us that she had been following our "helpful" Indian guide down the stairs when he turned on her, grabbing both her hands with his one, and tried to force his other hand up her shirt. Paul had been so surrounded by Indians, that he didn't even see the cowardly pervert make his escape from the building's entrance.

Alison's attacker had left behind his heavy, one-speed bicycle, so Paul and I set up a stakeout for the next couple of hours. Before too long, another young man whom we didn't recognize came along to collect the bicycle. At first we wouldn't let him take possession of the bike and tried to make the manager of the hotel understand what was happening, but it was to no avail. We finally had to let the bike go because we weren't a hundred percent certain that it was the same bike the young scoundrel had ridden. We realized there was little hope of catching this fellow who at first had pretended to be kind and hospitable; we just had to write it off as another unfortunate experience and lesson learned.

Dinner that night did little to lift our spirits; it was the same typical Indian fare—a cuisine that did little to stimulate appetites. The thought of any more curried rice, dahl, or chicken biryani was beginning to make my stomach do somersaults. I recalled that one of the guidebooks we had read said that if you had a hankering for good Indian food, you may not find it in India. We were finding this to be sadly true, and we were also becoming aware that we didn't quite fill out our clothing as we had before entering the Third World.

Our breakfasts usually followed the same pattern and were probably the culinary highlight of our day. There was always a vendor close by selling hard-boiled eggs, bananas and oranges were plentiful, and I always seemed to have a stash of some Lorna Doone-like cookies called Sucrose Biscuits—a brand name that would make dentists in the United States do back flips. Add to these a couple of handfuls of peanuts from the ubiquitous peanut vendors, and there you have the breakfast of champions that sent us on our merry way each morning.

We eventually found ourselves back on National Highway #3 heading towards Agra and the Taj Mahal, and here we had a difference of opinion. I felt that we should stay on the National Road because it seemed to be much better maintained, but Alison and Paul wanted to head northwest toward Udaipur on the secondary roads which had proved so far to be a bone-jarring ordeal.

"Don't you think we oughta stay on the main highway; it's a heck of a lot smoother and a more direct route," I reasoned.

"That's true, Al," Paul countered. "But secondary roads carry a lot less traffic and the cities of Udaipur and Jaipur are supposed to be well worth seeing."

What Paul had said made sense; I knew that sometimes I had the tendency to favor the more direct course at the expense of missing something that was really worth seeing. Still, I had my doubts. But the next morning when we reached the cut off from Highway #3, I cast those doubts aside and we pointed our wheels northwest in the direction of the cities of Udaipur and Jaipur. Had I known what was going to happen later in the day, I might have begged Alison and Paul to stay on the main road, for this would be a day that would very nearly end in tragedy—the kind of tragedy that snuffs out a life—in this case, mine. In truth, it was about the closest I have ever come to exiting this world and entering the next.

As soon as we turned off Highway #3 toward Mandu, an ancient fortress city that we planned to visit on the way to Udaipur, the road immediately disintegrated into a bumpy, potholed tooth-rattler, just as I feared it would. There was little satisfaction in knowing that I had been right, for my hands had to cling like a pair of vices to the handlebars just to keep the bike under control and upright. Much to my trusty Miyata's relief, however, the road smoothed slightly as we started climbing a range of hills and low mountains that still separated us from the vast plain of northern India's great river, the Mother Ganges.

In addition to the bad complexion of the secondary roads, they were also extremely narrow, most of them not much more than one lane in width. This provided many "interesting" situations when trucks were either passing or coming towards us. The truck drivers of India, as in Egypt, appeared to be a group of speeding, horn-honking maniacs who fancied themselves as jockeys sitting astride their six-thousand-pound horses. They constantly blew their horns and expected and required that you give them the whole road, even if there was plenty of room for them to move off to one side.

I'd gotten into the foolish habit of holding my ground as long as possible when an oncoming truck was deliberately hogging the whole road, and I would defiantly try to wave him off to the side. One truck on this day will forever live in my memory. I held on to my rightful spot on the pavement as the huge mechanical beast approached, waving frantically for the madman behind the wheel to give me space. I thought I had left myself plenty of time to bail out if it came to that, but the truck was moving much faster than I judged correctly. Bearing down on me at somewhere between forty and fifty miles per hour, the Indian behind the wheel was a supreme bastard, for he did not alter his course in the slightest, even though there was enough room to move off to the side and he could clearly see me.

In that last split second, I could even see a smile on his face as I realized in paralyzing horror that he was going to hit me. I remember the blurred image of a huge fender, a tremendous "whoosh," and the contact of truck and bicycle as he tore through my rear pannier, ripping the outside pocket to a shred and spraying the contents across the roadway. The next thing I heard was a clack, clack, clack, clack, . . .because he had driven my rear pannier into my spokes.

"Goddammit!" was the only thing I managed to bellow. "Paul, Paul!" Alison screamed from up ahead, "Al's been hit."

She raced back to where I was to find me shaking and seething in rage.

"My God, Al, are you all right?"

"Holy shit, did you see what that son of a bitch did?" I blurted. "God, I'd like to catch that bastard and pull him out of his truck and beat him to within an inch of his life. God, I can't believe it—he actually hit me, he really hit me."

After letting loose with every expletive at my command, I calmed down enough so that I could start picking up my toilet articles which now littered the road; they had been in the outside pocket of my pannier which had a slice clean through it. That was really the only damage done to the bicycle, but I knew that I was lucky to be alive. Just a fraction of an inch closer, and the truck would have caught my leg or handlebars, pulling me beneath the wheels of the speeding vehicle. I also knew that the driver of that truck would have splattered me across the roadway and not batted an eye or slowed his truck one iota. What was one crumpled and mangled body in a land of nine hundred million bodies— even a foreign one at that. I fervently hoped that somewhere in hell there was a special place for the Indian truck driver with a smile on his face. For the remainder of our ride to Mandu, I simultaneously pedaled and shook, pedaled and shook, haunted by the image of my crushed and bleeding body sprayed across a lonely country road in central India.

As if to balance out the bad with the good, when we arrived at the ancient site of Mandu, we found the best accommodations that we had encountered so far in India. It was a lovely tourist lodge with very clean and modern rooms with an attached bath. It was situated in a beautiful setting on a plateau overlooking a lush valley. The peaceful and serene panorama surrounding us helped to soothe my shattered nerves, and after touring the ancient ruins of Mandu the following morning, I was able to climb back on my bike without shaking like the Tin Man from the Wizard of Oz.

The next couple of days were fairly uneventful when compared with the happenings of my close encounters of a terrifying kind. We gobbled up the kilometers between Mandu and Dahar and then Dahar and Ratlan in fairly quick order, sailing along with a brisk tailwind. In fact, it was about the first favorable tailwind that India had coughed up for us so far.

Throughout this part of the country we noticed that many of the riverbeds were bone dry. This area had been suffering from an extended drought, and consequently, many of the poor peasants had to sell off their animals and sometimes drift into the larger cities looking for work. This is the problem that Bombay must deal with, because the hope of a job attracts peasants from all over that part of India. They end up living in the squalor of the shanty colonies that I saw on the outskirts and even in the heart of Bombay.

In some of the towns and villages, we had also come upon an interesting custom. This just happened to be the marriage season in India—yes there is a season for marriage—and in the larger towns a building or a large tent would be decorated with thousands of bright colorful lights which resembled an out-of-control Christmas display. All those who are ready to tie the Hindu knot will do so in the same setting at this time of year. There is a marriage parade with drums, clarinets, and decorated cars, and at night it is illuminated by neon light carriers who are followed by a portable generator. Everyone dances, jumps around, and has a good ol' time as the bride and groom are the center of attention in the parade.

* * *

We finally left the central state of Madhya Pradesh and entered the state of Rajasthan, and as soon as we did, the roads seemed to improve noticeably. Madhya Pradesh is one of the poorest states of India, and it had certainly been reflected in the condition of their highways. Those roads were also proving a real challenge for our tires and tubes. Of course, now that I was without a pump my wheels were making every effort to seek out and run over any and all junk in the roads that would result in the telltale hiss of a flat tire. This meant that if I was going to use my tubes and not one of Paul's spares each time my tires began hissing at me, I would have to find a shop with an air compressor that would fit my Schraeder valves.

As soon as we arrived in the town of Bansware, I set out on one of my search-and-inflate missions. I found a shop with an air compressor and set to work fixing my tube and tire, but before I was even half finished with the task, I had no less than thirty Indians standing silently around me, watching my every move—standing, staring, gawking, getting in my way, slowly closing the noose around me; they seemed to have no concept of privacy or personal space.

"Leave me alone! Doesn't anyone know what the word privacy means?" I shrieked at my startled fan club who jumped back about two feet. That made me an even more curious object for inspection and the circle became ever tighter. At last I finished patching and inflating and then burst out of the human cocoon that threatened to suffocate me, running over a few toes and feet in the process.

The following day when we entered the town of Salumbar we were once again engulfed by mobs of Indians. In the south the people had been fairly shy and reserved as they stood around us and stared, but now there seemed to be a noticeable shift in our reception. Here in the town of Salumbar the attitude and behavior of the people was much bolder, especially that of the children. They followed us around, intentionally getting in our way as we tried to buy our food in the town's bazaar. Milling about us, some of the youngsters thought it was great fun to push a friend so that they would bump into us. They were a constant nuisance and it was a relief to make it back to the sanctuary of our lodgings for the night.

We made the city of Udaipur with little difficulty the following day, but my entry into the city would not have been complete without a flat tire. Because it is surrounded by a number of small lakes, Udaipur is appropriately called the Lake City. The city lies in a picturesque valley bounded by gently undulating hills and a number of good-sized peaks. The small bodies of water which extend in every direction give one the impression of being on an island. One of the main attractions to be found in Udaipur is the Lake Palace which occupies every square inch of a miniature island in the middle of one of the lakes. Formerly the palace of the Maharajah of Udaipur, it is now a luxury hotel and has a claim to fame in the western world for being used as one of the settings for the James Bond film, *Octopussy*. Since it was now a luxury hotel, that meant the cuisine would be tailored to the western appetite. It had seemed an age since our stomachs had been surprised by any food they might recognize, and so we declared an all-out western-style pigout. A small boat ferried us out to the Lake Place and there we dined in opulent surroundings befitting a five-star hotel. It was a meal fit for a king—a western king at that—and when we got up from the table we were sure that we had died and gone to heaven. We were also aware that this one meal had cost the equivalent of a week's wages for the typical Indian laborer. But for the time being we were able to sweep our guilt feelings under the proverbial carpet, and after our meal we wandered through the exquisitely kept grounds and wondered at what must have been the luxurious lifestyle of India's maharajahs.

We took a break from the daily grind of our miles and spent the following day touring some of the sites of the Lake City including the City Palace which was actually a series of palaces all connected together—another one of the Maharajah's places in which to kick around. In the evening we enjoyed the pastel colors that descended over the gentle Vale of Udaipur. The outstanding meal and the day's layoff had helped to replenish our reserves and ready us for the push to Jaipur.

* * *

The temperatures had become much cooler now as we proceeded farther north across the Indian subcontinent. The sun hung noticeably lower in the sky, but the days were still warm and sunny while the nights and early mornings quite chilly. It reminded me of late summer or early fall in Ohio when the seasons cannot decide which way to turn. We cast long shadows as we pedaled over the Indian landscape, and the early winter sun bathed all in a golden glow: the peasant farmers plowing their fields with their wooden implements unchanged by the twentieth century, the women in their brightly-colored saris walking along the road with bundles of firewood balanced atop their heads, the plodding oxen and ox carts carrying the season's extra produce to the village bazaar.

Only about thirty-six miles north of Udaipur we happened upon a very nice tourist bungalow. It had spacious rooms and a comfortable atmosphere with well-kept grounds, and so we decided to sojourn here for the night rather than push on.

That evening I took a walk by myself and fell into a reflective mood and thought about how unique and different these past months had been and how in the years to come, I would look back on this time as a very special period in my life.

On toward the Pink City of Jaipur we trekked, through the cities of Bhim and Ajmer over semi-desert stretches of eastern Rajasthan that were reminiscent of our great southwestern United States. Barren hills and valleys were dressed in cactus-like plants that spoke of little precipitation in this northwestern state of India.

* * *

Friday, December 20, would be a day that would completely change the complexion of the rest of my trip. Again disaster lay lurking for me, but my encounter this time around would deal me a harsh blow. I had little inkling of what was to happen as we started our eighty-mile ride from Ajmer to Jaipur.

We at last emerged on to the broad flat plains of north central India, and the level expanses beckoned us with the promise of a swift, almost effortless ride—a promise that was fulfilled. The wind was no hindrance on this day, but really our ally. The miles fell victim to our spinning wheels as we cruised at seventeen, eighteen, twenty miles per hour. The warm December sun shone brightly from a cloudless sky. By early afternoon our destination lay only about fifteen miles distant. As we pulled from our last rest stop and soda break, we resumed our riding formation, one drafting behind the other. I was bringing up the tail, Alison was in the middle, and Paul was in the lead. As we again hit a cruising speed of about sixteen or seventeen miles per hour, a truck stop loomed up ahead. Just as we pulled even with the trucker's wayside, for a reason that was unknown to me at the time, Paul hit his brakes and Alison in turn hit hers. When riding in formation, a second's inattention can mean trouble. That's all it took, for my front wheel plowed into the rear of Alison's bicycle and sent me veering off out of control into the oncoming lane. Lady Luck dictated that day that there should be no traffic coming from the opposite direction, but my bike seemed to leap almost by itself into the air, doing a complete flip upside down, and bike and rider came down with a tremendous crash on the unforgiving pavement. This time, however, the mount fared much better than the rider. In fact, my bicycle sustained hardly any damage at all—cushioned once again by the bulky panniers— but I had landed almost full force on my elbow and I rose from the pile of bicycle and dislodged equipment, bruised, bleeding, and with a throbbing elbow that hung listlessly at my side. I was in a daze—almost a state of semi-shock—and did not quite comprehend yet what had happened. A score or so of excited Indians raced out from the truck stop to help Alison and Paul scrape me and my bicycle and equipment up from the pavement. Eventually I regained enough of my senses to begin checking to see if all my other parts and those of the bikes were still attached. It wasn't actually until a couple of weeks later that I learned it had been one of India's many stray dogs that had caused Paul and Alison to hit their brakes. Man's best friend had really done a number on me this time.

Still in a daze and a great deal of pain, I got back on my bicycle and we rode very slowly the last few miles into Jaipur. However, I could only ride with my one good arm while my left arm dangled helplessly at my side. Stopping quickly was next to impossible, and when we entered Jaipur I had to run a gauntlet of cars, trucks, pedestrians, taxis, and carts with only one arm to thread the needle and hit the brakes. Alison and Paul tried to run interference for me, but a couple of near misses almost took me down again. I winced in pain every time some thoughtless idiot cut me off and forced me to come to an agonizing halt. I would curse in anger and frustration at the effort required to brake, keep my balance, and get going once again. Luckily Jaipur has a plethora of hotels geared toward the tourist industry, and it did not take us long to locate one. That evening we settled in to watch my elbow balloon out of proportion to the rest of my anatomy. We were able to secure some rare ice from the management, but even so, it seemed to do little to stem the tide of the swelling in my elbow. I didn't know exactly how serious the injury to my elbow was, and I prayed that it was only a bad bruise.

Because of my accident we decided that it would be best to hole up in Jaipur for two or three days to see some of the sights and give my elbow a chance to recuperate. Jaipur is known as the pink city because of the pink sandstone used in construction of many of its buildings. Unlike most other Indian towns and cities, it was laid out with an eye to city planning, and consequently, the streets form a grid network and many of the roads are broad and spacious, giving one the feeling of openness. Because of my swelled arm we opted for a bus tour of the city's highlights instead of trying to do it on our own. We visited the City Palace and its museum, the Amber Palace high atop a hill overlooking Jaipur where the maharajah and maharani lived in splendor, and an amazing observatory which featured the world's largest sundial which is supposed to be accurate within two seconds of local time.

By the end of the second day I was still in a great deal of pain and I could not put any pressure on my left arm; I knew it was time to seek out a doctor. The hotel's management gave me the name of a physician, and while there the doctor performed what seemed like a thorough examination.

He twisted my arm this way and that and poked around here and there in a very doctorly fashion.

"There is appearing to be no damage to the bone," he diagnosed in Indian English. "But you do appear to be having quite a bit of hematoma. I will be prescribing some medicine to help reduce the swelling, and then I believe that you will be fine."

With this relieving news he sent me on my way, but the good doctor's diagnosis would come back to haunt me later. I never questioned the fact that he didn't suggest that an x-ray should be taken; all I knew was that he told me what I wanted to hear—that my arm was only bruised and that I was going to be OK.

That afternoon Alison and I sat down to lunch in the hotel's small dining room. As we nibbled on our chicken sandwiches and talked about the events of the last few days, she began to cry softly.

"I feel so bad about what happened, Al," she choked. "I feel like it was my fault; if I just hadn't hit my brakes so hard, maybe you would have had more time. Gosh, I'm really sorry."

"Hey now, you can't really blame yourself," I consoled. "It was an accident pure and simple, and there's really nobody to blame. It could have been the other way around. I've just got to roll with the punches."

The next day was December 24, Christmas Eve, and our thoughts turned to home and family. No, it didn't seem much like Christmas, here in Jaipur, India. Where was the soft blanket of snow and the frost on the windows, the songs of the season, and the happy lights that twinkle and dance in the chill night air. Where was the spirit of warmth and togetherness that makes this a special time of the year. It was hard to feel any of that half way around the world. And in a sense, maybe it would have been wrong to. Because one part of Christmas, the material part, seems almost obscene in a land where so many people have virtually nothing. Again the same question begged to be answered: Why do we in the U.S. have so much and the people of India so little? There was really no coming to terms with India's poverty, not when I thought of the land of plenty to which Alison,

Paul and I would return. It is just the way things are in an unfair world. Somehow we had lucked out in that huge celestial lottery which determines into which land and culture one will be born.

In the wee hours of Christmas morning, somewhere around 4:00 a.m., we three gathered sleepy eyed around the phone in the hotel manager's office. Paul then placed an international call to Kent, Ohio, U.S.A., and before too long he was talking in excited and joyful tones to his family as they celebrated Christmas Eve. After Paul's family hung up, they contacted my family who were about a hundred miles away in Toledo and told them to expect a call at any time. When it was my turn it took only a short time for the call to go through, and sure enough, there were the ecstatic voices of my mother and father and the rest of my family. Since there was a ten-and-a-half-hour difference between Jaipur, India and Toledo, Ohio, they too were in the midst of their Christmas eve celebration. I talked to each of my family members in turn, and I tried to make light of my accident and not let on that I was more than a little worried about my arm. Though I would miss out on this year's exchanging of gifts, this was certainly the best gift that any of us could have given each other—to hear one another's voices half a world away.

On Christmas Day we decided to ride; it was time to give my arm a trial run. I wrapped my arm tightly in a couple of ace bandages for extra protection and support, and we set out for Agra and the famed Taj Mahal. It was still pretty painful, but bearable and so we forged onward. As I rode I was forced to support myself mostly on my right arm, and soon that arm became quite fatigued. We put in seventy-four long miles to the Midway Tourist bungalow halfway between Jaipur and Agra. My one good arm and two legs that had to compensate for my crippled left wing were almost completely spent when mile seventy-four clicked over.

We were beginning to suspect that latitude had something to do with Indian manners and hospitality, because the farther north we rode, the more aggressive and obnoxious the behavior of the children seemed to be. In the south they had been in awe of us and our machines, but here they ran and chased after us, trying to grab on to our handlebars and packs, screaming and babbling, and if we stopped, they were all over us like flies, pulling our levers and putting their hands where they didn't belong. This type of attitude and behavior was causing me to become less tolerant of India and her people. I could feel a hardening in my attitudes toward India's backwardness and ignorance of such things as sanitation and cleanliness, and even common-sense safety habits on the highways and city streets. You see buses, taxis, and trains bursting at the seams with people hanging on every which way. If one falls off—well, that's one less mouth to feed. Maniacal truck drivers try to pass with oncoming traffic clearly in view, blowing their horns all the while and expecting all other vehicles and living things to get out of their way.

The social fabric itself seems to promote this backwardness. The ancient Hindu system of caste relegates people to a particular station in society based solely on the accident of their birth into a lower or higher caste. In some respects it appears to be a formalized way for the privileged and powerful few to keep the masses of India in their place. For those poor souls of the lowest caste or with no caste at all (those considered to be "untouchable"), according to the Hindu tradition, this life at best provides the opportunity to build up a little good karma so that they may be born into a higher caste in their next life. One has to wonder, too, about the sacred cows of India, many of which are emaciated skeletons and would make a good advertisement for bovine anorexia nervosa. The cities and towns seem to be full of strays that wander wherever they please, often sitting down right in the middle of traffic. People nonchalantly drive around them or step over them, or step in what they leave behind. Although on one occasion I did see an Indian shop owner give a sacred cow a boot in his sacred ass for deciding to feed on a choice piece of garbage in front of the shop.

The various governments of India also probably contribute to the snail's pace of change. It's true that India has the largest democracy in the world, but it also has the largest boondoggle of red tape and paperwork. The government seems unable, and in some cases unwilling, to deal with the immense problems faced by India's masses. One traveler I talked to said that he had met Mother Theresa in Calcutta and she said the government gives her nothing and would rather have her out, and those like her who are trying to do some good out of their concern for humanity and on their own initiative.

Probably one of the most difficult things to deal with on a personal level was the complete lack of privacy we were afforded by the Indian people. It was not only a problem in the towns and villages, but we could be in the middle of the country taking a break and minding our own business, and pretty soon we would have three or four people standing or squatting (the ol' Indian squat) around us and our bikes, just as if they were invited guests to our rest period. I just had to keep reminding myself of their background and mine and try to understand—but the treatment we were receiving was making that difficult.

About forty miles from Agra we visited the bird sanctuary at Bharatpur which is a wetlands type of haven for a multitude of bird species. It is a peaceful and serene natural setting, but our accommodations for the night at the Forest Lodge which was within the park were a real rip-off. We paid the outrageous sum of three hundred rupees for our room and we partook of their fifty-five rupee buffet which was one of the worst I'd ever had, even considering it was Indian food. The whole deal, except for the beauty of the sanctuary, was a real loser.

We wheeled into Agra and managed to locate a place to stay with some degree of difficulty. This was the high-tourist season and things appeared to be pretty booked up all over the city. The accommodations we found were more toward the outskirts of the city and probably would have fallen into the "lower end" category. In fact, it was necessary to bundle up in our sleeping bags before we went to bed because heat didn't seem to be a standard feature of our hotel—and the nighttime temperatures here in north central India were pretty darn chilly; it was, after all, late December.

Because we were only going to be in Agra for a day, and again because of my arm (the pain had diminished only slightly and I had to walk around with my arm cocked at a perpetual sixty-degree angle), we decided another bus tour would be the best bet for seeing the highlights of Agra. We first traveled about forty KM west of Agra to the deserted city of Fatehpur Sikri. This was a city that was built by Akbar, one of the greatest of the Moghul emperors. As the legend goes, Akbar visited the holy shrine on this site with the hope that he would be blessed with a son, for all his offspring so far had been of the female persuasion. Allah smiled on him— the Moghuls were Moslem rulers, not Hindu—and granted him a son. In thanks, he erected this city, his new capital, on the site, and today it is a magnificent and well-preserved example of the Moghul Empire at its height. However, it only served as his capital from around 1570 till 1586 when it was abandoned because of problems with providing the city with an adequate water supply.

Akbar, whose reign was contemporary with Elizabeth I of England, was probably one of the most enlightened rulers of his time, or any time. He came to the throne at the age of thirteen, and by the virtue of his conquests, superior organizational skills, and wise and tolerant leadership, he brought the Moghul Empire to the height of its power and achievement. He gained a well-deserved reputation for religious tolerance which should be a lesson for many of the militant Islamic leaders of the world today. Even though a Moslem, he was very tolerant of other religions and invited representatives and scholars from Christianity, Hinduism, Judaism, and Buddhism to his court to discuss the different belief systems. He even tried to devise a theology of his own incorporating all the best ideas from the different religions. He also lifted the taxes which the Moslem rulers of India had imposed on the Hindus for centuries which helped to ease tensions between the two groups. He used to say that we all live under the same sky, receive the same sunshine, drink the same water—so should any one religion be better than the others?

After Fatehpur Sikri it was on to the Taj Mahal. Though words are inadequate, one must say that it is surely one of the most beautiful buildings anywhere in the world. It was built by Akbar's grandson, Shah Jahan, as a tomb for his beloved wife, Mumtaz Mahal, who requested a fine tomb on her deathbed. It took twenty years to build and attracted the best artisans from all over India and Europe as well. It was his intention to build an identical tomb in black stone as his own, but before he could even begin, he was deposed by his stick-in-the-mud son, Aurangzeb, who imprisoned his father in Agra Fort where he had a clear view of his beautiful Taj which was the last sight he saw from his deathbed. Today Shah Jahan and his wife are entombed under the Taj Mahal.

* * *

The end of 1985, December 29 and 30, brought us to the end of our ride across the subcontinent. When we arrived in the capital of Delhi, we decided we'd had enough of India. This would be our terminus and here we would look into booking our flights for Thailand and Southeast Asia. The ride up from Agra featured some of the best roads in India as evidenced by the modern road-surfacing equipment that we saw in action along the way. When we arrived in New Delhi, it proved to be quite a surprise when compared to other Indian cities—broad, tree-lined avenues, attractive, modern buildings; a central park in the middle of Connaught Place; and a host of western-style eateries that would go easy on our stomachs. After riding over thirteen hundred miles from Bombay to Delhi, it gave us a feeling of coming out of the wilderness. New Delhi, of course, is not really Indian, but a relic of the British Raj—a grand and impressive reminder that, at least for a few centuries, the sun never set on the British Empire.

For the next two weeks our home base would be the Hotel Asoka, a huge concrete shell of a building that provided the basic necessities, although heat once again appeared not to be one of them. Also in the area of heat, or lack of, hot water for a shower could only be had early in the morning, and even then it might only last for a couple of minutes.

During our first days in New Delhi, we visited just about every western-style restaurant in an effort to remind our tummies that all was not lost and there was hope for a better tomorrow. I became a regular at Wimpy's, a British transplant that specialized in hamburgers—or rather lamburgers—fries, and shakes; we filled up on pizza; and one of our favorite stops in the evenings was Nirulla's, an ice cream parlor that served up hot-fudge sundaes which left us in a state of blissful Nirvana.

Since our bicycles were stashed in our hotel rooms seven floors up, we did a lot of hoofing it along the highways and byways of India's capital. Every day at least two or three times we made the considerable trek from our hotel to Connaught Place, New Delhi's central hub—a huge traffic circle out of which radiated numerous streets like the spokes of a wheel. Around the central park in the middle of Connaught Place were located the major banks, airlines, and travel agencies and so here we spent a good deal of time searching out the best travel bargain for our flight to Thailand and points east. One afternoon I was lounging on the grass in the heart of Connaught Place enjoying the warm winter sunshine when I was approached by a young Indian man carrying some kind of a wooden box slung over his shoulder.

"Hello," the dark young man called. "Would you like to be having your ears cleaned out?"

I was a little taken aback by his offer.

"Uh, well, gosh," I eloquently replied. "Geez, I really think my ears are fine right now, thank you very much."

I had seen this operation being performed on the streets and really didn't quite understand what it was all about until the moment of this strange offer. It seemed to be a thriving business here in Delhi, but I knew that having some Indian excavate around in my ears for wax and other foreign debris was not high on my list of things to do. I was quite certain that anything he pulled out of my ear would surely have my eardrum attached to it. He accepted my rejection of his service gracefully and moved on in search of another customer whose ears really needed a good swabbing out.

Alison, Paul, and I brought in the New Year of 1986 in the capital of India. It will be one that I will never forget—but not for the usual reasons. Yes, there was wild celebrating on the streets of Delhi—firecrackers, dancing, singing, the honking and blowing of horns. But for me personally, the New Year came in not with a bang, but with a whimper. I did not feel at all like celebrating on this festive occasion, not with my arm still swollen and aching away, a recurrent case of diarrhea staging a successful comeback, and a bad cold beginning to work its way into my system. I retired to my hotel room long before the magic hour and when the New Year sneaked into my darkened room, I flipped on the light, peeked at my watch, introduced myself to 1986, flipped off the light, and went back to a fitful sleep.

Our arrangements for our flight to Thailand were at last set, but now it looked as though those arrangements would have to be changed. There was something very much wrong with my arm; I was still in a good deal of pain, I could not put any pressure on it, the swelling was still there, and I could not straighten out my arm any more than half way. It was time to seek out another doctor before proceeding any further. I placed a call to the American embassy and they recommended a Dr. Chalwa whom I visited that same afternoon. The doctor was a large man with a beautiful red turban wrapped around his head indicating his Sikh background. He examined my elbow for only a moment.

"You should definitely have x-rays taken of your elbow," he said without any hesitation. "I will arrange for you to have x-rays taken tomorrow at the East-West Medical Center."

He gave me directions to the medical center, but the next day I searched high and low for the correct address with no luck. In frustration I dragged myself up and down the roadways, some of which were not indicated accurately on my map of the city. I had just about convinced myself that I should put things off until we arrived in Bangkok, when somehow I ended up on the street that was the object of my quest. (As events will reveal, it was quite fortunate that I did not give up my search.) I entered the East-West Medical Center, which was really more of a small clinic than a large hospital, and laid bare my photogenic elbow for the x-ray technician.

The following day in a meeting with Dr. Chalwa, the x-ray he held before me showed an ominous black line all the way through the bone of my lower elbow penetrating right into the joint—a clean fracture all the way through. The words of the doctor in Jaipur who had first examined my arm came back to me: "There doesn't appear to be any bone damage." I was bitter, but now I was also scared. What additional damage had been done to my arm by riding a couple of hundred miles with a fractured elbow and also by the gap of two weeks separating the accident and the discovery of the severe nature of my injury?

The orthopedic surgeon, Dr. Arora, happened to be on hand that day and he too inspected the x-rays.

"Tell me, what have you done to yourself?" he asked.

His choice of words didn't add to my peace of mind, but I related the story of my accident, my visit to the doctor in Jaipur, and the painful ride from Jaipur to Delhi. He was amazed that I had been able to ride that distance in such a condition.

"You should have an operation on your elbow as soon as possible," Dr. Arora recommended. "You might want to consider flying home for treatment, or we can do the operation for you right here. But whatever you decide, it should be done quickly, for the longer you wait the more arthritic trouble you may have with your elbow in future years. It has already been two weeks since the injury to your arm."

Could this mean the end to my world tour? To have come so far, cycled so many miles, endured so much, and now to be stopped by a fractured elbow. I couldn't let that happen, and so my decision was quick.

"I would like to have the operation done here as soon as possible, Dr. Arora," I said. "I've come too far to give up on my trip now."

The doctor understood my determination, and so he explained how he would insert two stainless steel pins into the fractured bones and then wire them tightly together. He would then prepare a soft cast that would afford a little more mobility than a hard cast because of my intentions to carry on with my journey.

"You must be very careful," he cautioned, "to not ride for at least four weeks to give the bones in your elbow time to heal. Even that may not be enough. If you ride too soon, you could interrupt the healing process and do more damage to your arm."

I began to have second thoughts about my decision the next Monday when I arrived at the medical center for my operation. My experiences at the center would not instill a great deal of confidence in any would-be western patient. It was a little unsettling when the nurse sent me to a semi-outside bathroom (there were four walls, but I could look up and see the sky) for a urine specimen.

Just before the operation Dr. Arora stopped in to see me and his quiet confidence eased my fears somewhat, aided by the sedative I was given which sent me floating about the hospital ward. Next, a team of nurses and Dr. Arora were standing over me and the bright lights of the operating room illuminated all.

"Please begin counting backward from ten," one of the nurses smiled as she placed a kind of mask over my nose.

I smiled back and began: "Ten, nine, eish, sepen, si ...."

What could have been only a couple of minutes later, I roused from a semi-stupor long enough to note that I was back in my room with a heavily-bandaged arm and a raw throat. Dr. Arora stopped in sometime later and told me the operation had gone very well and that I should get a lot of rest, which I proceeded to do.

Alison and Paul visited later that afternoon—at least I think they visited—and told me they would be back the next day when I was a little bit more with the program. The following afternoon their smiling faces were a happy sight. After their welcome visit, I thought about how fortunate I was to have Alison and Paul here for their moral and physical support. They could have flown on to Thailand on their own, but I believe that never even crossed their minds. The bond between us had been forged by sharing and enduring some difficult times and experiences; we had had our frictions and disagreements, but we were friends and they knew I needed their help.

That evening I opted for the "western-style" meal which turned out to be two pieces of dried toast with no butter or jam and something that resembled jello. My disenchantment with Indian medical care mushroomed the next day as I waited in the lobby ready to be discharged. I stood there supporting my bandaged arm with my good arm, waiting for someone to make a sling for me, or tell me what to do, or show some kind of concern for making sure I got on my way Ok. I finally had to ask what was supposed to happen next, and only then did I get any assistance. Before I left I placed the entire bill for my operation on my Visa card and was surprised to find out that the operation cost only around five hundred dollars which I hoped would be covered by my school system's medical insurance which was still in force even though I was on a sabbatical leave. I wondered what the same operation would have cost in the United States. At least that was one mark in the plus column for medical care here—it was cheap! But nevertheless, I was happy to be out of the East-West Medical Center.

The day after I was released from the medical center we loaded up our bicycles and, against doctor's orders, rode out to Delhi's international airport for our flight to Bangkok, Thailand. While I negotiated the busy roads with one arm, Paul rode in front and Alison brought up the rear in an effort to shield me from traffic and any sudden stops. I knew that if I went down in the condition I was in, it would probably mean the end of my world tour once and for all. Never was there a more careful rider than I on those miles out to the airport. We must have made quite a sight as we wheeled out of the city—an invalid cyclist with a heavily bandaged arm suspended in air sandwiched between two cyclists who kept wary eyes on the surrounding cars and trucks.

We made it to the airport in good order without too much jostling of my arm, and when it came time to board our plane, we did so with a sense of relief; we had survived India—although in my case, just barely. None of us felt sorry to leave. This country had been a challenge to our physical stamina, but even more to our spirits. The poverty, the filth, the teeming cities and towns, the fishbowl-like quality of our cycling experience, the internal clash of guilt and pride at being an American—all seemed to drag us down and make us question our purpose and even the right to do what we were doing. In spite of this, however, we had met many wonderful people who had shown us great kindness and hospitality. India has a mystical quality about it. Its unique and exotic sights, sounds, and smells remain with you and almost seem to beckon one to come and sample them again. The landscapes are beautiful and enchanting, and color the portrait of your memory with soft brush strokes and gentle hues.

Although India had been a challenge and a hard way to go, it was good to have had such an experience in order to appreciate better the difficulties our overcrowded little planet faces and also to never take for granted how blessed we Americans really are.

EIGHT

Southeast Asia—Depression

Arriving in Bangkok was like being delivered from the abyss. It is a huge, sprawling metropolis that has all the trappings of the west: super highways, monumental traffic jams that would do New York City proud, Kentucky Fried Chicken, Japanese imports, Pizza Hut, multi-level shopping malls, Dunkin' Donuts, and of course, that ambassador of lightening American cuisine—McDonald's. In fact, what surely must be the largest Ronald McDonald in the world stands commandingly in front of the huge McDonald's restaurant in central Bangkok. The two very ancient cultures of India and Thailand seem to be following different paths into the twenty-first century; one under a full head of steam in the effort to modernize and the other moving ever so slowly into an uncertain future, still handcuffed by the traditions of its past. However, judging Thailand by its capital (and many judge Bangkok less than favorably) could be a mistake, for the country is said to be one big city and a lot of country.

Finding a place to stay in Thailand's capital was not a problem. Bangkok had been one of the main centers of R&R for U.S. troops during the Vietnam War, and many of the establishments that had at one time catered to the recreational needs of men at war now catered to the R&R of travelers and tourists from around the globe.

Our search for a place to stay was made even easier by a hotel locator desk at the airport, and in no time at all we had our lodgings reserved in central Bangkok. It was a hotel geared toward the budget-minded tourist, but the rooms were clean and there was even a pool in the central court.

Although clean, my room fit into the saltbox-size category; standing in the middle, I would have been able to just about touch either wall if I could have stretched out both arms. And I would readily discover that Bangkok's steamy January temperatures would make the lazy ceiling fan overhead a dire necessity. Air-conditioned rooms could be had, but for a pretty penny, or rather a "beautiful bhat"—more bhat than I cared to pay. Besides, at this point in my trip I was into suffering; over the next couple of weeks in Bangkok I would have my share of that.

My first couple of days in the huge metropolis were spent mostly in my cubbyhole of a room trying to regain some of my strength and vitality. I felt exhausted and very down. The operation and its aftereffects and the hassle and stress of the flight from India had drained me. The reserves that I had up to that point been able to call upon, were no longer there. I was exhausted, but sleeping was difficult. Though I was taking pain medication, my elbow constantly throbbed and it was nearly impossible to find a comfortable position for my arm. The only thing that seemed to work for a while was to suspend my arm in midair with a sling which I hitched over the back of a chair positioned next to my bed. When I ventured out of my room it was usually for meal time, and then I would join Alison and Paul at a nearby restaurant which was an amazing smorgasbord of Thai, Chinese, Japanese, and Korean cuisines. But then it was back to my room. Alison and Paul would try to cheer me up, but I continued to draw even more inward with the pain and worry over my arm and the frustration at not being a whole and healthy cyclist.

Adding even more to my depression and worry was a visit to the Adventist hospital where the orthopedic specialist, Dr. Thrasher, (an American), examined and x-rayed my arm.

"Well, Alan," Dr. Thrasher reassured as he scanned the x-ray, "things look to be pretty good. I don't think the jostling your arm has received since the operation has done any harm."

I was relieved to hear this welcome piece of information, but then he said something that was very upsetting.

"However, I just wish your surgeon in Dehli had drawn the two fractured pieces of bone together a little tighter with the wires and pins." he said pointing to the fracture line in my elbow. "I think it will probably be fine, but there is a technique I sometimes use that would have allowed a more speedy use and rehabilitation of your arm. I would have used a stainless steel screw that would have drawn the two bones together tight as a drum. But as I said, things will probably turn out fine and you should have almost full use of your arm—I would say about ninety per cent."

I didn't want to hear this. I didn't want to hear "probably Ok." I didn't want to hear "almost", and I didn't want to hear "90%." After making an appointment to see Dr. Thrasher in one week, I left the hospital feeling very angry and worried. Was I damaging myself for the rest of my life? Should I have quit my world tour and flown home for the operation? Why hadn't Dr. Arora used the technique described by Dr. Thrasher? Why me? As I made the long trek back to the hotel, I cursed India and its medical care, the dog that had caused my accident, and rotten fate which had decreed this to happen. (When I eventually returned home to Toledo, Ohio, my doctor told me that Dr. Arora, my Indian surgeon, had done a nice job on my arm.)

After my visit to the hospital, my spirits hit rock bottom. I made the effort to visit some of the wondrous sights of Bangkok—the Buddhist temples, museums, and palaces— with Alison and Paul, but my heart wasn't in it. And my two friends, after three days in Bangkok, were ready to tackle the long journey down the Malay Peninsula. There was no way I could go with them. I had an appointment to see the doctor the following week, and it had only been a couple of weeks since the operation. Trying to travel now would damage the healing process of my fractured elbow. Alison and Paul had done all they could do for me, and now it was time for them to move on.

They packed up and rode off on the morning of January 16. We agreed that we would try to join up farther south on Koh Samui, a tropical resort island in the Gulf of Thailand. They would cycle the three-hundred mile jaunt down the coast, and after I saw the doctor the following week, I would catch a bus and meet them on the island. That was the plan, but plans often times run afoul, and I knew I might not see them again. As they pedaled off, I felt very sad, but also bitter and jealous—feelings that I tried to suppress, but couldn't. My injury had been the result of an unfortunate accident, but I found myself blaming Alison and Paul. I was envious of the fact that they were cycling out of Bangkok in good health, and I was stuck here alone in my miserable condition. I knew these feelings were completely unjustified, but I couldn't shake them.

Week one in Bangkok drifted into two, and my isolation and bitterness deepened. I rarely ventured out of my room, and when I did it was only to get something to eat. My arm felt thick and swollen and sore, and pain pills were the only thing that allowed me to get some rest in my steamy little enclave. And sightseeing was out of the question. I didn't have the energy or desire to make the effort; I hated being in exotic Thailand and feeling this way—not being able to cycle and experience the country the way I wanted, healthy and able-bodied. The entry in my journal for January 20 read: "Goddamn, I'm so disgusted."

On one of my forays onto the streets of Bangkok, I was surprised to see the smiling faces of seven American astronauts splashed across the front page of an English-language newspaper. The bold headlines, however, were not of glad tidings. The space shuttle, Challenger, had exploded during liftoff, taking seven American heroes to their tragic deaths. This did little to cheer me up.

On my second visit to the Adventist hospital I received much the same news from Dr. Thrasher. He tried to reassure me that my arm would probably be fine—again "probably"—and told me that I should be as careful as possible given the circumstances of what I was doing. I thanked him for his evaluation and care, and then went on my way to make bus reservations for the next day. With my second visit to Dr. Thrasher behind me, there was no longer any reason to remain in Bangkok. I needed to escape from the city where I had become a prisoner of my depression and self-pity. The tropical island of Koh Samui three hundred miles to the south would hopefully rejuvenate my body and my spirit.

My experience with the bus journey to the island of Koh Samui made me swear that I would never again take another bus in Thailand. Near to my hotel a travel agency sold me a ticket on a bus line to take me south, telling me the bus would pick me up right there at the agency which was only a minute from my hotel. How convenient, I thought. I was there at the appointed time but to my dismay, it was not a large bus, but a minibus that would shuttle me and all my equipment and bicycle to the waiting tour bus. The driver who looked like the equivalent of a beer-guzzling, Sunday-afternoon television sports jockey, stopped for my pickup in the middle of the daily traffic jam that clogs all of Bangkok's main thoroughfares. As I threaded my way through the sea of traffic with my bike and all my gear, punishing my fractured elbow in the process, I was a little relieved to see only two other people in the minibus. The driver helped me get my bike on top of the bus with the delicate touch of a linebacker for the Chicago Bears, and away we sped. Not to the bus station, however, but on a three-hour journey around hot, sultry Bangkok to pick up two, four, six, ten, fourteen more human beings with all their luggage, and all of it—human and non-human—crammed into and on top of the minibus. Much of the equipment on top, of course, found its resting place on top of my bike, and not placed there gently. At about this time in our Bangkok tour I had an insane desire to allow my foot to make an impression in the very copious ass of our Thai driver. Once at the bus station, which was probably a fifteen-minute bike ride from my hotel, the next problem was how to stuff my bicycle into a very small compartment in the side of the tour bus. After watching the porters turn it this way and that, I finally had to take off both wheels and stack everything in a pile of frame, wheels, cables, and packs. Once on the bus itself about five hours after I left the tour agency, I was amazed to find an "in-flight" attendant and a TV at the front playing some Thai program that the majority of foreign passengers couldn't understand. I and my fellow "sardines" were packed into our seats which seemed to be half the size of an airplane seat, making it impossible to stretch out; sleeping was out of the question.

Amazingly, the next day my bicycle and I were delivered intact to the island of Koh Samui, off the east coast of Thailand. The bus was shuttled onto a car ferry that arrived at the island around noon. By that time I felt as though I had been through the war, and I wanted nothing more than to find a soft mattress to curl up on. I pedaled into the main village of Na Thorn and almost immediately heard the call of some familiar voices.

"Hey Al, over here!"

It was Alison and Paul sitting in one of the local restaurants sipping a couple of cool brews. They had just arrived on another boat and were relaxing before they set out to find a place to crash among the many bamboo-hut communities that dotted the shores of the island. Their smiling faces were a welcome and wonderful sight, and the bitter feelings that had troubled me melted easily away. In happy tones we compared our experiences of the last week and after we each had downed another beer or two, we set out together to find our own little piece of paradise.

* * *

Miles of deserted, white sand beaches, swaying coconut palms, emerald and azure waters reaching to the horizon, beach bungalows steps away from the soothing rhythm of the Gulf of Thailand—the island of Koh Samui. It is a true tropical paradise, a place to relax and enjoy the pleasures of doing nothing except maybe walking the beaches, taking a dip in the warm waters of the Gulf, or watching the moon-glow reflected in the night sea. The shores of the island are punctuated by small communities of thatched-roof huts that provide any would-be Robinson Crusoe with the basic necessities of a tropical existence. At the heart of each little community is a combination cafe, restaurant, bar, and activity room where you can chow down on anything from spicy Thai dishes to good ol' American hamburgers or sip on a tall, cool concoction of rum, fruit juices, and fresh pineapple. In the evening, after a day of intense relaxation, guests gather in the bar/restaurant for the nightly video presentation—"Rocky" and "Rambo" seemed to be popular—or take a barefoot stroll through the cool sands to watch moonbeams shimmer and dance across the surface of the sea.

After only two tries, we found our own little beach-front paradise where we had to pay the "outrageous" price of fifty-four bhat, or about six dollars a night. The sea was only about fifty paces from our bamboo and thatched huts, and each night it sang a gentle lullaby to send us off to sleep. For eight days we whiled away the hours relaxing, sunning, beach combing, and in my case, trying to mend.

In spite of all this, what should have been an idyllic sojourn on the island of Koh Samui could not be that for me. My arm refused to let me forget. It continued to hurt and ache—especially at night—and I began to rely too much on at least part of a sleeping pill to help me drift off to sleep. Not being able to sleep normally, dress normally, and ride normally depressed me greatly, and always in the back of my mind was the question of whether or not I would be damaging my arm permanently by choosing to carry on with my world tour.

On February 1, about four weeks after my operation, we caught the ferry boat back to the mainland of the Malay Peninsula to continue our ride south to the Thailand-Malaysia border. It was still too early for me to ride, but I was determined to forge on with Alison and Paul. It's impossible for me to describe in words how I felt at the end of these first two days back on the road and have everyone understand what I'm talking about. One would just have to experience it. I can't remember feeling worse at any time on the trip. A special set of circumstances combined to leave me in a state of near exhaustion. It had been five to six weeks since I last rode in India—quite a long layoff requiring another break-in period.

The well-conditioned body that I brought out of Europe had been under assault by living and cycling in the Third World for the last three months. The operation itself and my short recuperation period seemed to have wreaked havoc with my bodily systems, and my weakened arm meant that the rest of my body would have to compensate, thus making all my other healthy parts sore and fatigued. And riding under the hot, tropical sun sucked the moisture and salt right out of me, causing my stomach and legs to knot up in cramps. Ninety-four long miles on the first day and eighty-three even "longer" miles on the next left me feeling like the Grim Reaper had come a knockin' at my door.

When we arrived in the town of Songhla and located a hotel in which to crash, it was all I could do to lug myself and my gear up to our room where I unceremoniously collapsed in a heap on the bed and temporarily checked out of this—world consciousness. When I awoke, Alison and Paul were in much the same position. It didn't take us long to decide that there would be no riding the next day. I had nothing left, and Alison and Paul were dead tired too. We declared the next day an official rest day, which is about all I managed to do. I spent most of the day in our room feeling weak and drained, only going out to get a bite to eat at one of the busy roadside food stalls. During the night I would make my customary trip to the bathroom to straddle the porcelain pit or Asian squat toilet, and when I turned on the light I was treated to the spectacle of a mad dash to the toilet drain by an army of huge, black cockroaches—real heavy weights that would relegate their American cousins to the light-weight division.

The day's rest gave our bodies a chance to regroup some of their forces in preparation for the coming assault, and early the next morning we found ourselves back on the road again with the first light of dawn at around 6:15 a.m. We decided that it was the only way to attempt to beat the fierce tropical climate. Even so, by eleven o'clock we were bicycling in a slow cooker, and by the time we reached our destination of Pattani at mile sixty-six, I felt once again like it was time to cash in my chips.

The following day proved to be a repeat, but the head winds from the southeast, our direction of travel, became even stronger. Now, in addition to my arm, I had to contend with a sunburned and blistered lower lip and a rather uncomfortably situated blood blister on my rear end where derriere comes in contact with bicycle seat. If all this gives you the idea that cycling in tropical paradise is not really paradise at all, you may have something there!

It took us six days to make it to the south of Thailand, and now before us lay Malaysia, land of rubber plantations and countless tropical beaches. In spite of the physical discomforts on our trek south from the island of Koh Samui, we had found the Thai people to be outgoing and friendly, but not overbearing like the Egyptians, nor lacking a complete sense of personal space and privacy like the Indians. Thailand is sometimes called the Land of Smiles, and it was easy to see why. One day as we stopped for a rest break, a woman came rushing out of her house with a pitcher of cool water for us. We placed our hands together and bowed in the Buddhist custom, trying to express our gratitude to this smiling angel of mercy. And a number of times I was waved over by the police, not for speeding, but because they just wanted to find out who I was and where I was headed. When they heard the word "American," they broke out into huge smiles and seemed to marvel at the idea that I was bicycling through their country. Each time this happened they gave me ice water from their cooler, and one officer gave me a large piece of watermelon. Treatment like this from the friendly Thais helped to ameliorate somewhat the large and small aches and pains that were part and parcel of our trip into the south.

On this leg of our journey, however, there seemed to be a growing distance between me and Alison and Paul, both figuratively and literally. I tended more and more to keep to myself, and they likewise. And on our long days of riding, we rarely cycled together; they were usually somewhere far up ahead while I brought up the rear, sticking to my own determined pace. At times they really seemed to be pushing it, and I had neither the energy or desire to keep up. More and more I began to think seriously about Malaysia and the long miles of tropical sun and heat. Was it time to get out of Asia and find a part of the world that would be more amenable to my mending arm and weakened condition?

We crossed the river leaving Thailand behind and entered Malaysia. There was no bridge, so the ferry boat chugged its way across the liquid boundary between the two countries. We continued on the short distance to Kota Bahru, the first large city on the east coast of malaysia. It was here that I broke my news to Alison and Paul.

"Well guys," I began, "I think this is going to be the end of the line for me in Asia. This has really been hard cycling for me with my arm and the heat and all. I think maybe I'm going to look into catching a train down the rest of the peninsula to Singapore and then try to book a flight to Australia or New Zealand."

"Well Al, whatever you feel is best for you," Alison replied. "We're going to miss you."

"Ya know, I think I'll miss you guys too."

And we truly would, but I think we each sensed that maybe it was time to make the split. And so, once again I gave Alison a good-bye hug and shook Paul's hand, and thanked them for all their help and friendship and wished them all the best. It's true that our last weeks had been strained, but we had been through much together in Africa, India, and Southeast Asia, and as they rode off, I was sorry to see them go. This would be our final good-bye. (I would not see them again until over a year later in Columbus, Ohio. It would be a happy reunion to say the least.)

I arrived by train in Singapore at the southernmost point of the Malay Peninsula. This jewel of the East appeared to be the garden spot of all Southeast Asia, maybe all of Asia. It's a city of tall skyscrapers, multi-level shopping malls galore, and western, fast-food establishments like McDonald's and Burger King—yes, the hamburger wars now have an eastern front! And it's a city that even by western standards is immaculately clean. Of course, a hefty fine provides somewhat of an incentive for not using the environment as a trash can, as the rest of Asia is wont to do. Singapore is really more of a city-state—a small island at the tip of Malaysia. It is independent of its neighbor to the north, although for a short time in the mid sixties it was a part of the Malaysian confederation.

I spent the first couple of days in Singapore trying to decide which course I should take. The homesick part of me kept pleading "get back to the U.S. of A." while the adventurous side kept urging "on to Australia and New Zealand." I finally settled on a compromise by eliminating

Australia because of its immense size and distances, not to mention the mid-summer temperatures, and opting for New Zealand. I'd heard so much of New Zealand's pristine beauty and the friendliness of her people that I would hate to miss it after having come so far.

I made my good-bye toast to Asia at the Raffles Hotel, that monument to Britain's hospitality during her colonial period in this far-flung part of her empire. This is where the Singapore Sling was invented by a Raffles bartender. And so, with an eight dollar (Malaysian) Singapore Sling in hand, I made a toast and a quiet prayer of thanks to the great deity of all bicyclists who allowed me to survive bicycling in the Third World. During this time, more than any other, I had truly been out on a limb.

* * *

New Zealand is a country that can only be described as an outdoorsman's paradise. It has just about everything in the way of geography to offer: tropical beaches, high mountain peaks, excellent ski fields, abundant trout streams, and scenery that is a feast for the eyes. It is also a land of three million beef cattle, six million dairy cows, seventy million sheep, and only three million Homo sapiens, meaning there are about twenty-six sheep for every man, woman, and child as the brochures and tour guides eagerly point out.

My plane touched down in Auckland, New Zealand's largest city, and on the fifteen-mile ride from the international airport into the heart of the city I had to do something that I had not done for what seemed like quite a while—dig out my woolly pull-ons from the depths of my panniers and bundle up. Here at thirty-six degrees south latitude it was mid-February and the New Zealanders were enjoying the swan song of their summer while the chilly temperatures hinted at the approaching change of seasons. Coming from the tropical heat of Southeast Asia to the chilly climes of New Zealand's North Island was no small switch, and it took a while for me to get used to the idea of being cold. My first few cycling miles in New Zealand also made it abundantly clear to me that I was no longer in the Eastern

World. Though I was still in the Eastern Hemisphere, everything my eyes beheld spoke of the West—the neatly sculptured landscape of farms and pastures; the brick and wood-framed houses dressed in colorful flower boxes and surrounded by tidy yards; the faces of the people that I passed along the way. A sense of being home replaced the aura of strangeness that had been so much a part of bicycling through Africa and Asia. And yet, I knew I was still a half a world away from my hometown of Toledo, Ohio.

When I arrived at the youth hostel in the heart of Auckland, it proved to be a melting pot of international travelers hailing from all corners of the globe: Europeans, Americans, Australians, Japanese, and of course, New Zealanders. Everyone was engaged in their own special adventure and had a story to tell of things they had seen and experiences they had had. Some were short timers who were hitting the high points of the Lands Down Under in the space of three or four weeks, and some like me had been on the road for many months and traversed great distances.

During my first couple of days in Auckland I did a lot of thinking. I was very much torn between seeing the treasures of this beautiful island nation and hopping a plane that would whisk me eastward to the west coast of America. I was anxious to hit the shores of the USA; to return to my own country and face the last challenge of my world tour— the transcontinental ride from California to Ohio. But I knew full well that I might not pass this way again; it would be foolish to give up the opportunity to see some of Nature at her finest.

So into the heart of New Zealand's North Island I pedaled, covering close to ninety miles on the first day out. I glided over gently rolling terrain painted in varying shades of green and brown. Tidy farmsteads punctuated the patchwork quilt of earth, and everywhere one gazed—sheep. I'd had a two-week layoff since last riding, and by the time I reached mile ninety and my destination of Huntley, I was dead tired. But it was a different kind of tired. In Thailand the tropical heat had drained me of just about every ounce of strength. But ninety miles in New Zealand felt like ninety miles in the U.S.—you were dog-tired, but something you could bounce back from. And too, there was the same sense that I was again bicycle-touring and not fighting for survival.

New Zealand is a country for adventurers and travelers—young, old, bikers, mountain climbers, skiers, white water rafters, and bushwalkers. Adventure tour agencies and outfitters abound, offering every conceivable outdoor excursion. They have an excellent and well-run network of youth hostels used extensively by foreigners and New Zealanders alike. And I took advantage a number of times of a travel feature that the U.S. could learn from. They have a unique system of motor camps which furnish you with a miniature wood-frame cottage with enough space for a couple of beds and storage. Since there are common bathrooms, showers, and kitchens, there is no need for plumbing. Consequently, the tiny cottages must be inexpensive to build and maintain, and that results in a cost to the traveler that brings a smile to the pocketbook. In fact, they really are more like campgrounds with permanent wooden tents. And most have activity and game rooms where guests can congregate in the evening and trade stories of the day's travels and adventures.

In the city of Rotorua I found amazing evidence of New Zealand's hot spot on the Pacific Ocean's Rim of Fire. Here the land hisses and groans and belches forth super-heated geysers of water—messages from Mother Earth's seething interior. Boiling mud pots bubble and gurgle, while blue-green pools of one hundred eighty-degree water invite only those with a desire to test the fate of a Maine lobster. And all around, trails of unearthly steam waft skyward from vents in the earth's cracked outer skin. If a time traveler from the Middle Ages were deposited in the middle of this natural wonder, he could only assume that he had entered the realm of Satan.

Rotorua, in addition to being a good imitation of hell and its environs, is also one of the main centers of the Maori tribe who were the original Polynesian inhabitants of this beautiful island. The warden of the youth hostel was a friendly chap and very helpful, like most of the New Zealanders I met so far, and he directed me to the Maori cultural center. Here I found many fascinating displays on the Maori people and their culture. And in the evening I attended a fun and exciting display of Maori singing and dancing that showcased the rich heritage of this handsome Polynesian people.

The next few days I spent exploring the heart of the North Island, but not alone, Riding along the shores of Lake Taupo, New Zealand's largest lake, I once again met two American cyclists. Joe and Dave were slightly crazy, but fun, and together we headed farther south to Tongiriro National Park, a beautiful area whose two permanent residents happen to be one dormant and one active volcano. We spent a day hiking, or "bushwalking" as the Kiwis call it, covering quite a bit of ground by foot instead of by wheel.

Joe and Dave planned to continue south toward Wellington and the South Island—but I wouldn't be going with them. Although my arm was getting stronger, long hours in the saddle still made everything hurt more than usual because of the increased pressure I was forced to put on my good right arm. It was nearly impossible to find a comfortable riding position that would last for very long. And my deliverance from the Third World had not been entirely successful, for it seemed that some little tropical bug had hitched a ride out of Asia. Every seven days or so my little parasite hitchhiker liked to kick up his heels and do a dance through my intestines, keeping me running in more ways than one. My periodic love affair with the toilet bowl and slowly mending arm weakened my resolve, and I finally gave in to the urge that was calling me home. Before I knew it, I found myself on a train bound for Auckland and the Qantus Airways office. It didn't take long for Qantus to clear me on a nineteen-hour flight through to San Francisco, via Sidney and Honolulu, and so there it was—the end of some of the greatest challenges I had faced on my trip. I had survived my passage through eleven foreign countries, five of them struggling to emerge from a Third World poverty, disease, and overpopulation. But I knew the challenges were by no means over with. When I set down in San Francisco, there would still be a sizable chunk of real estate that separated me from Toledo, Ohio. Somehow, though, it didn't matter. All I knew was that I had been away from my native shores for what seemed an eternity, and I was finally going home.

NINE

There's No Place Like Home

For the last nine months I had pictured myself stepping triumphantly off the plane in San Francisco, once again on U.S. soil. A brass band draped in red, white, and blue would be playing the Battle Hymn of the Republic, Governor Celeste of Ohio would be there energetically pumping my hand, and President Reagan would be smiling broadly at the end of the long, red carpet. But strangely, that long-awaited feeling of triumph wasn't there. In its place was a vague sense of disappointment in myself for having undercut my goals somewhat. I had trained through Malaysia, not cycled at all in Australia, and only spent a few weeks in New Zealand. I did my best to convince myself that my fractured elbow had a lot to do with not cycling as much as I had planned in this part of the world, but I just couldn't shake the feeling of short-changing my goals.

Nevertheless, my feet were once again on American terra firma, and it was a good feeling to be home. It had been nine long months since my eyes had beheld a familiar face—excepting Alison and Paul and my other riding companions—and the first familiar and very welcome face to greet me at San Francisco International was that of my good friend, Doug Palmer. Doug and I went back a long way through college fraternity days and the post-graduation struggle to determine the true direction of life's highway. He had left Toledo in the mid seventies, finding a need for his considerable engineering skills in Birmingham, Alabama, and eventually heard the call of the California mystique. He located a nice house in the East Bay community of Pittsburg

(Yes, there is a Pittsburg in California) and began his climb up the corporate ladder to a position of senior engineer in a company that deals in environmental concerns.

I saw his face before he saw mine; in fact, my good friend walked right on by me without taking note of a weathered bicyclist, bicycle and packs. Doug and I always good-naturedly kidded each other about suffering from what we called anal inversions (that situation when one has a tendency to have one's head up one's rear end,) and here was excellent grist for the mill!

"Uh, Doug, over here," I beamed in his direction.

"My God, Big Al, it's you. Brother Thompson, welcome home to the good ol' U.S. of A. God, it's great to see you."

"And you don't know how good it is to see a familiar face," I grinned.

As we shook hands warmly, enjoying the moment of reunion, Doug's happy expression turned to one of concern.

"My gosh, Al, you've lost so much weight. How are you feeling?"

"Actually, I feel pretty good right now, D.P.," I reassured my good friend. "I should stay that way as long as my little Asian parasites refrain from doing back flips through my intestines. Let's just say that Asia and my stomach did not become best of friends. In fact, I think I've discovered the ideal weight-loss program. It requires about nine months, however."

"Well, I can see that we're going to have to fatten you up considerably before you tackle the last part of your ride across the United States—you can count on that!" declared Doug.

For the next two weeks I did just that as I divided my time between relaxing in Doug's comfortable home and gorging myself on all those goodies that I had craved while traveling in Africa and Asia—Hostess cupcakes, quarter-pounders with cheese, and chocolate milkshakes. When not engaged in those two worthwhile pursuits, I made trips to the local bike shop where they were re-spoking my back wheel which had taken a lot of punishment over the last seven thousand miles. And on the weekends when Doug had some free time from his job, we made excursions to some of the local sights around the Bay Area: Fisherman's Wharf, Ghiardelli Square, and the Napa Valley which was shrouded in early spring showers.

One can only stand so many days of relaxation and gorging, especially after having been on the move for so many months, and so after two weeks' time, I knew I was ready to think seriously about forging ahead into the last leg of my journey. Doug graciously offered to drive me down to Los Angeles from whence I would begin the long ride back to Ohio. Starting out farther south would hold out the promise of warmer temperatures in this early spring of 1986, although it would be no guarantee against Jack Frost nipping at my nose as I would discover in the days ahead. I took him up on his offer, and on our journey south I had a chance to show Doug some of the beautiful sights south of San Francisco that he had not yet had the opportunity to see, like the Monterey Peninsula and probably one of the most spectacular pieces of real estate anywhere in the world— California's Big Sur coastline. We located a motel in the small town of Palmdale on the edge of the Mohave Desert just a little west of Los Angeles. There we crashed for the night after our twelve-hour meandering drive down the coast, and the next morning I performed my ritual of loading my bicycle, one that I could surely do in my sleep. I grasped Doug's hand in farewell and tried to express my gratitude for his hospitality, kindness and friendship. Words were hard to come by, and none were really needed. As I straddled my bicycle facing east and the Mohave Desert, I again experienced those feelings that had been my companions so often over the last year: apprehension, excitement, a tinge of fear at setting out on my own once again. There was also a new emotion—the anticipation of home and family. Twenty-five hundred miles distant, granted, but it was a distance my mind could comprehend. As I pedaled southeast out of Palmdale, I cast one final glance over my shoulder to see Doug waving a final good-bye from the front of the motel. My good friend had provided me with a much-needed respite for the final challenge which now lay before me.

* * *

I soon found myself heading into the great southwestern desert of California. The sky was cloudless, the air was warm and becoming warmer, the land desolate and barren. Still, I was surprised at the number of homes of one sort or another that populate this arid region of the country. These desert dwellers obviously prefer the stark beauty of this unforgiving environment to the more hospitable environs of other parts of the USA. As I was slowly becoming attuned to this new landscape, so different from that of New Zealand, my forward progress came to a screeching halt about fifteen miles outside of Palmdale. A close inspection revealed that my luggage rack had again broken and the support strut jammed into the freewheel. This was the same rack that had broken about eight months before in Spain. I was amazed that it had made it this far and very lucky that this had not happened about fifty miles out into the desert—or worse, half way across the Indian subcontinent.

Ever the economist, I sought out a hardware shop conveniently close by and drilled the necessary holes to get me on my way. This minor delay cut considerably into my mileage for the day and mile fifty-five found me at the town of Victorville about ready to call it quits. However, the only campground in the vicinity was a KOA and I almost choked when the camp manager told me that it would be twelve dollars for a small piece of dirt on which to throw my tent. "Thanks, but no thanks," was the only thing that came to mind as I pedaled away, determined to pitch my tent on a free piece of real estate. But then I remembered the layers of sweat that had been accumulating on my body under the warm desert sun, and that inviting-looking pool back in the KOA campground, not to mention the nice hot showers that sent steam spewing out the bathhouse windows. And from out of nowhere a little voice persuaded me.

"OK, Al, you've suffered quite a bit over the last nine months; it's time to ease up a little. Hey, you're right—it's not cheap, but it's the best thing right here and now. Go for it!"

I thanked the little voice for the wise counsel, and headed directly back to the KOA. Even so, as I was pitching my tent on my six by ten, twelve-dollar piece of dirt, I swore that I would never again pay that outrageous price for a place to park my bicycle and tent.

Under a sky sorely lacking in white, puffy things I pushed farther into the Mohave. A stubborn side wind protested my forward movement until my route swung around to a more easterly direction. Now the winds transformed their protests into encouragement and the last twenty miles of an eighty-four-mile day—my second day of desert riding—passed almost effortlessly beneath my wheels. Still smarting from the twelve-dollar piece of ground from the previous night, I knocked on the door of a friendly old couple who lived on the outskirts of the small desert community of 29 Palms.

"Hello there," I greeted the two elderly desert dwellers. "My name is Alan and I'm on my way to Ohio by bicycle— the last leg of a world bicycle tour. Would you mind if I pitched my tent somewhere in back of your house. I wouldn't need much—just a little water and maybe the use of your bathroom."

"Say now," the old gent smiled, "we'd be more than happy to have you pitch that tent anywhere you want out back. Just throw it up out there in between the cactus plants and Joshua trees. And let us know if we can get ya' anything! And, oh yea, welcome to 29 Palms!"

After establishing my impromptu camp and showering under my handy dandy water sack, I sat down to a dinner of tuna fish salad sandwiches which became the subject of my customary disappearing act. While I munched—no, make that devoured—my host came out to chew the fat awhile.

"Say young feller," how old are you anyway?" he asked. "My wife and I were talkin' in the house and we were bettin' that you're probably in your twenties. Is that about right?"

That brought a huge smile to my face and a considerable boost to the ol' ego. When I told him I was really in my mid thirties, he was amazed and very much impressed. Of course, this kindly old gent and his wife were on the far side of seventy-five, so it's a wonder they didn't suggest I was somewhere in my mid teens. As they say, it's all relative.

* * *

Up to this point in my ride across southern California's Mohave I had not felt completely alone. Every now and then I would happen upon a small island of habitation—an isolated mobile home surrounded by sage and cactus plants or a small cluster of homes standing firm together against the harsh desert environment. Even when no dwellings were in sight, which was a good part of the time, the endless file of telephone poles alongside the roadway with their singing wires was a reminder that civilization had not totally forsaken me. But on March 25, even these small tokens of humanity vanished.

> Before me lay the heart of the Mohave Desert. Desolate and barren, it is a land that bakes during the summer and simmers in the spring and fall. Even those who prefer to dwell in the desert have not penetrated this forbidding piece of earth. Ahead of me stretches the sole indication of man's presence, a thin ribbon of highway that melts into the far horizon. A swift tail wind sweeps me out into the middle of this no-man's land and then abandons me. Now the pedaling is difficult and the sun seemingly has forgotten it is only early spring, and not the middle of summer. As I inch my way toward Granite Pass, a dry and windswept desert passage high above the Mohave, I feel as though I will not make it. It becomes difficult to swallow and I almost have to peel my lips from the front of my teeth. At last, almost within reach! I am here, at this godforsaken summit, and amazingly two angels of mercy happily greet me in the forms of Ralph and Marie in their newly-purchased camper van stocked full of cold beer. I receive their blessing of an ice-cold Budweiser, offer my never-ending thanks and promise them my first-born child, and then begin my descent down into more nothingness. As I close in on mile one hundred, I spy two bright spots up ahead that appear to be bobbing up and down in the shimmering desert heat. The bright spots materialize into Paul and Brian, two

hikers with bright orange backpacks, each with a huge red and white umbrella attached to the back of their packs. The umbrellas provide moving shade as they trek across the heart of the Mohave. They are on a transcontinental hike to Virginia and hope to make it by Christmas. Just as people have been amazed at my travels, I too am amazed at their undertaking and the challenge that lies before them. We talk for nearly a half an hour, sharing our tales of the road, drawn together by our like experiences and the similarities of our challenge against the elements. As the sun nestles toward the horizon, we exchange goodbyes and wishes for good fortune. Twilight dances on the desert, and at mile one hundred and one I arrive at tiny Vidal Junction. I establish my camp a little way off the road and settle back to watch the moon ascend its celestial ladder, casting a soft glow over a small blue tent, a bicycle, and a very tired rider.

* * *

"Would ya' come over and have a beer with me?" said the voice from the side of the road as I headed toward Parker, Arizona, on the border with California. The voice was coming from grizzled ol' Bob Mann, a prospector hereabouts who looked as though he had not quite struck the mother lode yet.

"Well, that's mighty kindly of you Bob, but I just downed a whole bottle of Gatorade a piece back," I replied.

"Well hell, have one anyway," he insisted. "I can tell a man doin' the work you're a doin' needs more than a little ol' bottle of that there Gator stuff. Yes siree', I got me about sixteen claims staked out along yonder. Rich, hell, I'm bankrupt, but I'm gonna' work them claims as long as I can. Say, let me shake your hand—never shook the hand of someone who's been round the world before!"

"Well thanks, Bob—best of luck to you. Bye now, and God bless ya'!"

This colorful character constituted California's farewell committee as I approached the first major milestone of my trans-America ride—the mighty Colorado River and the California-Arizona border. In this year of firsts for me, here was another first, for it was the first time I had set foot—or wheel—in the vast state of Arizona. This great state, as well as many of the great states to follow, would show me the meaning of good ol' American hospitality. In the small town of Sonale while I was taking a bit of nourishment at the sole restaurant, a friendly fellow questioned me about my bicycle and trip. Don Welton lived in the next small town of Wenden, and after I finished giving Don the spiel on my trip, I asked him if he might have a place for me to pitch my tent for the night.

"Hey now, you're more than welcome to pitch your tent in our yard," Don enthused. "It's not large—we live in a mobile home park—but I think you'll have all the room you need. We're right on the outskirts of town—you can't miss it. I'll be waitn' for ya'."

I rode the five miles to Wenden and found Don and his wife Dot relaxing in the shade of their mobile home. As I was pitching my tent on a soft piece of grass in their side yard, Don came over to inspect my progress.

"Say now, you're more than welcome to stay in our spare trailer. It's got a comfortable bed, a small TV—all the comforts of home. At least that will save you one night from sleeping on the hard ground," he said with a twinkle in his eye.

"You know Don, I just may take you up on that generous offer. These days, anytime I get to sleep in a real bed, it's a treat. Thanks a million!"

It not only had a comfortable bed and a TV, but also a nice little shower stall and a small kitchen. After I took advantage of the shower and put the small kitchen to good use, I joined Don and his wife and occupied an empty lounge chair on the small carpet of green that surrounded their mobile home. We sat and watched the desert dusk erase the colors of the day and talked into the evening hours, exchanging our past histories, and before I retired Don pointed out a range of hills to the west behind which General Patton trained his armored divisions for action in North

Africa during World War II. In the morning I was up early, but so were Don and Dot with a tasty breakfast of bacon and eggs. I thanked my kind and generous hosts for their great hospitality, and as I pedaled away, I thought how these two were a nice introduction to the state of Arizona.

Even taking into account kind people like Don and Dot Welton, it would pay one to remember that this is the wild and woolly west. In fact, one might say there are a few rednecks inhabiting these parts, and it would be best for that one to hold his tongue around here if tempted to speak out in favor of gun control or against the NRA. I found this out after I rode the forty-five miles to Congress, a small town of about five hundred souls. It proved to be a rather tedious grind because of a nasty head wind, and so I decided this would be my stop for the night if I could find a good place to pitch my tent. As I was sitting in front of the local grocery consuming my daily ration of junk food and contemplating my situation, I heard a voice behind me growl.

"Hell of a place to park that thing!"

The growl came from a thick-necked, thick-bellied pseudo John Wayne type and he was referring to my bicycle which was parked innocently on the sidewalk in front of the store, not really blocking the way, but requiring maybe one or two extra steps to get around. This I was going to point out to this obvious reincarnation of Duke Wayne until my eyes settled on his camouflaged holster with a menacing-looking handgun slung around his waist à la Billy the Kid. Luckily, he was quickly in and out of the store and away in his pickup truck with shotgun rack and shotgun plainly visible through the back window—probably in a hurry to get back to the business of protecting his land from the omnipresent Red Menace.

The owner of the grocery then told me of the community park and that I could camp there if I was looking for a place for the night. What he didn't tell me of was the park's guardian and "watch dog" whom I met immediately upon my arrival. As I was pulling my bike up next to the park shelter, Robert, a little old fellow a few years shy of seventy came over to give me the official inspection. Robert was caretaker of the park and lived right there in a small room attached to the lavatories. Apparently, whether or not I would camp on this night in this particular spot depended on if I looked "Ok." Anyone whose appearance was too "shabby, long-haired, dirty or sleazy" would not be welcome. I must have passed muster because he pointed out where I should pitch my tent. Robert told me about how busy he was and how much work he had to do around the park, even though he spent the remainder of the day talking to me and expressing some of his views on life and politics:

> "Yup, I think we oughter take one of them A-bombs and drop her right in the middle of Red Square. And what's more, I'd like to be the one to do it! Never did trust them Ruskies. Yup, there's a lot of free women and free sex down in that town. Hell, you don't even have to go to Las Vegas. Yessiree, I'm up here all by myself to look after this here park. The only thing I have to rely on is my karate, and that's one thing I use full go!"

As darkness fell, Robert and his shadow, Bruce Lee, went off to listen to his police radio, and I to my tent.

* * *

The immense spaces of our great southwest—what grand vistas to behold; and what a challenge for the legs of any touring cyclist! My days seemed to be a series of ups and downs over the semi-arid hills and mountains of central Arizona. One minute in desert-like conditions, and a half hour later climbing through alpine meadows and fragrant pine forests. From Congress to Prescott to Cottonwood, up and down and over and under. On the one hand I was growing weary of the constant grades day after day, but at the same time, I could feel myself getting back into shape after the past few months of injury, recovery, and spot riding. I could feel my strength returning as I attacked each new grade with a vigor that had been drained out of me in India and Southeast Asia.

As I was climbing into Flagstaff at seven thousand feet on April 1, I could hear the rolling thunderheads behind me, and the menacing skies above unleashed a cold mountain shower that caught me short of my goal. I located the youth hostel in downtown Flagstaff and settled in for the night and the next day—a self-proclaimed day of rest after eight days of riding. This one day hiatus was to become two, for the temperatures here at seven thousand feet took a nose dive and soon the "white-tinged rain" was being whipped about in blizzard-like conditions, making sure that my escape from Old Man Winter during the last year would not be a total success. From the warmth and coziness of the hostel's parlor I looked out on a winter wonderland that to me seemed so strange, and thought about how only a week ago I had been sweltering in the dry heat of the Mohave Desert.

Due north of Flagstaff lies one of the greatest natural wonders to be found anywhere on our tiny but beautiful planet—the Grand Canyon. This was now my destination and though Jack Frost was very much my companion on this day of April 3, I chose to ride anyhow. Once again, my journal entry will speak for me:

> The air this morning is frigid; yesterday's snow lingers on; and I find it hard to crawl from the warmth and security of my down sleeping bag. Pedaling northeast out of Flagstaff under the shadow of the towering San Francisco Peaks, the arctic air knifes through my layers of protective clothing making me aware that these are the coldest conditions I've experienced in my ten months of riding. In spite of the cold air and a biting head wind, I still sweat and become all the more chilled when upgrade turns inevitably into downgrade. On one of the upgrades my wheels run off the pavement into the soft gravel, and unbelievably, down I go once again. I am going slow this time, but I land on my fractured elbow. I am gripped more by fear than by pain as I pick myself up from the roadside gravel— fear that I have re-injured my elbow. But luckily, I landed on my arm a little below the

fracture. Still, it scares me and I determine to buy some kind of protective pad for my elbow at first chance. By day's end I am tired and sore—and still short of my goal. I must choose between camping out in the chilly climes of northern Arizona or the snug security of a motel room. The same little voice speaks to me again. I opt for the motel room.

The following day only about a half day's ride brought me through the portals of Grand Canyon National Park. I'd seen much over the previous ten months, but nothing that could surpass the Grand Canyon for beauty and majesty. One is humbled when standing on the rim, gazing out over one of nature's most magnificent creations and trying to comprehend the forces of erosion that have sculpted this breathtaking display. The steep canyon walls with their rainbow strata are a storybook telling of the geologic history of this part of the great southwest. And the author of this fantastic record, the Colorado River, snakes far below at the bottom of the mile-deep gorge, twisting this way and that, most always hiding from the wondering eyes far above, but sometimes offering a rare glimpse of its muddy, brown face. It is truly a wondrous sight!

That night I stayed at the small youth hostel in Grand Canyon Village, and to my surprise I discovered that at this American youth hostel, I was the only American. There were Japanese, Aussies, Kiwis, Germans, and Dutch. And there was Jane, a cute little button of a gal from New Zealand who was traveling around the U.S. on her own by bus. She had a terrific sense of humor and when I told her about my trip and that I had just come from New Zealand, she became all excited and expressed her admiration for what I had accomplished so far. I must admit to feeling a little let-down when she talked about her boyfriend back in Kiwi Land, but I also realized it made little difference since she lived in the Southern Hemisphere and I in the North. Still, it was enchanting to talk to a young lass with such an effervescent personality and a zest for life. The fact that she was bold enough to set out on her own and take on the United States made her all the more enchanting. I said good-bye to Jane in the morning and pedaled away hoping some day I would meet a girl like her with the same enthusiasm and adventurous spirit.

I had just pulled into Desert View, the eastern exit for Grand Canyon National Park, in order to answer my stomach's call before my ride back down to the city of Cameron, my jump-off point for the push eastward. As I adjusted the packs on my bicycle I heard from behind me a familiar voice ask, "Do you ever have to get off and walk that thing up a hill?" I turned to get a look at the source of the familiar voice, and the face was familiar too. The familiar voice and face continued to ask me about my trip and bicycle until finally a vision of Walton's Mountain was projected upon the TV screen in the back of my brain. Yes, I knew this voice and face—it was Ike Godzy, or more properly, Mr. Godzy, owner of the general store in the television show *The Waltons*. His real name is Joe Connally and he was genuinely interested in my trip and experiences. I explained the purpose of my trip and gave him one of my Ride For World Hunger pledge cards and he said that he would be more than happy to send in a contribution to the Red Cross for African famine relief. We conversed a little while more and then his daughter Erin snapped a picture of me and Mr. Godzy. I rode away not a little flustered and flattered that a television celebrity had approached me in order to find out what the heck I was doing with a loaded-down machine such as mine. I also contemplated how his TV personality—the kindly general store manager and long-suffering but patient husband of Cora Beth—seemed to match his real-life personality—that of a nice person!

How many times had I been totally drained at the end of a day, my legs feeling like silly putty, every muscle pushed to the limit? One evening in eastern Arizona found me in this condition after traversing a portion of the Navaho Indian reservation—a land of stark beauty, but rugged terrain, consisting of one steep mesa leading to the next steep mesa. Three butt-busting climbs and a wind that was less than cooperative brought me to the end of the day and, thankfully, a free campground on the top of Second Mesa. My whole body felt much like a quivering bowl of jello. The following evening, having covered another not-quite-so-strenuous sixty miles of the land under the control of the Navaho Nation, I came to the small reservation town of Ganado and immediately addressed the problem of where to position my tired person for the night. After knocking on a couple of doors with no response, I wheeled into Ganado's good-sized educational complex which appeared to also contain housing for, I assumed, the teachers of the system. My assumption proved correct and while cruising past one little group of apartments a friendly-looking fellow waved to me from his backyard.

"Are you looking for a place to stay tonight?" he called.

"Well, I must admit that is my sorry condition right now," I replied. "If you have a small patch of ground in your yard where I could pitch my tent, that would. . ."

"Hey, forget about camping out tonight. I have an extra bed and you're welcome to stay here tonight. My name is Ed Bender and I'm the assistant principal at Ganado High School."

Ed proved to be a terrific host, offering me a hot shower, a warm and comfortable bed, and the fruits of his cupboard.

"Help yourself to anything you find in the kitchen," he smiled, knowing intuitively that he had here in his house one hungry bicyclist.

After cleaning up and filling my tummy, Ed and I sat and talked. He wanted to hear all about my trip and I wanted to know what it was like to teach on an Indian reservation and what were some of the unique problems that educators faced. Ed also explained that he is married, but that his wife works in Flagstaff, so they take turns commuting between Flagstaff and Ganado on the weekends. Ed suggested that in the morning I come over to the school complex to have a look around, and this I readily took him up on. The next morning he introduced me to the junior high principal who took over for Ed as tour guide, and he showed me around his building and further expanded on the problems of teaching in the Navaho world. We popped into a social studies class and soon I found myself in front of a group of students for the first time in about ten months. We rolled my bicycle, with all its gear attached, right into the classroom and I told this collection of curious brown faces about some of my experiences over the last year. Because I realized their knowledge of the outside world might be limited, I tried to mention some things that they might easily recognize.

"How many of you have heard of an ancient king by the name of King Tut?" I asked, thinking that just about everybody's hand would shoot up. Silence. Blank looks. Finally one little boy raised his hand and said that he thought that it had to do with a country called Egypt. This one question demonstrated well a point that both Ed and the junior high principal had made. The world of these native American youngsters is defined by the boundaries of the Navaho reservation, and they have little knowledge of the world outside of those boundaries. Nor are many of them motivated to learn about that outside world, for it would have little value or effect on the reservation. Some of the children still live in traditional Navaho shelters deep in the heart of the reservation and rarely ever make it to school. I thought of my own classroom and the vast gulf that separates this world from the world of midwest suburbia.

With the noon hour fast approaching and still sixty miles to cover, I bade farewell to the students and the junior high principal and thanked Ed for his great generosity and hospitality and set out for the Arizona-New Mexico border.

* * *

New Mexico is a vast and beautiful state. Its beauty lies in its vastness. From the semi-arid regions of the south and west to the alpine meadows of the central Sangre de Cristo range of the Rockies, to the grasslands of the high plains in the east, its immense open spaces help one experience the awe the early explorers must have felt as they came in search of the golden cities of Cibola. It is a land that had been home for centuries to the prehistoric Indians, the Anazazi, or Ancient Ones, to be followed by their descendants, the Pueblo Indians, and eventually the semi-nomadic tribes of the Great Plains. Over this territory have also flown the flags of Spain, Mexico, the United States and of course, the state flag of New Mexico. It is indeed a land of beauty and history. As I cycled across this great state I was treated to a variety of accommodations. There was the motel in Gallup, the side yard of a citizen of Grants where I pitched my tent, the Sigma Phi Epsilon fraternity house in Albuquerque (I was a Sig Ep at the University of Toledo), the youth hostel in Santa Fe, and a safe spot right at the feet of the dead Christ and Mary in St. Joseph's Catholic Church in Springer. My last stop in New Mexico was the border town of Clayton where Tim Connally flagged me down to find out where I was headed on my bicycle. He ended up inviting me to stay in a spare bedroom in his house which was temporarily rented for him by Shell Oil, his employer. Tim explained to me that he did title work for the mineral rights to the land. He had also cycled cross country, so we traded stories, shared some pizza, and found a lot in common about which to shoot the breeze.

Making it across New Mexico also meant leaving the Rocky Mountains behind. On the day I wheeled out of Santa Fe to make my final climb over the southern tip of the Sangre de Cristo, the winds were at gale force, and luckily they were with me. As I crested Glorieta Pass and battened down the hatches for a downhill run, the slingshot gusts of wind literally catapulted me out of the Rocky Mountains and onto the high plains of eastern New Mexico. At one point bicycle and rider hit a top speed of forty-four miles per hour. When I looked down, the highway became an asphalt blur inches below my feet and I couldn't help but contemplate the consequences if this seemingly fragile collection of metal tubes, wheel rims, and cables chose to come apart at that very moment. With the grace of God and technology, my Miyata held together and I headed toward my short but sweet crossing of Oklahoma's Panhandle.

* * *

An unsettled darkness had already fallen. Streaks of lightening illuminated angry clouds that rode the gusty winds above. Still my pedals kept spinning as they had been doing for the previous eleven hours. By that time, it was almost mechanical. As I pulled into Dodge City, Kansas, in the darkness, the rain began to fall and through my glazed eyes I saw that my odometer had registered one hundred sixty-five miles—fifty-five miles more than I had ever done before in a single day. Winds with muscles had sent me scudding across the high plains from Boise, Oklahoma to Dodge City of Boothill fame. For endless flat stretches I sat atop my two-wheeled mount pedaling almost effortlessly, but yet cruising at a phenomenal thirty-two miles per hour. The tall grasses that lined the highway's corridor were almost completely horizontal in my direction of travel, and I experienced the eerie sensation at thirty miles per hour of silence—no sound of the tremendous wind that was all about me, for I was moving easily with it. This was no gentle breeze; this was one helluva tail wind! Though I was pleased with my personal record mileage, I made a promise to myself that this would be the one and only day that I ever ride one hundred sixty-five miles!

* * *

It appeared that my limited fame was spreading before me, for during the week that I traversed Kansas' flat expanses where a single hill can be a lonely kind of guy, I was interviewed no less than three times (really two in Kansas and one in Missouri). On Monday, April 21, in the central Kansas town of McPherson, I stopped in at the local bike shop in order to find a replacement for my thrice-broken rear pannier rack. Though there was no replacement rack to be had at the shop, the girl in charge was so interested in my trip that soon she was on the phone to the local newspaper and before I knew it I was answering the questions of a local journalist. The very next day in Emporia, Kansas, I again visited a local cyclery in my continuing quest for a new rear pannier rack, and soon some local reporters popped into the establishment asking, "Where is the cyclist with the loaded down bicycle?" After answering their questions the reporter and her photographer hopped into their car and followed me out into the countryside for some action cycling photos. Unfortunately for the photographer who was riding in the trunk shooting out the rear, the hood of the trunk insisted on closing on his head as he was trying to snap his pictures of me cycling nonchalantly behind, causing him to find a more stationary position as I came breezing by. Once more on Friday in the historic town of Lexington, Missouri, as I was sitting in the local Dairy Queen sipping a soda, a fellow approached me with a recorder and microphone and wanted to know if he could interview me for the local radio station. By this time, an old hand at interviews, I replied, "Sure, fire away!"

During this week too, I continued to learn about the true meaning of American hospitality. In Larned, Kansas I benefited from the kindness of a fellow chimney sweep, Darrell Jordan who invited me to occupy the couch in his mobile home. In addition to my teaching job, I also had run a part-time chimney sweeping business for a number of years, and Darrell had done a number of short bicycle tours, so there was never a doubt about where I was going to stay that night. And then in Raytown, a suburb of Kansas City, I stopped to ask directions at a real estate office and the proprietors, Jim and Annabelle Hybarger, without hesitation invited me into their comfortable home for the night and took me out for a fantastic home-style chicken dinner and a tour of downtown Kansas City. Mid-American hospitality had so far lived up to its reputation!

* * *

Once upon a time eleven months and nine thousand cycling miles ago, I had said a difficult good-bye to my family and friends. Now, in crossing the Mississippi River, Mark Twain's Hannibal, Missouri nestled into the banks of the mighty river below me, I realized that my journey was nearing an end. The images of the past year seemed far away, and yet close at hand, and they tended to blend together so that it became difficult to recall exactly where I was at what time. In fact, sometimes I had difficulty remembering where I was just a few days before. Regardless, the overall impression that hung with me was having come a long way and having seen and experienced much of this wonderful but troubled globe of ours.

"You must be getting soft," I told myself as I glided through Illinois and Indiana, closing the distance between me and Ohio. For my "you've-suffered-enough attitude" made it not too difficult to make use of more frequent motel stays during the final days of my journey. But as I pulled into Attica, Indiana late in the evening with one hundred and one miles showing on my odometer, there was no such comfort to be had. So I found myself again wondering where to throw my tent for the night when I ran into Jerry and Sarah Mattern who were out walking with two-year old Mark and five-year old Elizabeth. They immediately made no bones about inviting me into their home for a night's slumber in a soft bed. Jerry and Sarah were also touring cyclists and I think quickly recognized the sorrowful look on my face. Again the kindness of strangers, who didn't remain that way for long, came to my rescue and snatched me from the grips of what promised to be a very chilly night.

And then there was Rob Schoenefeld working in a pizza shop outside of Fort Wayne, Indiana who, with the exuberance of a sixteen-year-old teen-ager, immediately invited me home to meet his family and camp out in his backyard if I so desired. I was soon adopted for the evening by Rob, his parents, Jerry and Karen, his little brothers, Brian, and David, sister Carey, and their very friendly golden retriever, Dallas. As I wolfed down a couple of hot dogs, chips, and cake, I told them of my travels, and Rob, who also loved cycling, swore that he was going to do something similar in the future. In the morning, Rob, in the true spirit of education, decided to skip his morning classes and ride with me as far as the eastern side of Fort Wayne, and I was glad to have the company for that short time. He was really a nice young man and was truly excited about having a "world cyclist" as a guest for a night. We shook hands and said good-bye and I pointed my front wheel east for the second- to-the-last time of my world bicycle tour.

* * *

JOURNAL ENTRY—MAY 6, DAY 327, LAST DAY

The last day—a day that I've thought about so often over the last 326; a day that, at times, I had serious doubts I would ever see, especially after each of my accidents and my near brush with death at the hands of an Indian truck driver. How do I feel? Happy, sad, disappointed, reflective, proud. Happy that it's over and that I will be reunited with my family and friends; sad that this small but so different slice of my life is ending; disappointed that in my desire to come home to the USA I didn't do justice to New Zealand and Australia; reflective about all that I've seen; proud of having survived these last eleven months. I also have a sense of pride in the United States. Having experienced so many countries and cultures, some of them ancient, and having seen the tremendous problems that many of them face, I have a real appreciation for what we have been able to accomplish as a nation and a people in the short span of our history. It makes me wonder what it is that has enabled us to achieve such a high standard of living compared to so many other countries. Is it our natural resources? Our people? Our mix of ethnic backgrounds and rich diversity? Our ability to tolerate and accommodate new ideas and ways of doing things? Our commitment to a free, open, and democratic society? This sense of pride is tempered by a degree of guilt when one travels in the Third World: guilt for being such a rich country while so many others are struggling to feed, clothe, and house their people; guilt for having been one of the lucky ones to be born into this rich land. This sense of guilt underscored by my ride through the fertile farm lands and past the comfortable-looking homes of the small and large towns of Middle America. How fortunate we are here in the United States!

Now, as I cycle the last miles of my twenty-five thousand mile journey, nine thousand of those miles atop my faithful companion beneath me, the brooding skies and streaks of lightening overhead seem almost a fitting conclusion to this very strange year. The images of the previous three hundred and twenty-six days play across my mind in a sequence of exhilarating highs and depressing lows. The day I said good-bye to my family and friends is forever fixed in my memory. As I pedaled out of Promenade Park and looked over my shoulder for a last glimpse of my parents, I weighed my chances of making it back to see them again, and the odds frightened me. I remember the pain of the four hundred miles of hills and mountains through Pennsylvania on my heavily-laden bicycle and at the same time, the beauty and solitude of a quiet campground tucked into the hills of Appalachia. I will never forget the wilting heat of cycling across the Iberian Peninsula in mid-summer, and also feeling at home in Toledo, Spain, the city of El Greco and our sister city. The spectacular beauty of the French Riviera and Côte d'Azur is a lasting impression, as is standing in quiet awe in front of Leonardo's *Last Supper*. I recall gazing up at towering Mt. Vesuvius from the excavated streets of ancient Pompeii and musing about how the citizens of this once-thriving Roman city must have felt as the angry volcano announced its fateful reawakening. My memory casts a golden glow when I think of my visit to Olympia, Greece and how special this place is for us as it was for the Greeks of the Golden Age. Against the backdrop of the Pyramids and the Taj Mahal, the poverty and disease of Africa and India come rushing back to me: the victims of leprosy and polio pulling themselves along the pavement, the emaciated beggars on the streets of Bombay, the little girl with no shoes dressed in dirty rags pulling on my arm, the makeshift hovels that are home for thousands. My day on an Indian movie set will certainly stay with me. When I administered torture to the movie's star and later swung back and forth over the set in a helicopter, I remember thinking, "Can this really be happening?" I once again see my bicycle and me sprawled across the Indian road-way in a tangled mass of equipment and rider with my fractured elbow throbbing at my side and I can feel the apprehension as I stared at the operating room ceiling waiting for the surgeon to begin his work. I remember the lush vegetation and tropical heat of Thailand, the cool, green beauty of New Zealand, and the friendliness and hospitality of so many people as I traversed my own country from California back to Ohio. Now, as I pedal into Secor Park on the outskirts of my hometown and I see the happy, sweet faces of my family and friends amid the balloons and champagne, I know that I am back home, My Home, Toledo, Ohio.

THE END